Zhe Li

AF286671

**Design and Analysis of Robust Kanban System
in an Uncertain Environment**

WISSENSCHAFTLICHE BERICHTE

Institut für Fördertechnik und Logistiksysteme
am Karlsruher Institut für Technologie (KIT)

BAND 81

Design and Analysis of Robust Kanban System in an Uncertain Environment

by
Zhe Li

Dissertation, Karlsruher Institut für Technologie (KIT)
Fakultät für Maschinenbau, 2013
Referenten: Prof. Dr.-Ing. Kai Furmans, Prof. Dr. Stefan Nickel

Impressum

 Scientific
Publishing

Karlsruher Institut für Technologie (KIT)
KIT Scientific Publishing
Straße am Forum 2
D-76131 Karlsruhe

KIT Scientific Publishing is a registered trademark of Karlsruhe
Institute of Technology. Reprint using the book cover is not allowed.

www.ksp.kit.edu

Print on Demand 2013

ISSN 0171-2772
ISBN 978-3-7315-0117-6

Design and Analysis of Robust Kanban System in an Uncertain Environment

Zur Erlangung des akademischen Grades eines

Doktors der Ingenieurwissenschaften

der Fakultät für Maschinenbau
des Karlsruher Instituts für Technologie (KIT)
genehmigte

Dissertation

von

M.Sc. Zhe Li

Tag der mündlichen Prüfung:	18. Feb. 2013
Hauptreferent:	Prof. Dr.-Ing. Kai Furmans
Korreferent:	Prof. Dr. Stefan Nickel

Vorwort

Ich möchte mich bei meiner größten Quelle der Unterstützung bedanken: Prof. Dr.-Ing. Kai Furmans, meinem Doktorvater. Ohne seine Unterstützung und Anleitung wäre diese Arbeit nicht möglich gewesen. Ich bin sehr dankbar, dass er dies sowohl akademisch als auch persönlich zeigte. Er hatte immer ein offenes Ohr, gab mir wertvolle Ratschläge, hat meine Arbeit im Detail gelesen, und mir geholfen die Schwierigkeiten im Leben einer ausländischen Studentin zu bewältigen.

Ich möchte Prof. Dr. Stefan Nickel, meinem zweiten Gutachter, für seine Anregungen und Kommentare zu dieser Dissertation und seiner Bereitschaft, das Koreferat zu übernehmen danken. Ich möchte auch Prof. Dr. Gisela Lanza danken, sie ist die Vorsitzende meiner Mündlichprüfung, und gab mir viele hilfreiche Ratschläge.

Ich danke zutiefst meiner liebsten Freundin und Kollegin Judith Weiblen. Sie hat mir eine unschätzbare Hilfe und Freundschaft gegeben, seit meinem ersten Arbeitstag am IFL. Ich bin ihr dankbar für alles. Ohne Judith und ihre Familie, hätte ich nicht so schöne Erfahrungen im wunderbaren Deutschland gehabt. Mein tiefer Dank geht auch an meine Freunde und IFL Kollegen Melanie Schwab, Martin Veit, Christoph Nobbe, und Eda Özden. Sie boten immer großzügige Hilfe und warme Ermutigungen, sowohl in meinem akademischen als auch persönlichen Leben. Ich möchte auch meinen anderen IFL Kollegen für die gute Arbeitsatmosphäre danken.

Meine chinesischen Freunde Yan Xiaoxing, Yang Qian, und meine Cousine Sun Jia, haben mir in dieser schweren Zeit sehr geholfen. Sie waren immer da, um mich aufzumuntern und mir Mut zu machen. Ich möchte auch meiner Deutschlehrerin Carmen Reck danken. Ihre Freundlichkeit und Beratung waren mir eine wertvolle Hilfe die deutsche Kultur zu erlernen.

Ich bedanke mich bei dem Chinese Scholarship Council (CSC) und dem Karlsruhe House of Young Scientists (KHYS) für die finanzielle Unterstützung während meiner Promotion am IFL.

Mein letzter und herzlicher Dank geht an meine Eltern, die immer für mich da waren, und für alles.

Karlsruhe, Februar 2013 Zhe Li

Kurzfassung

Zhe Li

Entwicklung und Analyse eines robusten Kanban-Systems in einem unsicheren Umfeld

Das traditionelle Supply Chain Management hat das Ziel System billiger und schlanker zu gestalten. Die Kanban-Steuerung ist dafür eine unterstützende Methode. Jedoch hat die Kanban-Steuerung auch Beschränkungen. Einerseits reduziert sie die Kosten der Operation für die Supply Chain, andererseits erhöht sie aber auch die Verletzlichkeit des Systems. Insbesondere wenn die Umgebung nicht stabil sondern volatil ist, ist diese Beschränkung offensichtlich. Moderne Supply Chain Operationen müssen verschiedene Risiken eines unsicheren Umfeldes überstehen. Deshalb ist es sinnvoll eine robuste Supply Chain, die mit den Unsicherheiten der Umwelt umgehen kann, zu entwickeln. Da dieses Thema von großem Interesse ist, haben sich in den letzen Jahren viele Forscher und Praktiker damit beschäftigt.

In dieser Arbeit wird eine robustes Kanban Modell vorgestellt. Das Modell zielt darauf ab, das Supply Chain System mit einem Mechanismus für unterschiedliche Risiken auszustatten und eine gute Leistung in einem unsicheren Umfeld zu erhalten. Die Anwendung des hier entwickelten robusten Kanban Systems sind praktisch, und das Modell kann leicht an ein breites Anwendungsspektrum angepasst werden. Die Arbeit besteht aus vier Hauptteilen.

Zuerst, wird ein konzeptionelles Modell des robusten Kanban-Systems entwickelt. Dann wird ein Simulationsmodell erstellt, um das konzeptionelle Modell umzusetzen. In diesem Modell wird der Mechanismus zur Reaktion auf Risiken des unsicheren Umfeldes bereits berücksichtigt. Durch Änderung der System-Konfigurationsparameter auf drei

Ebenen, kann das System schnell und effektiv auf unterschiedliche Risikosituationen reagieren. Die Änderung der Parameter können systematisch von über die operative Ebene (z.b. Änderung der Kanban-Anzahl), zur taktischen Ebene (z. B. Änderung der Maschinenbetriebszeit), bis hin zur strategischen Ebene (z. B. einen Ersatz-Anbieter oder einen neuen Server auswählen) eskaliert werden, um die Risiko-Auswirkungen zu mindern und die Störungen des Systems zu vermeiden.

Im zweiten Teil, werden Methoden der Parametrierung entwickelt, um geeignete Parameterwerte für den Risiko-Mechanismus zu finden. Die Parameter sind für die Konfiguration des robusten Kanban-Systems und die Umsetzung des Risiko-Mechanismus auszuwählen. Ein MINLP (mixed integer nonlinear programming) Modell wurde entwickelt, um die Basiswerte und die Abgrenzung der 3-Ebene einstellbaren Konfigurationsparameter zu wählen (einschließlich der Kanban-Anzahl, Maschinenbetriebszeit, Server-Anzahl und Ersatz-Lieferanten). Einige Ansätze wurden benutzt, um geeignete Parameterwerte des Risiko-Mechanismus zu schätzen.

Im dritten Teil, wird ein vergleichendes Experiment mit den Kanban-System Simulationsmodellen vorgenommen. Einige Risikoszenarien werden angenommen, und anschließend wird die Leistung des hier vorgestellten robusten Kanban-Systems mit den Leistungen von zwei aus der Literatur bekannten Kanban-Systemen (Traditional Toyota Kanban-System, Inventory-based adaptive Kanban-System) verglichen. Basierend auf den Vergleichsergebnissen, bestätigt sich, dass durch das robuste Kanban-System eine Leistungssteigerung in einem unsicheren Umfeld gewonnen werden kann.

Im letzten Teil, wird ein Simulations-basiertes facktorielles Experiment durchgeführt, um die Wahl der Basiswerte der Steuerparameter zu verbessern. Zunächst wird ein faktorielles Experiment entwickelt; dann werden sogenannte Response Surface Methoden angewandt, um die optimalen Parameterwerte (optimal im Sinne des besten NetProfit Ergebnis) herauszufinden. Mit den neuen Parameterwerten kann die Leistung des robusten Kanban-System noch weiter verbessert werden.

Abstract

Zhe Li
Design and Analysis of Robust Kanban System in an Uncertain Environment

Traditional supply chain management focused on making the system cheaper and leaner. In this direction, the Kanban mechanism is a representative control policy pursuing cost-efficient features for the material flow system. However, the adoption of the Kanban mechanism increases the system vulnerability while reducing the cost of operating the supply chain, especially when the environment is not stable. Modern supply chains are subject to various risks in an uncertain environment. Therefore, to build a robust supply network, which can deal with the environment uncertainties, has obtained wide attention among researchers and practitioners in recent years. In this study, we proposed a robust Kanban system model for the supply chain system based on the Kanban mechanism. The model aims at helping the supply chain system deal with various risks in an uncertain environment. The proposed robust Kanban system model and its application methods are practical to use, they can be easily extended to a wide range of applications.

The work in this dissertation is composed of four parts.

Firstly, a conceptual model of the robust Kanban system is designed, and then a simulation model is built to implement the design ideas. The robust Kanban system uses a risk-response mechanism to handle risks in an uncertain environment. The system can respond quickly and effectively to a variety of risk situations by adjusting a series of system configuration parameters. In order to mitigate the impact of risks and help the system recover from disruption, the response actions are taken systematically from an operational level (e.g. change Kanban number), a tactical level (e.g. adjust machine service time), or a strategic level (e.g. use a backup supplier, start a new server).

In the second part, we introduce methods for determining suitable parameter settings. The parameters are used for specifying the robust Kanban system configuration and implementing the risk-response mechanism. A mixed integer nonlinear programming (MINLP) model is developed to decide the basic values and ranges of 3-level configuration parameters (including Kanban number, machine service time, server number, and backup supplier supply proportion). And a set of estimation approaches are used to find suitable values of the control parameters that are used in the risk-response mechanism.

In the third part, a comparative experiment is carried out based on Kanban system simulation models. Given a variety of risk scenarios, we compare the performance of the proposed robust Kanban system and two other Kanban systems from previous literature (Traditional Toyota Kanban system, Inventory-based adaptive Kanban system). Based on comparison results, we confirm the performance improvement made by the robust Kanban system in the uncertain environment.

In the last part, we perform another simulation-based experiment to find better settings for the control parameters that are used in the risk-response mechanism. We design a factorial experiment, then use response surface methods to determine optimal factor setting (that generates maximum Netprofit in a given region). Using the new parameter setting, the performance of the robust Kanban system can be further improved than using the former estimation-based factor setting.

Contents

Kurzfassung   **iii**

Abstract   **v**

1 Introduction   **1**
    1.1 Motivation 1
    1.2 Problem statement 4
    1.3 Overview of the study 8

2 Literature review   **11**
    2.1 Supply chain risk management 11
    2.2 Development of Kanban systems 14

3 Robust Kanban System model formulation   **27**
    3.1 Preliminary 27
       3.1.1 Kanban-controlled supply chain system 27
       3.1.2 Design questions for risk-response mechanism . . . 30
    3.2 Conceptual model description 36
       3.2.1 Assumptions 37
       3.2.2 Parameters and variables 41
       3.2.3 Risk-response mechanism 49
    3.3 Simulation model construction 69
       3.3.1 Preliminary 69
       3.3.2 Model construction 70
       3.3.3 Model verification 77
       3.3.4 Model validation 83

4 Methodology of parameter setting   **91**
    4.1 Decision of 3-level adjustable parameters 91
       4.1.1 Introduction of decision model (MINLP) 93

4.1.2   Constraints   96

4.1.3   Objective function   101

4.1.4   Model formulation summary   123

4.1.5   Model implementation: a numerical example   . . .   124

4.1.6   Define adjusting ranges of 3-level parameters   . . .   129

4.2   Estimation of control parameters in the risk-response mechanism   133

4.2.1   Control limits for monitor mi_inv   134

4.2.2   Control limits for monitor mi_rate   136

4.2.3   Smoothing weight factors and safety factor   138

5   Simulation experiment 1: compare Robust Kanban System with others   **143**

5.1   Design of experiment   145

5.1.1   Problem statement   145

5.1.2   Control factors   148

5.1.3   Response variables   150

5.1.4   Choice of design and conducting details   151

5.2   Result analysis   157

5.2.1   Result overview   158

5.2.2   In a stable scenario   162

5.2.3   In a demand++ scenario   167

5.2.4   In other scenarios   168

5.3   Result discussion   169

6   Simulation experiment 2: improve the risk-response mechanism setting   **179**

6.1   Design of experiment   180

6.1.1   Problem statement and experiment planning   . . .   180

6.1.2   Choice of factor ranges and levels: a pilot test . . .   184

6.1.3   Design of response surface model   190

6.2   Result analysis   193

6.2.1   Optimization with response surface model   193

6.2.2   Statistical analysis   198

6.3   Result discussion   203

7 Concluding remarks   **213**
    7.1   Work summary 213
    7.2   Application guidelines for the robust Kanban system . . . 216

Glossary of Notation   **223**

References   **227**

List of Figures   **235**

List of Tables   **237**

A Appendix for Chapter 5   **239**

B Appendix for Chapter 6   **255**

1 Introduction

1.1 Motivation

Traditional supply chain management featured cost-efficient policies, aiming to make supply chain activities leaner and cheaper. In this direction, the Kanban mechanism is a representative control policy; it implements the pull mechanism under the Just-In-Time philosophy. The Kanban mechanism is derived from Japanese Toyota Production System (TPS) (Monden 1983; Ohno 1988) since 1950s. It has been widely used in manufacturing and production systems. Using the Kanban policy, not only the movements of material (e.g. to release, produce, and transport the product), but also the material inventory at each stage can be controlled by Kanban cards. Besides, it is practical to implement the Kanban mechanism without causing much operating cost. Due to these "lean" features, the Kanban-controlled system works very well given a repetitive environment. However, it can hardly remain at a high performance level when the environment is uncertain. A main shortcoming of the Kanban system is the slow and limited response actions when risks occur in the environment.

Modern supply chains are subject to a variety of risks, the supply chains often operate in an uncertain environment. Especially in recent years, as the global competition increases, as the customers require more product variety, customization and shorter delivery time, the companies are forced to form more complex and larger supply chain networks in a worldwide range. This in turn leads to a highly volatile and uncertain environment for modern supply chain management. There are various risks that could happen to the supply chains. Some are small risks and happen frequently in daily supply chain activities, such as the customer demand fluctuation, the transport time delay, the machine process time variation. Generally, the impacts of the small risks are slight, the system can recover easily from these operational risks (Tang 2006a). By contrast, other risks are more serious and could bring severe consequences to the system. These risks are also referred to as disruptions, ranging from economic turbulence, natural disasters, plant fire to man-made strikes. Although these disruptions occur with very low probabilities, once they happen, the consequences are often catastrophic. It takes much more time for the supply chain system to recover from such disruptions and go back to the normal level. In the modern environment, supply chains have to face much more risks than before. Hence, the requirement of building a robustly designed supply chain against the various risks has become important and inevitable. Lee (2004) studied more than 60 leading companies, and suggested that the design of a triple-A (agility, adaptability, and alignment) supply chain was a crucial issue of successful supply chain management in the modern uncertain environment. The supply chain risk management has become an important part of the modern supply chain management; research in this field has received much attention in recent years. Supply chain risk management refers to "the management of supply chain risks through coordination or collaboration among the supply chain partners so as to ensure profitability and continuity" (Tang 2006a). In order to build a robust supply chain network and mitigate the impact of risks, a series of robust approaches is suggested and developed by researchers. The robust approaches for supply chain risk management can be classified into four primary types based on the management methods: supply management, demand management, product management, and information management (Tang 2006b). For instance, the backup supplier, product dynamic pricing, production postponement, and demand collaborative forecasting are four typical robust approaches from the four management aspects.

In supply chain management, the decision making activities group into three levels: strategic, tactical and operational levels (Ballou 1992; Schmidt and Wilhelm 2000) Strategic-level decisions characterize the framework of the supply chain system and define long-term plans, such as to determine the facility location or capacity, to select suppliers. In the tactical level, decisions are connected to medium-term, medium-range supply chain activities, like to plan the production schedule of a manufacturing plant for the next month, allocate the workload for service facilities, and assign transport routes for distribution centers. At last, the decisions at the operational level are about daily operation activities of the supply chain; they are usually repetitive and short-term decisions. To plan daily production schedules and transport activities, to forecast the daily customer demand, to monitor and control the inventory level every hour, are all instances of the operational-level decisions. Based on the 3-level framework, the robust approaches can be developed from strategic, tactical, and operational levels as well for supply chain risk management.

There is vast literature investigating robust models for modern supply chain design and operation. Many robust models have focused on the robust approaches from the strategic or tactical decision levels, such as to determine the facility location or the backup plant capacity (Lim 2009). A small proportion of robust models is formulated at the operational level, such as the modified Kanban system models, which can flexibly change the Kanban number in response to customer demand fluctuation (Takahashi and Nakamura 1999; Takahashi 2003). Particularly in the area of Kanban-controlled supply chain models, although some robustly designed Kanban system models have been presented in previous literature, most of them just deal with a simple typical risk situation: customer demand with slight fluctuation. Neither risk scenarios with severe demand fluctuation, nor risk scenarios with supplier-side or process-side (e.g. supplier material shortage, process machine breakdown) risks have been taken into consideration in the system operating environment. Moreover, in most of the previous Kanban system models, only the approach of adjusting Kanban number is adopted as the response action to deal with risk occurrences. To adjust the Kanban number can be seen as a typical robust approach for mitigating risks from the operational level. However, the robust approaches from strategic and tactical levels are seldom considered in these Kanban models.

From the literature study, we notice that there is a need to improve the design and development of robust Kanban-controlled supply chain systems, which can deal with diverse risks in the modern uncertain environment. The objective of this dissertation is to design a new robust model for a Kanban-controlled supply chain system. With the robust mechanism, the Kanban system will be able to handle a variety of risks (slight or severe risks; from a demand, process, or supply side) systematically and retain a satisfactory performance level, even in an uncertain environment.

1.2 Problem statement

The scope of study is a supply chain system which is operating based on Kanban-mechanism and facing a variety of risks in an uncertain environment. The supply chain is supposed to be a multi-stage single-product serial-line system. It contains five stages: a supplier at the upstream side, three manufacturer stages located in a sequential form in the middle, and a customer stage that generates demand orders randomly at the downstream end of the supply chain. At each stage, two types of Kanban cards (Production Kanban, Transport Kanban) are employed to move the material, transmit the information, and control the inventory. The risks considered in the uncertain environment include: slight or severe customer demand fluctuation (demand-side risk), raw-material supply shortage (supply-side risk), machine process time variation (process-side risk). Since raditional Kanban systems cannot achieve a good performance level in an uncertain environment while the modern environment is full of uncertain risks, a new robust mechanism for the Kanban-controlled supply chain system is proposed in this study with the goal of dealing with various risks. We name the new model the "robust Kanban system", it aims to mitigate the impact of risks and enhance the Kanban system performance in the uncertain environment.

Compared with previous Kanban system models, the risk scenarios considered in this study are more various and extensive. Besides the typical risk situation "slight customer demand fluctuation", other risks with slight or severe impacts, from a demand, process, or supply side, are included in this study. To distinguish the various risk situations better, we use four parameters to describe the risk features: location, extent, duration, and probability. With the four parameters, risks can be clearly described and measured, then proper risk-response actions can be taken referring to the risk parameters.

The proposed robust Kanban system features a newly designed risk-response mechanism. The mechanism employs two monitor items (a rate-balance monitor mi_rate and an inventory-balance monitor mi_inv) to monitor the operating status and performance of the Kanban system. When different risks occur in the environment, the system operating status will be affected accordingly. The status changes are reflected by the rate-balance or inventory-balance monitors. By observing the monitor values, the Kanban system can firstly detect the status changes timely and be aware of the impact of risks on system performance. Nextly, the Kanban system may adjust some of the system configuration parameters (such as machine-capacity parameter) according to the observed monitor values. Essentially, the risk-response mechanism is an adjusting-parameters mechanism. The robust Kanban system responds to different risk situations by dynamically adjusting a series of system configuration parameters. These parameters are designed to be flexible in the robust Kanban system; to adjust different parameters indicates the Kanban system takes different robust approaches in response to risks.

As mentioned in Section 1.1, there are four basic aspects of robust approaches in supply chain risk management (Tang 2006b): the supply, demand, information, and production management. Many robust approaches can be considered from the four aspects to design the robust Kanban system. Since in this work we study a multi-stage single-product serial-line system under Kanban control, the following robust approaches are selected as optional risk-response actions for the robust Kanban system design. They are:

- From the supply aspect: main supplier and backup supplier. The robust Kanban can shift material orders between a main supplier and a backup supplier. The backup supplier is supposed to be more reliable but expensive.

- From the demand aspect: dynamical pricing for product. The change of product price could affect the customer demand rate. So dynamical pricing is a method to cushion the demand variability, or balance the demand and supply. (To be noted, in this work the dynamical pricing method is not involved in the simulation model of the robust Kanban system.)

- From the information aspect: information sharing among stages. The supply chain partners can share the information about system operating status, such as inventory levels, machine process rates, supplier material supply rates, and customer demand rates.

5

- From the production aspect: 1) Flexible production rate. The Kanban system is allowed to adjust the machine process speed, the number of servers. 2) Dynamical inventory control. The number of cyclic Kanbans, buffer sizes, or inventory control limits can be changed in response to risks.

Besides considering the four management aspects, when we design response approaches for the robust Kanban system, the three decision levels (Ballou 1992; Schmidt and Wilhelm 2000) for supply chain activities are also taken into consideration. They are strategic, tactical, and operational decision levels, as introduced in Section 1.1. Here we employ the 3-level framework to classify the response approaches adopted in the robust Kanban system. As mentioned in literature, there are many parameters that can characterize the supply chain system configuration and measure its performance (Beamon 1999; Gunasekaran, Patel and McGaughey 2004). For example, the cyclic Kanban number and the inventory level are typical parameters used in Kanban systems. Since the objective model in our study is a Kanban-controlled supply chain system, and considering the above references, we select the following parameters as adjustable parameters used in the robust Kanban system: 1) Kanban number at each stage; 2) Machine process speed at specific stages; 3) Number of servers (service facilities) at specific stages; 4) Material supply proportion from the backup supplier. The values of adjustable parameters are allowed to change dynamically during the system operation; and the changes of the parameters correspond to the response approaches taken by the robust Kanban system in response to risks.

In Figure 1.1, we list the selected adjustable parameters (words in parentheses) based on the 3-level framework. To adjust the Kanban number is an operational-level robust approach taken from the production aspect. To adjust the machine process time is a tactical-level action, and is from the production aspect too. To change the number of servers is much more expensive than the former two approaches; it can be seen as a higher strategic-level approach that is also from the production aspect. Lastly, to change the material order proportion from the backup supplier is also a strategic-level action; it is from the supply aspect. Besides, when the robust Kanban system calculates the values of rate-balance and inventory-balance monitors, it implies the information is shared among supply chain partners, which is also a robust approach taken from the information aspect.

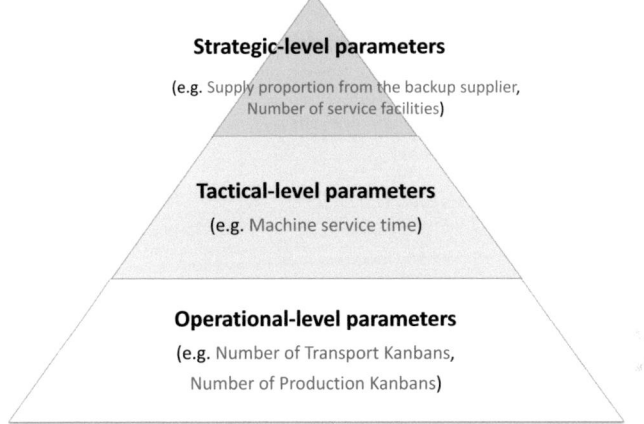

Figure 1.1: The 3-level adjustable parameters in Robust Kanban System

The risk-response mechanism of the robust Kanban system changes the system capability through adjusting the 3-level parameters. Given different risk scenarios, different parameters could be selected and changed (to different extents) to mitigate the risk impact. For example, when the risk situation is slight customer demand fluctuation (the demand rate is increased by 5%), then the action of increasing the Kanban number (operational-level parameter) will be a suitable response. If the demand rate is increased by 80%, in this situation a strategic-level action of adding a new server will be more effective to handle the risk. And between the two extreme risk situations, for a medium-extent risk situation where the demand rate is increased by 20%, a tactical-level response action of increasing the single-machine process speed will be a good choice. And when the risk situation is machine breakdown, to repair the machine or start a new machine will be selected as response actions. When the risk is material supply shortage, to purchase material from a backup supplier will be an effective method. In sum, the robust Kanban system can dynamically adjust a series of system parameters according to different risk situations, thus the impact of risks can be mitigated by changing the parameter values at the right time and to a suitable extent. Thus, the performance of the Kanban system can remain at a satisfactory level even in an environment with many uncertainties. This is the main difference and improvement made by the robust Kanban system, comparing with other Kanban systems.

1.3 Overview of the study

The dissertation is composed of seven chapters. Except the introduction part in Chapter 1, the remainder of the dissertation is organized as follows.

In Chapter 2, related literature is reviewed. We first review the robust approaches and models suggested by researchers to deal with a variety of risks for supply chain systems. Then the development of Kanban system models is reviewed in the second section. A series of typical modified Kanban system models developed by researchers are listed. The review of Kanban model development ranges from the traditional models that focus on minimizing cost, to the recent complex variation models that pay more attention to dealing with risks. At the end of this chapter, the limitations and extension of previous research work on Kanban systems are pointed out, which also shed light on this study.

Chapter 3 gives a detailed description of the proposed robust Kanban system model. With specifying the model assumptions and parameter notation, the robust Kanban system structure and its risk-response mechanism are described in a more accurate manner using mathematical notations and logical relationships. Then the conceptual model is implemented in the simulation environment. The work about the simulation model design and development is also presented in this chapter.

After the model formulation, we address how to decide suitable parameter values in the robust Kanban system. The parameters include the system configuration parameters and the risk-response mechanism-related parameters. The methodology for setting the parameters is presented in Chapter 4. First, a mixed integer nonlinear programming model (MINLP) is developed with the aim of determining suitable settings and ranges for 3-level adjustable parameters. Then, the methods for estimating the monitor control parameters used by the risk-response mechanism are introduced. Having defined suitable parameter settings, the risk-response mechanism can be then implemented in the robust Kanban system.

In Chapter 5 and 6, two experiments are designed and conducted respectively, based on the simulation model of the robust Kanban system. In Chapter 5, we do a comparative experiment. Three types of Kanban systems are built in the simulation environment: the proposed robust Kanban system, the traditional Toyota system, and the inventory-based adaptive Kanban system presented in previous literature. The aim of the experiment is to compare the performance of the robust Kanban system with the performance of other two Kanban systems when the environment is with risks. Through analyzing the experiment results, we can confirm the performance improvement made by robust Kanban system in a variety of risk scenarios.

In Chapter 6, we design a factorial experiment with the objective of improving the risk-response mechanism setting, so that performance of the robust Kanban system can be further improved. Response surface methods are applied in this experiment to approximate the relationships between the response variable "Netprofit" (in this work we denote the time-averaged net profit value gained by the Kanban system by "Netprofit") and the factors "monitor control parameters" that are used by the risk-response mechanism. Based on the response surface models, we can find optimal solutions for the factor value setting. With the improved parameter setting of the risk-response mechanism, the performance of the robust Kanban can be further improved in the uncertain environment.

Lastly, concluding remarks about this study are given in Chapter 7. We summarize the research work in this dissertation, and suggest some guidelines for applying the robust Kanban system in realistic problems.

2 Literature review

2.1 Supply chain risk management

Supply chain management has been extensively studied among researchers and practitioners for decades. During the early decades, companies and researchers mainly focused on how to make supply chains faster and cheaper to control the material flow. However, in recent years, as the global competition and customer requirement increased, the supply chains have been brought into a more challenging environment, where more complex network, product proliferation, and shortened product life are required. The modern environment contains various risks. Therefore, only pursuing faster and cheaper features is not enough for a supply chain system to thrive, even survive.

Lee (2004) studied more than 60 leading companies, and observed that the best supply chains were not just fast and cost-efficient; the design of a triple-A (agility, adaptability and alignment) supply chain became a crucial issue for supply chains to achieve a satisfactory performance in an uncertain environment. The supply chain risk management is an important part of modern supply chain management. Particularly in last ten years, there has been a large amount of research literature concerned with risk management. Some researches are done from a strategic-level perspective; they provide comprehensive frameworks for supply chain risk management, and propose strategic robust policies for the supply chains to mitigate the impact of risks (Chopra and Sodhi 2004; Kleindorfer and Saad 2005; Tang 2006b). Other researches are conducted from a tactical or operational aspect; they focus on some specific risk types and suggest response methods for dealing with the risks. For example, Jordan and Graves (1995) suggested tactical methods to improve manufacturing process flexibility, so as to cope with product demand uncertainty. Their work was further investigated by other researchers (Graves and Tomlin 2003; Tomlin and Wang 2005; Tomlin 2006; Hopp, Iravani and Xu 2010) to enhance the flexibility of supply chain network. Tang and Tomlin (2008) followed the robust strategies framework suggested by Tang (2006a) and further presented stylized models to show the improvement gained by flexible methods. Moreover, in other aspects of supply chain management, there are also many robust approaches and models developed by researchers to handle the various risk situations, such as inventory control (Parlar 1997; Askin and Krishnan 2009), facility location (Snyder and Daskin 2006), material procurement or revenue sharing contract (Cachon and Lariviere 2005; Martinez de Albeniz and Levi 2005). Note that some robust approaches presented in literature can be classified as strategic, tactical, or operational level methods, while other approaches are mixed with two or three levels' policies.

Tang (2006a) stated that supply chain risks could be categorized into two types: operational risks and disruption risks, according to the risk characteristics (such as extent and frequency). Operational risks refer to the inherent uncertainties such as daily customer demand fluctuation, material supply uncertainty, process or transport time variation. These risks happen more frequently to a supply chain than disruption risks, but their impact is relatively small. By contrast, disruption risks mean the large disruptions caused by natural or man-made disasters, such as earthquakes, floods, hurricanes, terrorist attacks, economic crises, and strikes. Although disruptions happen with a very low probability, usually their effects are catastrophic. Tang's risk classification provides a good reference for the risk measurement in this study.

The supply chains designed with robust features will be more competitive and profitable when working in the modern uncertain environment. Tang (2006a) pointed that the application of robust approaches would be accepted by firms only if two conditions are satisfied. The first is the system efficiency, which enables a firm to handle daily operational risks efficiently without causing much cost for backup policies. The second is the system resiliency, which enables a firm to sustain its operation during severe disruption risks and make it recover quickly from disruptions. The robust approaches applied in supply chain risk management can be also classified into several types. Tang (2006a) listed four management aspects for classifying the robust approaches: demand management, production management, supply management, and information management.

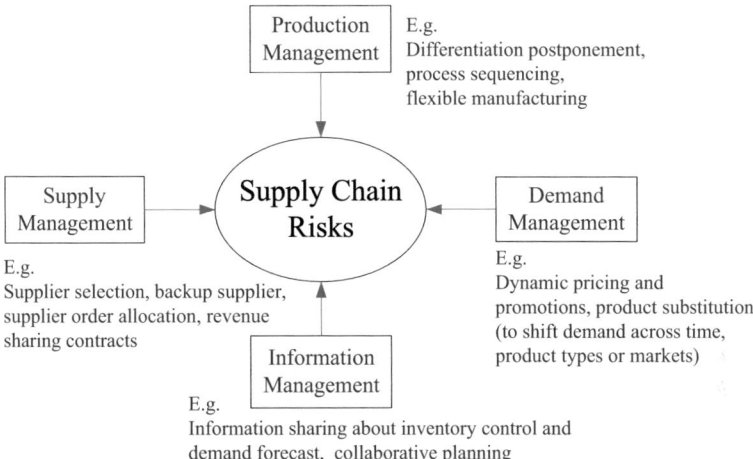

Figure 2.1: Robust approaches from 4 management aspects (revised based on Tang(2006))

In Figure 2.1, we illustrate the four basic management aspects and typical robust approaches of each aspect (the diagram is revised based on Tang's study (Tang 2006a)). For example, to set backup suppliers, to allocate material supply orders between different suppliers according to their prices or reliability, to make revenue-sharing contracts between the supplier and the manufacturer to improve their cooperation, are typical robust approaches in the supply management aspect. The changes of the product price and the sale promotion are both familiar measures the customers can see in the market, they are actually the robust approaches in the demand management aspect. In the production management aspect, especially when using the assembly line or mixed-model production line, the robust approaches such as the postponement of the differentiation point, the flexible process sequence or manufacturing modules will benefit the manufacturer's performance in the uncertain environment. The robust approaches in the information management aspect contain also a variety of types, the most famous and basic approach is information sharing. To share the information about the inventory status, the machine processing status, the customer demand changes among the supply chain members, will significantly reduce the bullwhip-effect (Lee, Padmanabhan and Whang 1997) and enhance the supply chain partners collaboration, finally improve the performance of the entire supply chain. The role of information sharing is especially important and valuable when the environment contains uncertainties. More information about the robust approaches from the four aspects can be found in Tang (2006a).

2.2 Development of Kanban systems

Different from the current trend of designing robust features for supply chains, over the past decades, traditional supply chains pursued fast and cost-effective features to control the material flow. For example, the Just-in-time (Groenevelt 1993) philosophy derived from Japanese Toyota Production system (TPS) (Monden 1983; Ohno 1988) since 1950s is a typical control policy in this direction. Kanban policy was designed with the purpose of reducing the waste and improving the production system efficiency. Later in western industries, the concept "Just-in-Time" was extended to a comprehensive philosophy "lean" (Krafcik 1988; Womack, Jones, Roos and Technology 1990; Zipkin 1991; Askin and Goldberg 2002; Arnold and Furmans 2006), with emphasis on improving efficiency of material flow, decreasing waste, preserving values with less work. Lean philosophy includes a set of lean manufacturing tools, such as cellular manufacturing, pull mechanism, total quality management, rapid setup, production leveling and so forth. The famous Kanban control policy (Kimura and Terada 1981; Zipkin 1989) is essentially a tool of the pull mechanism. Toyota Production System uses Kanban to control the material flow in a production line; Kanban cards are employed to authorize the production and release material into each production stage.

In a pull system, the supply or process at the upstream stage is determined by downstream demand information. By contrast, in a push system, the upstream-side production is decided depending on the demand forecast and former production plans. Comparing the pull and push systems, several advantages of the pull system can be observed over the push system. First, the pull system is easier to implement than the push system, because the push system requires forecast information and production plans in advance while the pull system does not. Secondly, the inventory can be easily controlled and bounded by the number of Kanbans in the pull system. Thirdly, there is less congestion in the pull system. So once some failures or changes occur in a pull system, to detect the changes is much easier than in the push system. More details about the comparison between pull and push systems can be found in Spearman's research (Spearman and Zazanis 1992; Spearman 1992).

Generally, the researches on Kanban-controlled systems (Berkley 1992; Dallery and Gershwin 1992; Huang and Kusiak 1996; Akturk and Erhun 1999; Kumar and Panneerselvam 2007) are concerned with the following issues: model a Kanban system using different techniques, compare pull Kanban systems with push systems, compare different variations of Kanban systems, determine optimal parameter settings of Kanban systems, investigate the Kanban system application in realistic problems, and so on.

The modeling approaches of Kanban-controlled systems can be classified into three basic types: deterministic model (e.g. mathematical programming, Toyota formula (Monden 1983)), stochastic model (e.g. queueing model, Markov chains), and simulation model. For example, Rees Philipoom et al (1987) investigated the factors which could affect the number of Kanbans in a production system; the number of Kanbans was determined depending on the Toyota formula. Then, Rees (1987) extended the Toyota method; it used the estimated lead time to adjust the Kanban number dynamically. Bitran (1987) formulated a mathematical programming model to determine the optimal parameter setting for a deterministic multi-stage assembly-structure Kanban system. Berkley (1991) considered the serial line dual-Kanban system as a generalized tandem queue, thus the queueing theory can be used to measure approximately the Kanban system performance. Buzacott (1989b) developed a linked queueing network model to describe Kanban system behavior. Hodgson Deleersnyder et al (1989) developed a discrete-time Markov process model to analyze the operation of the Kanban mechanism. George Mitwasi Askin et al (1993) built a continuous-time Markov model for a multi-stage multi-product JIT system; through analyzing the steady state of the model, the optimal Kanban number can be then determined. Frein Di Mascolo et al (1996) modeled a queueing network with synchronization

15

mechanisms for a single-product multi-stage serial line Kanban system. They proposed practical approximation methods to determine the parameters of each stage by considering each stage as a sub-system. Baynat, Dallery et al (2001) treated the Kanban system as a multi-class queueing network, and developed analytical approximation methods which can be used to analyze more general Kanban systems. Wang and Sarker (2006) modeled a multi-stage supply chain system which was operated under the JIT delivery policy as a Kanban system, then formulated a mixed-integer nonlinear programming (MINLP) model to the determine the optimal Kanban number, optimal batch size, and other parameters of interest.

Many analytical models and methods for Kanban systems, as mentioned above, are accompanied with simulation-based validation or experiment work. Besides, there exist also pure simulation-based researches concerned with Kanban systems. The simulation approach is quite useful when the studied model or problem is too complex, such as comparing the push and pull systems, comparing different variations of Kanban systems, or measuring the impact of different control factors in the Kanban system (Huang, Rees and Taylor 1983; Krajewski, King, Ritzman and Wong 1987; Philipoom, Rees, Taylor and Huang 1987; Bonvik, Couch and Gershwin 1997). King, Krajewski et al (1987) conducted comprehensive experiments based on simulation models to investigate the impact of various control factors in Kanban systems. Factors like setup time, lot size, production rate, worker flexibility, production structure and degree of standardization were suggested as high-impact factors by Krajewski; while inventory record inaccuracy, machine failure and vendor reliability were found less important than the former factors according to the simulation observation. These results suggest that the inherent nature of the manufacturing system is more important the production control methods in affecting the system performance. Couch Bonvik et al (1997) performed also extensive simulation experiments to compare the performance of several pull mechanism policies, including Kanban, bases tock, CONWIP, hybrid Kanban-CONWIP policies. Their study was carried out with a serial-line production system model; the environment contained constant or changing demand rates. After the experiments, they concluded that the hybrid policies would generally give better performance than other policies.

The success of Toyota Production System has triggered various development of the pull mechanism-based system. As illustrated in Figure 2.2, we summarize the development using a framework. The various modified pull systems are classified into different groups in the diagram. Among them, the "Kanban policy" (denoted by K) and "base-stock policy" (denoted by B) are two basic control mechanisms of pull systems. The other control mechanisms can be seen as variations based on the two basic mechanisms; they added some new features to the two basic mechanisms. In the following text, we will introduce the various pull systems with more details.

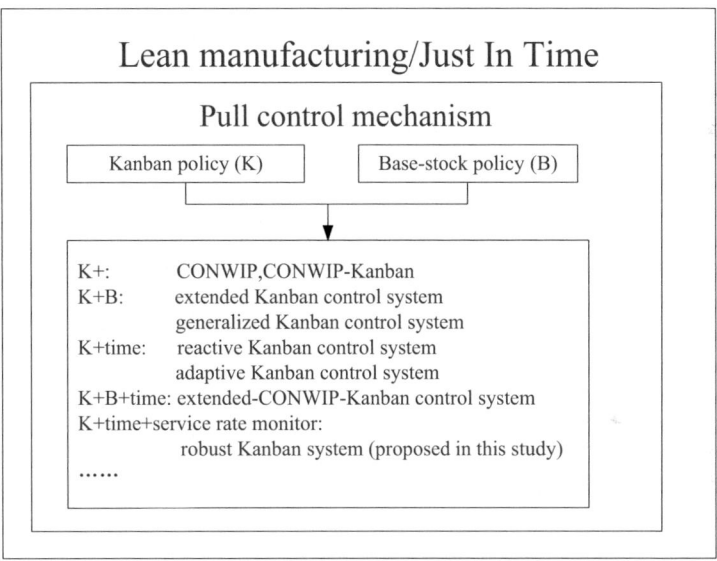

Figure 2.2: Variations of Kanban-controlled systems based on the pull mechanism

The Kanban policy is known as the most famous and typical tool of implementing the pull mechanism. Besides, many other control policies are also developed based on the pull mechanism. For example, the famous inventory control policy "base stock", is considered as an important policy of the pull mechanism as well. The base stock policy is derived from traditional inventory control models (Clark and Scarf 1960; Kimball 1988;

Axsaeter 2000). It can be seen as a special case of (s,S) policy (for the case s=S). In a pull system, the inventory in the output buffer of a stage is controlled within a specific range if using the base stock policy. Once the current inventory is found lower than the target level (base stock level), the upstream production or supply will be triggered to fill the gap.

The Kanban policy (K) and the base stock policy (B) are two basic and important tools of implementing the pull mechanism. Both of them have some advantages and disadvantages. With the Kanban control policy, the inventory at each stage is bounded by the number of Kanbans at that stage, and the production pace is controlled by Kanbans, too. Due to these features, the production cycle time and the inventory level can be easily maintained at a suitable level under Kanban control. These are the advantages of the Kanban policy. However, the disadvantages of Kanban systems also exist. Although the Kanban system can work well in a repetitive or stable environment, in the uncertain environment where the demand rate or process time is varying, the traditional Toyota Kanban system cannot retain a satisfactory performance level any more. It is because the Kanbans at each stage play two roles simultaneously: to limit the amount of Work-In-Process (WIP), and to provide inventory in the buffer to cushion the demand variability. When the environment is repetitive, the Kanban system can select a small Kanban number to operate the system in an efficient manner. Thus, the system can keep a low inventory level to cover the demand variability with achieving a high service level; and the inventory holding cost can be maintained at a low level due to the limited WIP amount. Therefore, the Kanban system can work efficiently in a stable environment. However, when the environment is uncertain like high variability is involved in demand or process, the Kanban system need to hold a high inventory level in the buffer to cushion the supply or demand changes. It therefore requires a large Kanban number. While on the other side, the requirement of reducing inventory cost still calls for a small Kanban number. The two opposite requirements about the parameter Kanban number cannot be satisfied together; therefore the Kanban system cannot perform well in the uncertain environment. In addition, the risk-response actions taken by the Toyota Kanban system could be slow and not effective, because the downstream demand information can be only transmitted upstream (from neighbor to neighbor) through the number and arriving rate of

Kanban cards. If the behavior of moving Kanbans is not quick enough, or the number of Kanbans is limited which cannot reflect the entire demand change, the response action delay will be inevitably caused. Also, as Lee (1997) stated, if we make inventory control decisions only based on the demand of the immediate downstream stage, the real demand change of customers will be distorted. Namely the Bullwhip effect will be caused. Besides, the response actions adopted by Kanban systems could be not effective for only the releasing or halting Kanbans actions can be taken in response to risks, which cannot significantly change the service rate.

The advantages of the base stock policy are also obvious. This policy can avoid the delay in transmitting the demand information from downstream to upstream stages (this is a disadvantage of the Kanban system), because the information about each demand order can be immediately sent to every stage upon its arrival at the customer stage. Then, the system can immediately adjust the current inventory level according to the received demand information. The response action can be taken quickly in response to the changes in the environment. This is the advantage of the base-stock policy. Nevertheless, the disadvantage of it is also noticeable. The amount of inventory at each stage cannot be bounded within an expected range when using the base-stock policy. This may cause the waste of keeping high-level inventory, especially when the environment is uncertain. Imagine that when a stage in the supply chain is blocked due to risks like machine breakdown. In this situation, the upstream stages will still produce redundant goods, regardless of the goods congestion occurring in front of the blocked stage; the redundant inventory will cause much cost of holding unnecessary inventory.

Seeing the advantages and limitations of the Kanban policy and the base-stock policy in the uncertain environment, many variations of the pull system are developed to combine the merits of Kanban and base-stock policies, with the aim of achieving a better performance level in the uncertain environment. As illustrated in Figure 2.2, a series of modified pull systems is given in the diagram. All the modified systems are designed based on the two basic mechanisms (Kanban, Base-stock) and meanwhile involving some new design features, such as to combine Kanban and base-stock policies (K+B), to use Kanban policy with considering the time factor (K+time), to integrate the Kanban and base-stock policies and the time factor together (K+B+time). In the following text, we will explain the design motive and control techniques of the Kanban system variations with more details.

Denoted by K+ in Figure 2.2, it means the modified Kanban systems that are built mainly based on the Kanban mechanism plus some small modifying features. The main disadvantage of the Kanban system is the delayed and limited response actions taken by the upstream stages when changes occurred in the downstream side. To overcome the limitations, Woodruff and Spearman et al. (1990) proposed a CONWIP (constant Work In Process) Kanban model. This new model can be seen as a special case of the original Kanban system, because it considers the entire manufacturing system as a single-stage Kanban system. Thus, the total number of WIP (Work In Process) is kept constant by the number of Kanbans which are cycling in the whole system. In the single-stage Kanban system, the demand information from downstream customers can be immediately transmitted to the upstream stages, then it triggers the release of new material into the system. Using the CONWIP mechanism in the Kanban system, the delay in transmitting downstream demand information can be avoided. However, with such centralized control policy, the operating details of each stage cannot be observed. It is to some extent like a push system, just the demand forecast information used in the push system is now replaced by the demand data in the CONWIP system. Therefore, the CONWIP system has the same shortcoming with the push system. Couch, Bonvik et al (1997) proposed a CONWIP-Kanban model combing the Kanban system and CONWIP together; but there still remains the shortcoming of demand information delay, especially when the customer demand is uncertain.

Based on the K+ systems, more complex and flexible pull system models were developed in the consideration of combining Kanban and base-stock policies (denoted by K+B in Figure 2.2), such as extended Kanban control systems (Frein, Di Mascolo and Dallery 1995; Dallery and Liberopoulos 2000) and generalized Kanban control systems (Buzacott 1989a). In these modified Kanban systems, the positive features of Kanban and base-stock policies can be combined. The production at each stage is now controlled by two parameters: the Kanban number and the target inventory level (base-stock level). The control mechanism of the extended Kanban control system is relatively less complex than the generalized Kanban control system. The demand information flow in the extended Kanban system is directly transmitted to each stage as global information. By contrast, in the generalized Kanban system, the demand information is transmitted from downstream stages to upstream stages one by one; thus the information delay is inevitably incurred (this is the limitation of the generalized Kanban system). However, the extended Kanban system has also drawbacks. For example, the value of parameter "Kanban number" at a specific stage should be greater than the value of parameter "base stock level" at the same stage, to ensure that the available Kanban number at that stage is above zero. This constraint to some extent narrows the range of Kanban number, because the Kanban number should be set always larger than the inventory level. In contrast, in the more complex generalized Kanban system, there are not such constraints.

In general, the modified pull systems are more complex than the systems using pure Kanban or pure base-stock policies in both design and application phases. Seeing the prosperous development of Kanban system variations, a lot of study concerned with comparing the Kanban system variations also emerged (Bonvik, Couch and Gershwin 1997; Duri, Frein and Di Mascolo 2000; Karaesmen and Dallery 2000; Liberopoulos and Dallery 2000; Geraghty and Heavey 2005). Karaesmen and Dallery (2000) did a performance comparison study about four pull systems: the Kanban system, the base stock system, the generalized Kanban system, and the extended Kanban system. It was claimed that the latter two systems did not necessarily perform significantly better than the former two systems for a specific scenario, because in some stable scenarios the two simple control policies (Kanban, base-stock) are very efficient in application. Nevertheless, the extended Kanban and generalized Kanban systems can achieve a good performance level over all scenarios. Namely, they are more robust than the two simple policies in an overall view.

Afterwards, Boonlertvanich (2005) developed a more general and deliberate Kanban model using also combined policies, it is called Extended-CONWIP-Kanban (ECK) control system. The ECK system uses Kanban, base stock, and CONWIP policies simultaneously to control the material flow. In the system, the parameters "base stock level" and "number of Kanbans" are designed to be adjustable during the system operation, which implies that the time factor is taken into account. Thus in Figure 2.2, this model is denoted by the type "K+B+time". Through comprehensive simulation-based comparisons and analysis, it was concluded that, with providing a more flexible and robust adjusting mechanism, the Extended-CONWIP-Kanban control system could perform better (higher service level, lower inventory level, less sensitive to the changes in the environment) than the previous modified Kanban system models. Boon-lertvanich's Kanban system model is more flexible and robust than the previous Kanban models for it contains the good merits of them.

However, there remain limitations of the ECK system. For example, the mechanism of adjusting-two parameters (total Kanban number, base stock level) used in the single-stage ECK system model can only response to some demand-side risks. The ECK system can change parameters "Kanban number" and "base stock level" as response actions to deal with the demand fluctuation risks. However, the environment may include not only demand-side risks, there are many risks from process and supply sides, such as the machine processing time variation, material supply shortage. Furthermore, although changing the parameters "Kanban number" and "base stock level" can help the system deal with slight operational risks, only adjusting the two parameters is not effective for handling larger disruptions. The limitations motivate the study in this dissertation. We propose a new robust mechanism for the Kanban-controlled supply chain system to deal with risks. The new model considers not only demand-side but also process-side or supply-side risks from an uncertain environment, and the risks include both disruptions and operational risks.

Except combining the Kanban policy and base-stock policy, other methods for designing more robust pull systems are also studied in vast literature.

Sanchez Moeeni at al (1997) employed the Taguchi robust parameter design methodology to determine the control factors and parameters for a multi-stage Kanban system which is operated in an uncertain environment. The study is carried out based on simulation, the techniques of experiment design and analysis are applied to analyze the factor effects on system performance. Variations in demand time, process time and material supply time are selected as noise factors for the experiment; the control factors are Kanban number, review period and container size at each stage. Depending on simulation experiment results, the robust parameter configuration for the Kanban system can be accordingly determined. Moeeni's work provided a new perspective for the decision-making on Kanban parameters. However, unlike other modified pull systems that add new features to the operating mechanism, Moeeni's model did not modify the original working mechanism of the traditional Toyota Kanban system. The model just selected the best parameter setting out of different possible combinations. It can be seen as a static parameter design method with the aim of optimizing the expected performance results across a range of risk scenarios, for the parameter values are held fixed during the system operation.

Different from the above static parameter design methods, some researchers developed dynamical parameter design methods for building robust Kanban systems. If the Kanban system can dynamically change parameters as the risk situation varies, the system performance would be robust to the risks in the uncertain environment. Thus, to design such a dynamical robust mechanism will be a promising direction for Kanban systems working in the modern uncertain environment. The researches from Takahashi et al (1999, 2003) and Tardif and Maaseidvaag (2001) followed this direction of dynamical parameter design. In both researches, the number of Kanbans is designed as a flexible parameter, which can be dynamically changed during the system operation. In another word, they consider the parameter "Kanban number" and the factor "time" simultaneously as control factors when running the Kanban system. The symbol "K+time" in Figure 2.2 just corresponds to this type of Kanban systems.

Takahashi and Nakamura (1999) firstly proposed a reactive Kanban system, which can dynamically change the Kanban number when monitoring the demand data series (exponentially smoothed demand interarrival time). They employed the concept "control limits" from traditional statistical control charts to define the upper and lower bounds of the normal demand interarrival time values. Later, Takahashi (2003) modified his demand time-based reactive Kanban control mechanism to build a new inventory-based reactive Kanban system. In the new Kanban system, the Kanban number is also supposed to be able to change dynamically in response to unstable changes in demand, just the data monitoring is taken depending on smoothed and scaled inventory level of finished goods. Control limits are also employed to define the normal range of the inventory level. If the inventory level is detected being out-

23

side the normal range, an unstable change is thought to be happening to the system; and the reactive Kanban system would correspondingly add/extract a Kanban into/from the Kanban system as the risk-response action.

Tardif and Maaseidvaag (2001) proposed another dynamical model, named inventory-based adaptive Kanban control system. The system can change the Kanban number at some time points. Upon each demand arrival, it will check the inventory backlog level of finished product, then decide whether to change the Kanban number. Similar to the above reactive Kanban system, in the active Kanban system there exist also an upper bound (Kanban extract threshold) and a lower bound (Kanban release threshold) for determining when to extract or release Kanban from/into the current Kanban system. Through numerical experiments, it was shown that the adaptive Kanban system could achieve a better performance level than the traditional Toyota Kanban system, if the Kanban system is built as a single-stage M/M closed queue model (M/M means the service time and demand interarrival time are both exponentially distributed). Sivakumar and Shahabudeen (2009) continued the study on adaptive Kanban system with extending the single-stage model to a multi-stage Kanban system, and they obtained similar conclusions.

The Kanban system models designed with dynamical parameters, such as the above-introduced adaptive and reactive Kanban systems, have attracted more research attention in recent decades. Nevertheless, the Kanban systems with dynamical parameter design have both pros and cons. The advantages of dynamical Kanban systems are obvious: the system parameters can be dynamically changed in response to different risk situations. However, the disadvantages of them are also noticeable: the parameters like "control limits" (to control the inventory level, or control demand interarrival time) can be set properly only when sufficient information is given. The information could be a large amount of simulation experiment results, or historical data in practice.

For example, in the above two dynamical Kanban system models, before one can successfully apply the adaptive or reactive Kanban systems, many simulation results need to be collected. In the reactive Kanban system, a great number of simulation runs should be conducted for each possible demand rate scenario, to generate the control limits curves. The experiment work is time-consuming, which makes the control limit parameters difficult to obtain. In the adaptive Kanban system, the thresholds of releasing and capturing Kanban (or the control limits of inventory level) are also determined based on enormous simulation results.

In general, a lot of experiment or simulation work will be done for determining the control limits. Especially when the working conditions are not sufficient (e.g. the working time is urgent, or the information of demand time and process time data are limited), the shortcomings of the dynamical Kanban system models will become more obvious. This is the main disadvantage of the above dynamical Kanban systems. Except the requirement of enormous simulation results, other shortcomings may also exist. For instance, the adaptive Kanban system is designed to adjust the Kanban number depending on the observation of the exact inventory level, but not the smoothed inventory level (which was used in the former reactive Kanban system). However, the observation of the exact inventory level may lead to over reactions in response to risks, because the exact inventory level may vary strikingly in a wide range. If we observe the exact inventory data just for a short time, the conclusion of detecting unstable demand changes could be wrong due to some accidental demand fluctuation. In contrast, if we observe the inventory data for a longer period with using some smoothing or average calculation methods, the smoothed inventory level will remain in a relatively small and stable range, then the information distortion caused by the demand variability can be reduced. Thus, we can get a more accurate judge on the inventory change and the system operating status. In sum, only observing the exact inventory level is not a good method for judging the system status, it may distort the real varying trend of customer demand. Hence, there is room for improvement for the current inventory-based monitor method.

As discussed above, the requirement of enormous simulation or experiment work in these dynamical Kanban system models limits their application in practice. On the other side, the limitation also provides a good direction for the future development of robust Kanban models. Can we design and apply a robust mechanism for Kanban systems to handle a wider range of risks, with less simulation work? This question is the motivation of the work in this dissertation. It sheds light on the work of developing a "lighter" (with less simulation experiments) robustly designed Kanban system, which can systematically and dynamically changing system parameters to hedge against more risks in the uncertain environment. The notation "K +time +service rate monitor" in Figure 2.2 just denotes the new robust Kanban system model proposed in this study. We will present the design and development procedures of the robust Kanban system model in the following chapters.

3 Robust Kanban System model formulation

In this chapter, we first introduce the design procedures of the robust Kanban system model, then explain how a Kanban system works with the proposed risk-response mechanism. The model is a multi-stage single-product supply chain system working based on the Kanban mechanism; a variety of risks is incorporated in the system operating environment. We first design a conceptual framework of the robust Kanban system, then build a simulation model to study its performance.

The rest of the chapter is organized as follows. First, in Section 3.1, we give a brief introduction of the background knowledge about the Kanban-controlled supply chain, and list questions about developing the risk-response mechanism. These can be seen as preparation work before the model formulation. Nextly, in Section 3.2, we describe the conceptual model of the robust Kanban system. The system structure and the risk-response mechanism are explained in detail. At last, in Section 3.3, we introduce the procedures of building the simulation model of the robust Kanban system.

3.1 Preliminary

3.1.1 Kanban-controlled supply chain system

Although the Kanban control mechanism was originally applied in production lines, it can be adopted in a wider range across the entire supply chain. As can be seen in Figure 3.1, a typical production line and a typical supply chain have similar system structures: a serial line composed of several functional stages. Both systems can be operated under the Kanban control mechanism. The main difference between them is that the supply chain system works in a more volatile environment with more risks. The supply chain spans a wider range across companies and factories. By contrast, the production line is located in a manufacturing plant where the environment is relatively stable. Since we aim to study a model of a Kanban-controlled supply chain system, a variety of risks is considered in the environment.

In this study, we use an abstract model to describe the Kanban system. Either the production line or the supply chain system can be seen as a special case of the abstract Kanban system model. The model is assumed to be a single-product multi-stage serial-line supply chain system under the Kanban mechanism; two types of Kanban cards (Production Kanban and Transport Kanban) are used at each stage.

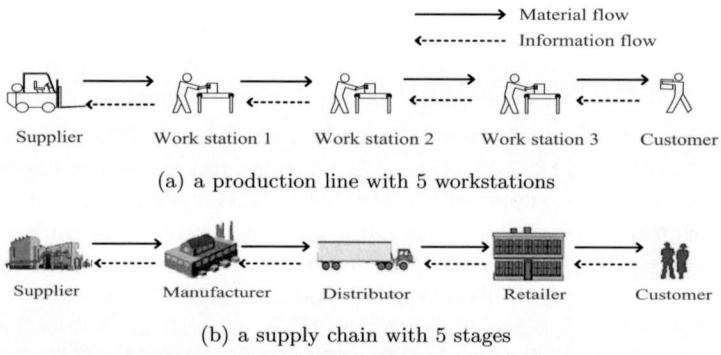

Figure 3.1: Examples of real-world Kanban systems

Figure 3.2 shows the abstract model of the robust Kanban system. Figure 3.2a) presents an overall structure of the Kanban system; and Figure 3.2b) shows the detailed mechanism inside Process-stage 3, it can be seen as a complex queueing network.

The Kanban system is composed of 5 sequential stages. The first stage (upstream side) is the supplier; it supplies material to its downstream manufacturer stages. The end stage (downstream side) is the customer, it generates demand orders of finished product. Inbetween are process stages. Each process stage involves a group of machines and workers to process the material; we call the functional group a "Workcell". Between adjacent stages exist an input buffer (for storing the halted ma-

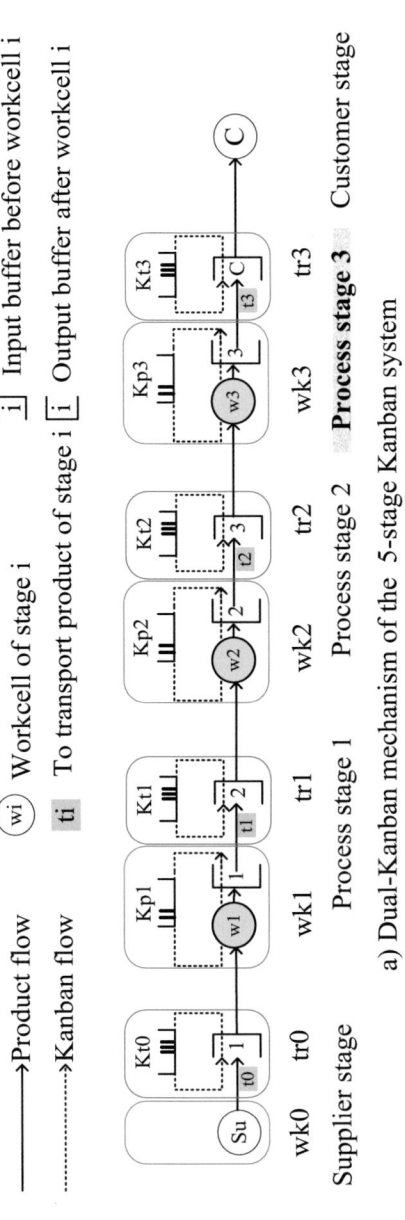

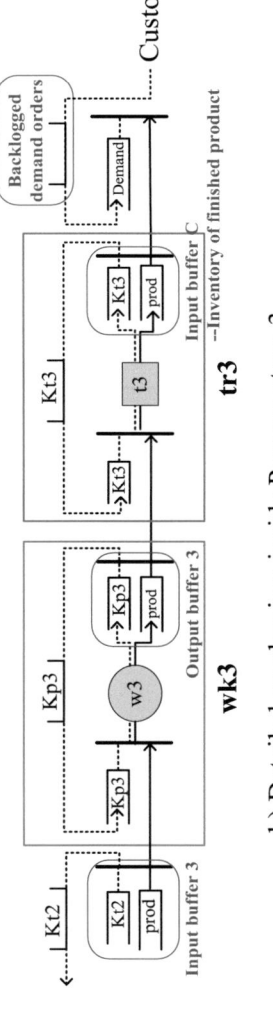

Figure 3.2: The abstract Kanban system model (serial line with 5 stages)

29

terial) and an output buffer (for smoothing the conflict between material supply and demand). All kinds of material movements in the system, (such as to release, to process, to deliver, and to halt the material) are controlled by Production Kanbans and Transport Kanbans.

Take a specific stage i as an example to demonstrate the dual-Kanban working mechanism (refer to Askin (2002)). The material is first released from the preceding stage i-1 to stage i and stored in the input buffer waiting for the process authorization. Then, with a Production Kanban's authorization, the material can be processed at stage i, then stored in the output buffer waiting for downstream demand orders delivered by Transport Kanbans. Finally, the material will be delivered to the succeeding stage i+1 upon a demand arrival. The material-transport between stage i and stage i+1 is defined as the transport module of stage i. Thus, each stage of the Kanban system contains two work modules: production module (wk_i, to process the material at Workcell i), and transport module (tr_i, to transport the material from Stage i to Stage i+1). The maximum inventory level in each buffer (namely the buffer size) is bounded by the number of cyclic Production Kanbans or Transport Kanbans at that stage. In particular, the size of input buffer i is limited by the number of Transport Kanban i-1; and the size of output buffer i is limited by the number of Production Kanban i.

The performance is even worse in a Kanban-controlled supply chain than in a Kanban-controlled production line, because the supply chain spans a wider range across different companies, more risks could happen in the environment. Therefore, the scope of our study is decided to be a Kanban-controlled supply chain system incorporating a variety of risks in the system operation environment. We aim to design a robust mechanism to help the Kanban system hedge against the various risks in the uncertain environment, to overcome the limitations of the traditional Kanban system.

3.1.2 Design questions for risk-response mechanism

In order to design the risk-response mechanism of the robust Kanban system, we should address the following questions as preparation work:

- "What kind of robust approaches should be adopted in the Kanban-controlled supply chain system?" We are concerned about how to select the suitable robust approaches for the system in a general view.

- "Which parameters of the system should be designed as adjustable parameters?" The values of such parameters are supposed to be able to change dynamically during the system operation in order to mitigate the risk impact.

- "How to change the adjustable parameters?" We are concerned about when and how much we should change the parameters, and what decision criteria should be followed.

If we can answer the above questions, the basic framework of the risk-response mechanism can be thus developed for the robust Kanban system.

Question 1: What kinds of robust approaches should be adopted in the Kanban controlled supply chain system?

To answer the first question, some robust approaches from literature are taken into consideration. Based on the four basic aspects of supply chain risk management (demand, supply, information and production management), we select the following robust approaches as preliminary for the robust Kanban system.

1. From the supply aspect: main supplier and backup supplier. Since the material supply shortage and interruption are potential risks, the dual-sourcing supply policy is selected as a robust approach to deal with supply-side risks. We assume that the material supply orders can be allocated between a main supplier and a backup supplier in the robust Kanban system, and the order proportion can be adjusted depending on the risk situation. The main supplier supplies material with a lower price but longer supply time, its supply is supposed to be uncertain with shortage or interruption. By contrast, the backup supplier is more reliable with shorter and reliable supply time, but its material is sold at a higher price. The backup supplier is seen as a strategic-level robust approach.

2. From the demand aspect: dynamical pricing. We can set dynamical prices for finished product sold in the customer market. Thus,

31

the customer demand can be reduced or increased by the higher or lower prices, which could cushion the conflict between supply and demand. (It should be noted that, the dynamical pricing is suggested here as an optional robust approach for the conceptual model of the robust Kanban system, but not executed in the simulation model.)

3. From the information aspect: information sharing among supply chain partners. The robust Kanban is designed to be able to share the information, such as inventory status, production status, supplier supply rates, and customer demand rates, among different supply chain partners. Thus, the information of any new changes at each stage can be transmitted timely to related stages, which improves the cooperation between supply chain partners.

4. From the production aspect: 1) Flexible production rates. The robust Kanban system is designed to adopt flexible production rates, which means it can dynamically change the machine service time and the number of servers (within a specified range) during system operation. When the environment varies, to adjust the production rate will be a good approach to reduce the conflict between supply and demand. 2) Dynamic inventory control. This method is executed based on the Kanban mechanism. When the environment varies, the number of Kanbans at each stage can be changed, thus the amount of inventory in buffers are changed in response to risks.

Some of the above robust approaches are more practical and economical in application. For example, to adjust the number of Production Kanbans in a workcell will cause much less cost and efforts than setting a new server (service facility) in the workcell. Different robust approaches have different control ranges and effects on the system. According to the decision ranges and effects, the supply chain activities can be divided into three levels: strategic, tactical and operational (Ballou 1992; Schmidt and Wilhelm 2000). Referring to the 3-level framework, we divide the proposed robust approaches into three levels as well (see Figure 1.1). Generally, the tactical-level or operational-level approaches are relatively easier and economical to carry out than the strategic-level approaches. The actions taken at the more detailed level will cause less implementing cost, and have smaller impacts on the system operation. For example, adding a new server is considered as a strategic-level approach, and increasing the number of cyclic Kanbans is an operational-level approach.

In between, reducing the machine process time can be seen as a tactical-level approach.

Question 2: Which parameters of the system should be designed as adjustable parameters?

In order to apply the proposed robust approaches in the robust Kanban system, some system parameters are designed to be adjustable during system operation. To change the values of the adjustable parameters means some system elements are modified correspondingly, which implies that related robust approaches are adopted in the system.

As demonstrated in Figure 1.1, the adjustable parameters of the robust Kanban system are selected from the strategic, tactical, and operational levels. The operational-level adjustable parameters are the number of Production Kanbans and the number of Transport Kanbans at each stage. To adjust the Kanban number is easier to execute and it costs less than adjusting other levels' parameters. Meanwhile, it can be seen as a robust approach taken from the production management aspect. In the tactical level, the machine service time is designed to be flexible. We assume that the machine service time can be changed within a reasonable narrow range. Through increasing or decreasing the machine process speed (the reciprocal of single-machine service time), the production rate at the stage can be accordingly modified in a small range, to cushion the conflict between supply and demand. The flexible production rate also represents a production-aspect robust approach. Different from the detailed operational- or tactical-level parameters, the strategic-level parameters characterize the entire Kanban system configuration. In the strategic level, the decision is about such as deciding a suitable supply proportion for backup suppliers, determining a reasonable number of service facilities or their locations. The change of strategic-level parameters has larger influences on the entire system. Implementing the strategic-level decisions will cost much more than implementing the operational- or tactical-level decisions. The adjustable parameter "supply proportion of the backup supplier" can be seen as a supply-aspect robust approach; and the adjustable parameter "number of service facilities" corresponds to a production-aspect robust approach.

Besides the design of 3-level adjustable parameters, in the robust Kanban system, the information about the system operating status (including the demand rate, supply rate, process rate at each stage, inventory and backlog level at each stage) is allowed to be shared among supply chain partners. Thus, the unusual changes and risks happening to the system can be detected and transmitted in time. This is an information-aspect robust approach; it is a very important and widely used approach in robust supply chain design.

In the robust Kanban system model, we plan to adopt the newly designed robust mechanism, called the risk-response mechanism, to control the operation of the system, and help the system deal with the risks in the uncertain environment. In sum, the risk-response mechanism is essentially an adjusting-parameter mechanism. It changes the 3-level adjustable parameters as response actions to mitigate the impact of risks, thus the Kanban system can still perform well in the uncertain environment. The behaviors of changing the 3-level adjustable parameters in the abstract robust Kanban system model can be interpreted as practical approaches in the real-world supply chain. The relationships between the adjusting actions in abstract and real-world Kanban systems are summarized in Table 3.1.

In abstract Kanban system	In Kanban-controlled supply chain
Change Kanban number	Catch/release a Kanban container
Change single-machine service time	Change machine process speed, overtime work
Change number of servers	Start/stop a machine or other service facilities
Choose a backup supplier	Shift material orders among suppliers, make a contract with new suppliers

Table 3.1: Risk-response actions in abstract Kanban system vs. in Kanban-controlled supply chain

Question 3: How to change the adjustable parameters?

After selecting the adjustable parameters for the robust Kanban system, we nextly address the third question: how to adjust the 3-level parameters at the right time and to a proper extent, namely when and how much to adjust the parameters? What are the criteria for us to make the changing-parameter decisions?

We employ two monitor items in the risk-response mechanism to observe and record the system operating status. They can provide useful references for the decision making on adjusting parameters. The first monitor item is inventory-balance monitor (mi_inv), it regularly monitors and records the inventory and backlog level of finished product at the customer stage. The second monitor item is the rate-balance monitor (mi_rate), it is defined as the ratio of demand rate to bottleneck-stage service rate (bottleneck stage is the stage with slowest process rate among all supply chain partners).

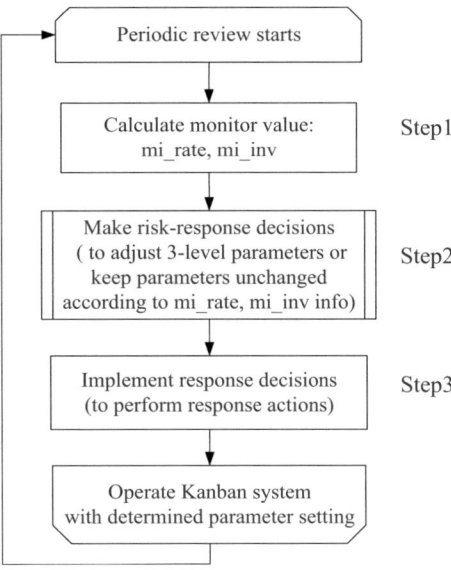

Figure 3.3: Flow chart of the working mechanism of Robust Kanban System

We expect to keep a low inventory level as well as a sufficient supply rate (the supply rate is larger than the customer demand rate) through monitoring the inventory and rate data. The two monitors can reflect real-time system operating status; by using them, the Kanban system is able to detect the risks in time. Then based on the monitor information, we further decide how to change the 3-level adjustable parameters. The decision includes whether or not to change the parameters, which parameters should be changed and to what extent. Through comparing the observed monitor values with predefined control limits parameters, we can finally decide how to change the parameters in response to risks.

During system operation, the information required by two monitors is collected constantly. The procedures of comparing monitor values with their control limits and selecting response actions are taken regularly at the beginning of each review period. A review period is a specific time length, during which the system status will be examined once. It could be set such as one hour, two days, or other values based on the manager's requirement. At the beginning of each review period, the decision "how to adjust 3-level parameters" will be made, then the selected response actions will be carried out from this time point till the beginning of the next review period.

A brief flow chart is given in Figure 3.3, to demonstrate the working principle of the risk-response mechanism of the robust Kanban system. The details about the monitors and decision criteria of the mechanism will be described in Section 3.2.3, after introducing the parameter notation.

In this section, we have answered three questions for designing the risk-response mechanism of the robust Kanban system. With the answers, the framework of the robust Kanban system can be established. In Section 3.2 and 3.3, we will give a more detailed and systematical description of building the robust Kanban system model.

3.2 Conceptual model description

Now we describe the conceptual model of the robust Kanban system in a mathematical form, so that the logic and quantitative relationships of system elements and the working mechanism can be interpreted more accurately. In Section 3.2, we first list the assumptions and restrictions used in the model. Then we introduce the parameters and variables that are used for the model formulation. Lastly, the working steps of the risk-response mechanism are explained in detail.

3.2.1 Assumptions

The assumptions used in the robust Kanban system are as follows:

—Overall assumptions

1 The supply chain system is a single-product, multi-stage (5-stage in the simulation model, including a supplier stage and a customer stage), serial-line system.

2 The system is operated in a finite time horizon, e.g. 5000 time units (in simulation clock).

3 This supply chain system is operated based on the Kanban control mechanism. Two types of Kanbans are used at each stage: Production Kanban and Transport Kanban.

4 At each stage, the number of Production Kanbans and the number of Transport Kanbans can be set arbitrarily. Different stages could use different Kanban numbers. The number of Kanbans at each stage is defined as an adjustable parameter in the robust Kanban system.

5 A demand order or a product unit will be attached with one Kanban card, namely, the Kanban container size is 1.

—Demand assumptions

6 Customer demand is generated at the customer stage (the end of the supply chain). The demand interarrival time is distributed in a stochastic and independent form, for example, the exponential distribution, uniform distribution, gamma distribution, etc. Every customer orders only one unit of product; bulk demand arrivals are not allowed in this model.

7 The customer demand order will be backlogged, if it cannot be satisfied immediately. The backlog order will be suspended in the waiting queue, until available product arrives.

—Supply assumptions

8 The origin of the material flow is the supplier stage. The supplier generates raw material and supplies it to the downstream manufacturer stages. The supplier material supply time is supposed to be either in a stochastic independent distribution like the demand interarrival time, or in a deterministic form with a constant value.

9 Two suppliers are supposed to be able to supply material in the robust Kanban system. One is the main supplier with a lower purchase price but longer material supply time; the other is the backup supplier with a higher purchase price but shorter material supply time. The robust Kanban system is allowed to change the material order proportions of the two suppliers. The supply proportion of the backup supplier is defined as an adjustable parameter in the robust Kanban system model.

—Process assumptions

10 The process time and transport time at each process stage (manufacturer) are supposed to be distributed either in a stochastic independent form like the demand interarrival time, or in a deterministic form with a constant value.

11 The setup time and setup cost are not considered in the robust Kanban system model. There is no batch production; the product is processed singly.

12 Each process stage contains two inventory buffers: an input buffer and an output buffer. The input buffer is put in front of the workcell, it is used to store the material that is delivered from the preceding stage and attached with Transport Kanbans. The output buffer is put behind the workcell for collecting the processed product that is attached with Production Kanbans. The input buffer size is bounded by the number of cyclic Transport Kanbans, and the output buffer size is limited by the number of cyclic Production Kanbans.

13 Each process stage includes two tasks: to process the product in the workcell, and to transport the product from the current workcell to the next workcell. Each task takes specific time and cost.

14 Each workcell is a functional group; it could contain some machines (servers) to process the product. All machines at the same workcell

are supposed to have identical capacities in normal status. The number of machines at a specified stage (usually the bottleneck stage) and the single-machine service time are designed as adjustable parameters in the robust Kanban system.

—**Risk assumptions**

15 The risks occurring in the robust Kanban system could be from three sources: demand side, process side, and supply side. A risk situation is measured with four parameters: location, extent, duration, and probability.

The aim of designing the robust Kanban system is to help the system deal with the various risks in the uncertain environment. Therefore, the risks situations should be clearly defined and described. We use four parameters to describe a risk situation: location, extent, duration, and probability. Using the four parameters, the various risk situations can be clearly distinguished and measured. Hence, a variety of risk situations can be assumed by giving different values to the four parameters.

The detailed explanations of the four risk-measure parameters are summarized in Table 3.2. The parameter "location" indicates the source of the risk; it tells us the risk is from the supplier, the manufacturer, or the customer side. The "extent" means how severe the risk is when comparing it to its normal level. For example, the unusual machine process speed is only 40% of the normal speed (we set Extent=40%). The parameter "duration" specifies how long a risk event will last consecutively. And the parameter "probability" measures how often the risk will occur, it means the proportion of the total risk-occurring time to the entire system operating time. The value of "probability" is dependent on how many times the risk events occur and the "duration" of each event. For example, a risk event "supply interruption" happened to the system. Suppose the system operating time is one year. If the risk event occurred 4 times during a year, and each time the interruption lasted 10 days, namely the "duration" is 10 days, and the "probability" is 10 days*4/365days=10.96%. Another example, if the "supply interruption" happened once in the year, and the event "duration" was 40 days, then the "probability" is 40 days*1/365days=10.96%. Although the total risk-

Parameter	Definition	Descriptive example
Location	Where the risk occurs, from the supplier, process, or customer stage	Unusual supply rate at the supplier stage, Unusual demand rate at the customer stage, Unusual produce rate at the process stage.
Extent	How severe the risk is (comparing to its normal level), slight, serious, or catastrophic	Normal demand rate $=10$ /hr; disrupted demand rate$=12$ /hr (slight risk 120% of the normal level); disrupted demand rate$=30$ /hr(severe risk, 300% of the normal level).
Duration	How long the risk lasts, the lasting time of consecutive risk events	The consecutive unusual demand orders (with shorter or longer inter-arrival time) last 100 hr, namely the risk duration is 100hr.
Probability	How often the risk occurs, the proportion of total risk-occurring time to the total system operating time	Suppose the system operating time $=5000$ hr ; the risk (consecutive demand orders with unusual interarrival time) occurs 2 times, each time the risk duration is 100 hr. Thus the probability is 100*2/5000=4%.

Table 3.2: Four risk-measure parameters in risk situation description

occurring time in the two examples is the same, the impact of the "supply interruption" risks in the two examples could be quite different. If the "supply interruption" lasts for a consecutive 40 days, the order backlog level (number of unfinished demand orders) will be much higher, than in the case where "10 days interruption" and "normal supply" alternate to appear for four times. Therefore, we use both "duration" and "probability" parameters to measure the time of risk occurrence.

Using the four risk-measure parameters, we nextly define the typical risk situations that may happen to the robust Kanban system. As mentioned in Assumpion 15, the risk scenarios considered in the robust Kanban system can be classified into three types: demand-side, process-side, and supply-side. And as listed in Table 3.3, the demand rate fluctuation at the customer stage, the machine service time variation at the bottleneck process stage, and the material supply rate variation at the supplier stage are selected as typical risk situations from the three sides.

Risk source	Risk example	Characteristic parameter
Supply side (upstream)	Uncertain material supply rate, material supply shortage or interruption	Supplier material supply time
Process side (bottleneck process stage)	variation of machine service time, machine breakdown	Machine service time
Demand side (downstream)	Customer demand rate variability	Demand interarrival time

Table 3.3: Three risk sources considered in the robust Kanban system

The location, extent, duration, and probability parameters of each risk situation can be specified, then we add the risk features into the normal demand, process, and supply data series. For example, we make some changes on the data series of customer demand interarrival time (e.g. in a short time length, we set the decreased demand time as 50% of the original demand time), thus the risk occurrence is reflected by the unusual changes of the demand time data.

With the above assumptions and parameter specification, the basic system structure and operating environment of the robust Kanban system have been defined. In the following text, we will systematically describe the system configuration and the risk-response mechanism, after introducing the parameter notation.

3.2.2 Parameters and variables

The notation of parameters and variables is introduced in this section. The notation lists 1, 2, 3, 4 present respectively the information of parameters, decision variables, status variables (including performance measures), and special parameters and variables used in the risk-response mechanism.

41

Notation list 1: parameters

Indices:

i	Index of supply chain stages, $i \in \{0, 1, \ldots, I, c\}$
sc	Index of risk scenarios, $sc \in ScenariosSet$

Deterministic parameters:

T	Total system operating time
t_{review}	Review period length
Ttr_i	Time of transporting product from stage i to stage $i{+}1$
$maxKp_i$	Maximum number of Production Kanbans at stage i
$minKp_i$	Minimum number of Production Kanbans at stage i
$maxKt_i$	Maximum number of Transport Kanbans at stage i
$minKt_i$	Minimum number of Transport Kanbans at stage i
$pricein_{main}$	Material purchase price per product unit from the main supplier
$pricein_{backup}$	Material purchase price per product unit from the backup supplier
$priceout$	Finished product sell price, per product unit
h_i	Inventory holding cost per product unit per time unit at stage i
b_i	Backlog penalty cost per product order per time unit at stage i
cKp_i	Cost of keeping a Production Kanban cyclic at stage i for one time unit
cKt_i	Cost of keeping a Transport Kanban cyclic at stage i for one time unit
$cStime_i$	Cost coefficient of using the given machine process speed per time unit at stage i
$cServer_i$	Cost of operating a server per time unit at stage i
$cSupplier$	Cost of changing the backup supplier supply proportion each time
sl_0	Target customer service level (=number of customer orders filled without delay / total number of customer orders)

Stochastic parameters:

t_d	Demand interarrival time at the customer stage, e.g. t_d follows an exponential distribution with mean t_d^{mean}
ts_i	Disrupted single-machine service time at stage i

tsu_{main}	Material supply time (per product unit) of the main supplier
tsu_{backup}	Material supply time (per product unit) of the backup supplier

As can be seen in Figure 3.2a), the robust Kanban system model is composed of 5 sequential stages, including a supplier stage and a customer stage. Let i index the system stages, $i \in \{0, 1, \ldots, I, c\}$, where $i = 0$ indicates the supplier stage, $i = 1, 2, 3, ..., I$ indicates the i-th process stage of the supply chain, and $i = c$ signifies the customer stage.

Except the customer stage that is responsible for generating demand orders, each of the remaining stages contains two functional modules: the process module (denoted by Workcell wk_i) and the transport module (denoted by tr_i).

Generally, we use deterministic parameters to specify the system configuration. The cost coefficients of operating service equipment $(c_{Kanban}, c_{stime}, c_{server}, c_{supplier})$ are designed as deterministic parameters. The inventory holding cost rate (h_i) and order backlog penalty cost rate (b_i) at stage i are also deterministic. Moreover, the allowable ranges of adjusting the 3-level parameters, the baseline machine service time $(Ts0_i)$ are defined as deterministic parameters, too. Their values are given based on practical situations or the designer's requirement. A complete summary of the deterministic parameters used in the robust Kanban system is given in Notation list 1.

We also employ stochastic parameters and variables to describe the risk situations in the robust Kanban system. A variety of risk situations is considered to represent the uncertain environment; they are indexed by the parameter sc, where $sc \in ScenariosSet$. We select some typical risk scenarios to compose the Scenarios Set. In this set, for example, demand+ signifies a "demand rate increase" scenario, supply- represents a "supply rate decrease" scenario. Since the risks could be from demand, process, and supply sides, we assume related characteristic parameters such as the demand interarrival time (t_d), actual machine process time at stage i (ts_i), supplier material supply time $(tsu_{main}, tsu_{backup})$ as stochastic parameters. The stochastic parameters used in the robust Kanban system are also summarized in Notation list 1.

Notation list 2: decision variables

Kp_i Number of Production Kanbans at stage i
         $Kp_i \in [\min Kp_i, maxKp_i]$, integer, e.g. $Kp_i \in [5, 10]$

Kt_i Number of Transport Kanbans at stage i
         $Kt_i \in [\min Kt_i, maxKt_i]$, integer, e.g. $Kt_i \in [4, 12]$

Ts_i Standard single-machine service time at stage i
         $s_i \in \{Ts_{\min}, Ts_0, Ts_{\max}\}$, discrete value, Ts_0 is a baseline value (constant) of the machine process time, e.g. $Ts_i \in \{80\%Ts_0, Ts_0, 120\%Ts_0\}$

Ns_i Number of in-use servers at stage i
         $Ns_i \in [Ns_{\min}, Ns_{\max}]$, integer, e.g. $Ns_i \in [1, 3]$

pr_{backup} Material supply proportion from the backup supplier, $pr_{backup} \in [pr_{low}, pr_{high}]$, continuous value, e.g. $pr_{backup} \in [0, 0.5]$. Define $T_{su} = pr_{backup} \cdot tsu_{backup} + (1 - pr_{backup}) \cdot tsu_{main}$, then T_{su} means the actual material supply time at the supplier stage

The variables used in the robust Kanban system include two types: decision variables and status variables. Decision variables refer to the variables whose values should be decided by the manager. In the robust Kanban system, four types of variables are designed as decision variables, they correspond to the formerly selected 3-level adjustable parameters. They are the Kanban number (Kp_i, Kt_i), standard single-machine service time (Ts_i), number of servers (Ns_i) at stage i, and the material supply proportion from the backup supplier (pr_{backup}). The information of the decision variables is summarized in Notation list 2.

Notation list 3: status parameters and variables

Status parameters:

t Current operating time, $t \in [0, T]$

n Index of generated customer demand orders, $n \in \{1, \ldots, N\}$

Status variables (directly observed):

$N(t)$ Number of generated customer orders at time t

$B(t)$ Number of unfinished customer orders (Backlog) at time t

$I(t)$	Inventory level (of finished product) at customer stage at time t
$IB(t)$	Inventory-backlog level of finished product at customer stage at time t, $IB(t) = I(t) - B(t)$
$Iin_i(t)$	Input buffer inventory level at stage i at time t
$Iout_i(t)$	Output buffer inventory level at stage i at time t
$I_i(t)$	$I_i(t) = Iin_i(t) + Iout_i(t)$
wt_n	Waiting time of the n-th customer order
$t_d(n)$	Demand interarrival time of the n-th customer order
$Q_{main}(t)$	Number of orders supplied by the main supplier
$Q_{backup}(t)$	Number of orders supplied by the backup supplier
$Kp_i(t)$	Value of Kp_i at time t
$Kt_i(t)$	Value of Kt_i at time t
$Ts_i(t)$	Value of Ts_i at time t
$Ns_i(t)$	Value of Ns_i at time t
$N_{su}(t)$	Counts of changing backup supplier proportion till time t
$T_{su}(t)$	Actual supplier material supply time at time t

Status variables (calculated):

$N(t) - B(t)$	Number of accomplished customer orders at time t
$N_{nodelay}(t)$	Number of customer orders filled without delay(waiting time=0) till time t

$$N_{nodelay}(t) = \sum_{n=1}^{n=N(t)} Y_n, \text{ where } Y_n = \begin{cases} 1, & if \, wt_n = 0 \\ 0, & if \, wt_n > 0 \end{cases}$$

$sl(t)$	Actual customer order fill rate at time t (proportion of the customer orders filled without delay), $sl(t) = \frac{N_{nodelay}(t)}{N(t)}$
$\overline{wt}(t)$	Mean waiting time of customer orders at time t, $\overline{wt}(t) = \frac{\sum_{n=1}^{n=N(t)} wt_n}{N(t)}$
$\overline{B}(t)$	Mean backlog level of customer orders at time t, $\overline{B}(t) = \frac{\int_0^t B(y)dy}{t}$
$\overline{I}(t)$	Mean inventory level of finished product (at customer stage) at time t, $\overline{I}(t) = \frac{\int_0^t I(y)dy}{t}$
$\overline{Iin_i}(t)$	Mean inventory level in the input buffer at stage i at time t, $\overline{Iin_i}(t) = \frac{\int_0^t Iin_i(y)dy}{t}$
$\overline{Iout_i}(t)$	Mean inventory level in the output buffer at stage i at time t, $\overline{Iout_i}(t) = \frac{\int_0^t Iout_i(y)dy}{t}$
$\overline{I_i}(t)$	$\overline{I_i}(t) = \overline{Iin_i}(t) + \overline{Iout_i}(t)$
$cost_{inv}$	Time-averaged inventory holding cost of the entire system

$$cost_{inv} = \sum_{i=1}^{i=I} h_i [\overline{Iin_i}(T) + \overline{Iout_i}(T)] + h_c \cdot \overline{I}(T)$$

$cost_{backlog}$	Time-averaged backlog penalty cost of the entire system $cost_{backlog} = b_c \cdot \overline{B}(T)$
$\overline{Kp_i}$	Time-averaged value of $Kp_i(t)$ over the whole operating time T, $\overline{Kp_i} = \frac{\int_0^T Kp_i(t)dt}{T}$
$\overline{Kt_i}$	Time-averaged value of $Kt_i(t)$ over the whole operating time T, $\overline{Kt_i} = \frac{\int_0^T Kt_i(t)dt}{T}$
$\overline{Ts_i}$	Time-averaged value of $Ts_i(t)$ over the whole operating time T, $\overline{Ts_i} = \frac{\int_0^T Ts_i(t)dt}{T}$
$\overline{Ns_i}$	Time-averaged value of $Ns_i(t)$ over the whole operating time T, $\overline{Ns_i} = \frac{\int_0^T Ns_i(t)dt}{T}$
$cost_{Kanban}$	Time-averaged operating cost of Kanban $$cost_{Kanban} = \sum_{i=1}^{I} cKp_i \cdot \overline{Kp_i} + \sum_{i=0}^{I} cKt_i \cdot \overline{Kt_i}$$
$cost_{stime}$	Time-averaged operating cost of machine service rate $$cost_{stime} = \sum_{i=1}^{I} \frac{cStime_i}{Ts_i}$$
$cost_{server}$	Time-averaged operating cost of in-use servers $$cost_{server} = \sum_{i=1}^{I} cServer_i \cdot \overline{Ns_i}$$
$cost_{supplier}$	Time-averaged operating cost of changing supplier proportions, $cost_{supplier} = cSupplier \cdot Nsu(T)/T$
$cost_{change3level}$	Time-averaged operating cost of 3-level adjustable parameters, $cost_{change3level} = cost_{Kanban} + cost_{stime} + cost_{server} + cost_{supplier}$
$cost_{purchase}$	Time-averaged cost of purchasing material from suppliers, $cost_{purchase} = [pricein_{main} \cdot Q_{main}(T) + pricein_{backup} \cdot Q_{backup}(T)]/T$
$Income_{mean}$	Time-averaged total income, from selling finished product to customers, $Income_{mean} = priceout \cdot [N(t) - B(t)]/T$
$Netprofit_{mean}$	Time-averaged total net profit of operating the robust Kanban system, $Netprofit_{mean} = Income_{mean} - cost_{purchase} - cost_{change3level} - cost_{inv} - cost_{backlog}$

Different from decision variables, status variables need not to be determined arbitrarily, their values are dependent on other parameters and variables. The status variables are used for describing the system operating status. We can calculate their values based on the relationships between system elements and the values of related parameters or variables. The system performance measures, such as the inventory level and the customer waiting time, are examples of status variables. If we simulate the Kanban system operation, some output data of system elements can be seen as status variables. For example, the number of product units stored in the customer input buffer, can be recorded as the status variable "inventory level of finished product". Besides the directly observed status variables, the values of some status variables can be known only after calculation, such as the total operating cost, which is a sum of several detailed operating cost items.

In Notation list 3, we summarize the status parameters and variables involved in the robust Kanban system model. Some status variables of them are selected as performance measures for the system, more explanations will be given in the following text.

In order to observe the system behavior, some status variables are selected as quantitative performance measures. Some are direct output data of system elements, and others are summary statistics. The performance measures are selected from two aspects. The first is the manufacturer's requirement. Manufacturers aim to minimize the cost of operating the entire Kanban system (e.g. $cost_{purchase}$, $cost_{change3level}$, $cost_{inv}$) and maximize the gained net profit. In the following work, we denote the net profit data by a response variable "Netprofit" (also $Netprofit_{mean}$), which refers to the time-averaged net profit obtained from operating the robust Kanban system. By contrast, the second aspect is the customer's requirement. The customers care about whether the system can provide satisfactory service. Here we define the order fill rate as the customer service level (β-type service level), namely, the ratio of the number of customer orders filled without delay to the total number of demand orders. The average customer waiting time $\overline{wt}(t)$, average order backlog level $\overline{B}(t)$, and the service level $sl(t)$ are the performance measures in view of customer's requirement. In Notation list 3, we listed all the status variables. Since some of them are selected as performance measures, we briefly summarize the information of performance measures in Table 3.4 for the sake of readability.

Aspect	Performance measures
Manufacturer's requirement	Main performance measure: $Netprofit_{mean} = Income_{mean} - cost_{purchase} - cost_{change3level} - cost_{inv} - cost_{backlog}$ (to maximize) Detailed performance measures: $\overline{Kp_i}, \overline{Kt_i}, \overline{Ts_i}, \overline{Ns_i}, \frac{Nsu(T)}{T}, \frac{Q_{main}(T)}{T}, \frac{Q_{backup}(T)}{T},$ $\overline{I}(T), \overline{B}(T)$
Customer's requirement	Mean customer service level $sl(T)$ (to increase or maintain) Mean customer waiting time $\overline{wt}(T)$ (to decrease) Mean order backlog level $\overline{B}(T)$ (to decrease)

Table 3.4: Summary of performance measures in the robust Kanban system

Notation list 4: risk-response mechanism related parameters and variables

Last but not least, we list the special parameters used in the risk-response mechanism. Here we first give a list of all the special parameters. Their functions and application methods will be introduced systematically in Section 3.2.3.

Status variables in the risk-response mechanism:

mi_rate	Rate-balance monitor, $mi_{rate}(t)$ means the value of mi_rate observed at time t
mi_inv	Inventory-balance monitor, $mi_{inv}(t)$ means the value of mi_inv observed at time t
$\widetilde{T}_{demand}(t)$	Exponentially smoothed value of demand interarrival time, for calculating mi_rate
$\widetilde{T}_{supplier}(t)$	Exponentially smoothed value of supplier material supply time, for calculating mi_rate
$\widetilde{T}_{process}(t)$	Exponentially smoothed value of bottleneck-stage process time, for calculating mi_rate
$\widetilde{T}_{transport}(t)$	Exponentially smoothed value of bottleneck-stage transport time, for calculating mi_rate
$\widetilde{I}(t)$	Exponentially smoothed value of inventory level at customer stage, for calculating mi_inv

$\widetilde{B}(t)$	Exponentially smoothed value of backlog level at customer stage, for calculating mi_inv

Parameters in the risk-response mechanism:

sf	Safety factor used to control the rate balance ($sf = 1 + \varepsilon \geq 1, \varepsilon$ is a small positive value)
sf_{dt}	Smoothing weight factor of demand interarrival time, $sf_{dt} \in [0,1]$
sf_{pr}	Smoothing weight factor of single-machine service time, $sf_{pr} \in [0,1]$
sf_{su}	Smoothing weight factor of supplier material supply time, $sf_{su} \in [0,1]$
sf_{inv}	Smoothing weight factor of inventory and backlog level, $sf_{inv} \in [0,1]$
ss	Safety stock level, baseline control limit of mi_inv
ss_{low}	Lower bound of ss, lower control limit of mi_inv
ss_{high}	Upper bound of ss, upper control limit of mi_inv
LCL_K	Lower control limit of mi_rate for changing Kanban number
UCL_K	Upper control limit of mi_rate for changing Kanban number
LCL_{Ts}	Lower control limit of mi_rate for changing machine service time
UCL_{Ts}	Upper control limit of mi_rate for changing machine service time
LCL_{Ns}	Lower control limit of mi_rate for changing server number
UCL_{Ns}	Upper control limit of mi_rate for changing server number
LCL_{su}	Lower control limit of mi_rate for changing backup supplier proportion
UCL_{su}	Upper control limit of mi_rate for changing backup supplier proportion

3.2.3 Risk-response mechanism

With the parameter notation, we can describe the working mechanism of the robust Kanban system better. The working mechanism contains two parts: the basic dual-Kanban mechanism, and the new risk-response mechanism.

The basic dual-Kanban working mechanism of the robust Kanban system is similar to that of a traditional dual-Kanban system. The difference is, some system parameters (decision variables $Kp_i, Kt_i, Ts_i, Ns_i, pr_{backup}$) are designed to be flexible in the robust Kanban system. Through adjusting the parameter values, the system capacity can be dynamically changed during operation to mitigate the impact of risks.

Recall the three questions about how to design the robust Kanban system: *1) Which robust approaches to apply? 2) Which parameters to change? 3) When to change and how much to change?*

In Section 3.1.2, the first and second questions have been answered. A risk-response mechanism was proposed to solve Question 3, but it was only briefly discussed. Now, after introducing the parameter notation, we will present a detailed description of the risk-response mechanism.

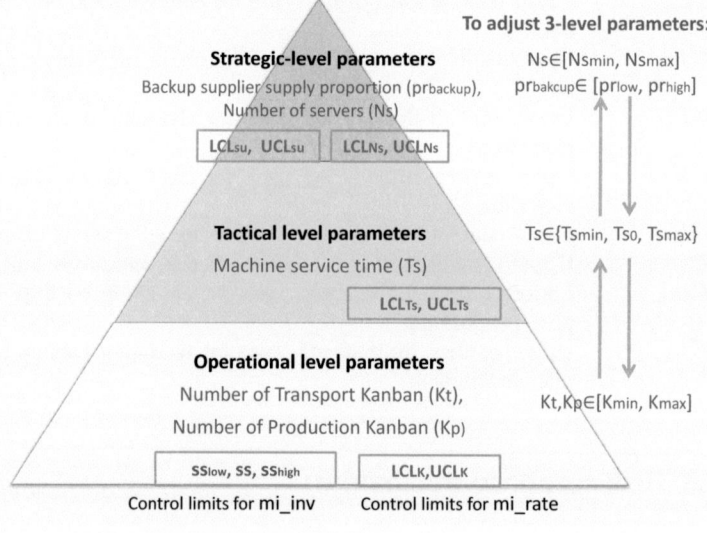

Figure 3.4: The risk-response mechanism of Robust Kanban System: to adjust 3-level parameters

Figure 3.4 gives us a general introduction of the risk-response mechanism. All important elements of the mechanism (including the 3-level parameters, the two monitors mi_rate and mi_inv, and the control limits parameters of monitors) are listed in the figure.

The 3-level adjustable parameters include not only the widely used parameter Kanban number (operational level), but also higher-level parameters like machine service time (tactical level), number of servers, and supplier order proportion (strategic level). Essentially, the risk-response mechanism is an adjusting 3-level parameters mechanism. Its working principle is to adjust the right parameters of the Kanban system at the right time and to a right extent, so as to reduce the impact of risks from the uncertain environment. Therefore, to know when to change and how much to change the 3-level parameters is a crucial issue of applying the mechanism.

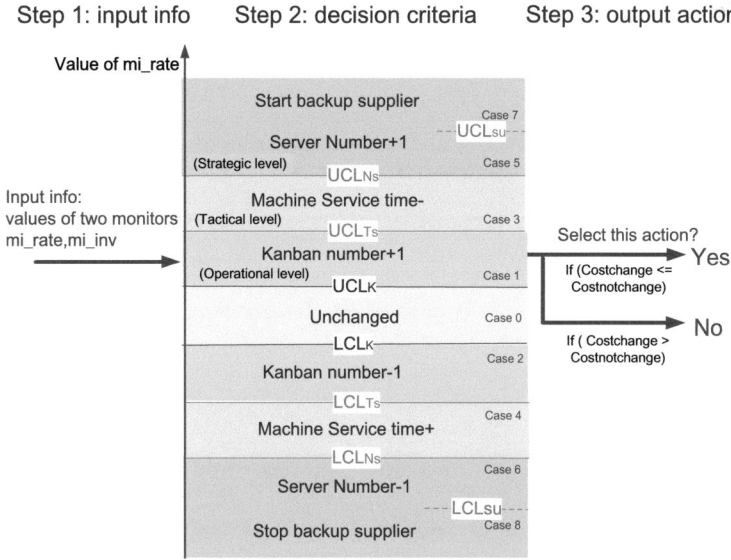

Figure 3.5: Control logic of the risk-response mechanism

In order to make proper decisions for adjusting the 3-level parameters, we employ a rate balance monitor (mi_rate) and an inventory monitor (mi_inv) and corresponding "monitor control limits" parameters (LCL, UCL series, ss series) in the risk-response mechanism. Recall the flow chart in Figure 3.3, the decision making process includes three steps in each review period: 1) observe the current system status to calculate mi_rate and mi_inv; 2) make decisions on how to change the 3-level parameters; 3) adjust selected parameters and continue to operate the system. Figure 3.5 illustrates the control logic and decision criteria of the risk-response mechanism. They will be explained in detail in the following text.

Step 1. Calculate monitor values

At the beginning of each review period, the system will collect required information, then calculate up-to-date values of mi_rate and mi_inv. The monitors are used for detecting unusual changes of system operating status in time. Required information includes the current inventory or backlog level of finished product, the slowest supply or process rate among all stages, and the current demand rate (or demand forecasting information).

The monitor mi_rate is defined as the ratio of the demand rate to the service rate:

$$mi\_rate = \frac{demand\ rate}{bottleneck\ service\ rate} = \frac{(smoothed)\ bottleneck\ service\ time}{(smoothed) demand\ interarrival\ time}$$

And the monitor mi_inv is defined as the inventory and backlog level of finished product in the customer input buffer:

$$mi\_inv = (smoothed)\ inventory\ and\ bakclog\ level\ of\ finished\ product$$

During the system operation, the values of mi_rate and mi_inv are regularly examined and updated in each review period.

Most Kanban system models presented in previous literature use only inventory-based indicators to monitor the system operating status. However, we employ two monitor items simultaneously in the risk-response mechanism to observe the system. This is a new feature of the robust Kanban system. We choose "inventory-balance" and "rate-balance" monitors to cooperate, because only using one monitor cannot reflect the system operating information sufficiently, and may mislead the decision on adjusting parameters.

For example, when enough inventory remains in the current period, a high value of *mi_inv* can be observed, which indicates no adjusting action need to be taken. However, at this moment a risk event "supplier material shortage" happens, thus another monitor *mi_rate* generates an unusual high value (because a low value of bottleneck-stage service rate is caused). If we only look at the monitor *mi_inv*, the risk event cannot be detected quickly, because the finished product inventory (which is monitored by *mi_inv*) will be able to reflect "supplier material shortage" only after the inventory shortages at all middle stages have been caused. Only after a long time can we detect the risk and take risk-response actions. Thus, the potential risk of order backlog will be increased, due to the delay of risk-response actions. By contrast, if we use *mi_rate* and *mi_inv* together to monitor the system status, we can still detect the supplier risk quickly. This benefits from the *mi_rate* that shares the process rate information among all stages.

From the above example, we can see that the monitor *mi_rate* can compensate the drawbacks of monitor *mi_inv* when monitoring the system status. Similarly, the monitor *mi_inv* can also supplement the rate information observed by *mi_rate*. Still use the "supplier material shortage" example. If we only observe the value of *mi_rate*, a response action of selecting the backup supplier is suggested to handle the risk, which may also take much operating cost. However, if sufficient inventory is stored in the system, to use the backup supplier may be not so necessary or urgent at this moment. At least we can wait until the next period, to see whether the material shortage is getting higher, then take suitable response actions. Therefore, if we can combine the information offered by *mi_rate* and *mi_inv*, a more suitable decision can be derived in response to unusual changes of system operating status.

Therefore, to avoid making biased decisions, we use two monitor items *mi_rate* and *mi_inv* simultaneously in the risk-response mechanism, to collect comprehensive information about the system operating status.

The calculation methods of two monitors are as follows:

$$mi_{rate}(t) = \frac{\max\{\widetilde{T}_{supplier}\left(t\right),\widetilde{T}_{process}\left(t\right),\widetilde{T}_{transport}\left(t\right)\}}{\widetilde{T}_{demand}(t)} \quad (3.1)$$

$$mi_{inv}(t) = \widetilde{I}\left(t\right) - \widetilde{B}\left(t\right) = \widetilde{IB}\left(t\right) \quad (3.2)$$

The parameters with tilde, such as $\widetilde{T}_{supplier}\left(t\right),\widetilde{T}_{process}\left(t\right),\widetilde{T}_{demand}\left(t\right)$ in Formula 3.1, and $\widetilde{I}\left(t\right),\widetilde{B}\left(t\right)$ in Formula 3.2, stand for the exponentially smoothed values (Holt 2004) of relevant system status data. Here we use exponentially smoothed data but not exact data to calculate the monitor values, because the smoothed data vary in a narrower range in comparison with the exact output data. The varying range of the smoothed data is relatively stable. If the smoothed data is found varying beyond the normal range, it is more reasonable to conclude that unusual changes have happened to the system. By contrast, the variation of exact data is much larger than that of the smoothed data, the variation may distort the true varying trend of the output data and lead to a wrong detecting-risk conclusion.

"Rate-balance" monitor

Three parameters $\widetilde{T}_{supplier}\left(t\right),\widetilde{T}_{process}\left(t\right),\widetilde{T}_{demand}\left(t\right)$ (we suppose the parameter $\widetilde{T}_{transport}(t)$ is constant) are involved in Formula 3.1 to calculate the value of $mi_{rate}(t)$.

$\widetilde{T}_{demand}(t)$ signifies the exponentially smoothed value of customer demand interarrival time at time t. Suppose at time t, the number of generated demand orders is $N(t) = n$, $\widetilde{T}_{demand}(t)$ can be denoted in another form $\widetilde{T}_{demand}(n)$ based on counting $N(t)$. $\widetilde{T}_{demand}(n)$ is calculated as shown in Formula 3.3:

$$\widetilde{T}_{demand}(1) = t_d(1) \quad (3.3a)$$

$$\widetilde{T}_{demand}\left(n\right) = (1 - sf_{dt}) \cdot t_d\left(n\right) + sf_{dt} \cdot \widetilde{T}_{demand}\left(n - 1\right), n = 2, 3, \ldots \quad (3.3b)$$

where $t_d(n)$ is the exact demand interarrival time of the n-th customer order (current data); $\widetilde{T}_{demand}(n-1)$ is the last smoothed value of $\widetilde{T}_{demand}(t)$ at $N(t) = n-1$ (historical data); and sf_{dt} is the smoothing weight factor used in the exponential smoothing method, it indicates the weight of historical demand-time data in the calculation. The domain of sf_{dt} is [0,1], its value is usually set at 0.7, 0.8, or 0.9 in practice. It is suggested that the value of sf_{dt} be decided depending on the realistic situation of the problem.

$\widetilde{T}_{supplier}(t)$ (also denoted by $\widetilde{T}_{supplier}(n)$) means the smoothed value of supplier material supply time at time t. It is calculated in the similar way of calculating $\widetilde{T}_{demand}(t)$. In Formula 3.4, sf_{su} is the smoothing weight factor of supplier supply time; $t_{su}(n)$ is the observed material supply time of the n-th material order at time t; the selected supplier could be either the main supplier or mixed with the backup supplier.

$$\widetilde{T}_{supplier}(0) = tsu_{main} \tag{3.4a}$$

$$\widetilde{T}_{supplier}(n) = (1 - sf_{su}) \cdot t_{su}(n) + sf_{su} \cdot \widetilde{T}_{supplier}(n-1), \ n = 1, 2, 3, \ldots \tag{3.4b}$$

As shown in Formula 3.5, $\widetilde{Ts_i}(n)$ represents the smoothed value of single-machine service time at process stage i at time t, suppose n service tasks have been accomplished at time t. Hence, it is also denoted by $\widetilde{Ts_i}(t)$. We calculate $\widetilde{Ts_i}(n)$ using an exponential smoothing method as well, where sf_{pr} is the smoothing weight factor.

$$\widetilde{Ts_i}(0) = Ts_i(0) \tag{3.5a}$$

$$\widetilde{Ts_i}(n) = (1 - sf_{pr}) \cdot Ts_i(n) + sf_{pr} \cdot \widetilde{Ts_i}(n-1), \ n = 1, 2, 3, \ldots \tag{3.5b}$$

Based on the obtained value of $\widetilde{Ts_i}(n)$, we can further estimate the average single-machine process time (the time for serving one product unit on a machine) for the entire workcell i by $\widetilde{Ts_i}(t)/Ns_i(t)$, suppose there are $Ns_i(t)$ in-use servers at Workcell i at time t. The workcell with the maximum $\widetilde{Ts_i}(t)/Ns_i(t)$ value is considered as the bottleneck workcell. Then, $\widetilde{T}_{process}(t)$, the smoothed average process time of the bottleneck workcell, is calculated by Formula 3.6:

$$\widetilde{T}_{process}(t) = \max_i\{\widetilde{Ts_i}(t)/Ns_i(t)\} \quad i = 1, 2, \ldots, I \tag{3.6}$$

Similarly, we can estimate the average transport interarrival time of the slowest transport module using Formula 3.7,

$$\widetilde{T}_{transport}(t) = \max_i\{Ttr_i/Kt_i(t)\} \quad i = 1, 2, \ldots, I \tag{3.7}$$

In conclusion, after knowing the values of $\widetilde{T}_{supplier}(t)$, $\widetilde{T}_{process}(t)$, $\widetilde{T}_{demand}(t)$ and $\widetilde{T}_{transport}(t)$, the value of monitor mi_rate at time t

$(mi_{rate}(t))$ can be finally calculated using Formula 3.1. Given a time point t in the total operating time, we first compare the service rates of different supply chain stages (including supplier, and all process stages with workcell and transport modules), to find out which part of the system is the bottleneck. The service time generated by the bottleneck part is then divided by the customer demand time, the obtained ratio is namely the value of *mi_rate*. Using *mi_rate* to monitor the system status, the risk source and extent can be perceived easily; it provides important reference for the final decision on adjusting 3-level parameters.

"Inventory-balance" monitor

Except the "rate-balance" monitor *mi_rate*, another monitor "inventory-balance" *mi_inv* $(mi_{inv}(t))$ is employed in the robust Kanban system as well to reflect the inventory status. The monitor *mi_inv* functions as the supplement to *mi_rate*, the value of $mi_{inv}(t)$ is calculated by Formula 3.2, where $\widetilde{I}(t), \widetilde{B}(t)$ signify the exponentially smoothed inventory level and backlog level, respectively. The calculation of $\widetilde{I}(t), \widetilde{B}(t)$ is similar to that of $\widetilde{Ts_i}(t)$, an exponential smoothing method is used with the inventory data series. Formula 3.8 and 3.9 give the calculation methods for $\widetilde{I}(t), \widetilde{B}(t)$ respectively. Here $I(t), B(t)$ are the exact inventory level and backlog level observed at time t, and sf_{inv} is the smoothing weight factor.

$$\widetilde{I}(t) = (1 - sf_{inv}) \cdot I(t) + sf_{inv} \cdot \widetilde{I}(t-1) \qquad (3.8)$$

$$\widetilde{B}(t) = (1 - sf_{inv}) \cdot B(t) + sf_{inv} \cdot \widetilde{B}(t-1) \qquad (3.9)$$

So far, we have explained the work of Step 1. It showed how the monitors *mi_rate* and *mi_inv* are calculated and updated during the system operation. Note that the smoothing weight factors are used here as predefined deterministic parameters, which implies their values should be decided before operating the system. The domains of the smoothing weight factors $sf_{inv}, sf_{dt}, sf_{su}, sf_{pr}$ are defined between 0 and 1. Take sf_{dt} as an example. When $sf_{dt}=0$, the smoothed result is equal to the exact newest data. When $sf_{dt}=1$, the result is always the oldest data. Except the two extreme cases, in other cases with $0<sf_{dt}<1$, the exponential smooth method will generate different results under different sf_{dt} values. The values of smoothing weight factors can be set freely between

0 and 1 depending on the designer's opinion; this enhances the flexibility of monitor calculation.

Step 2. Decision making criteria

In Step 2, we compare the observed monitor values to their control limits. If the monitor value is found beyond the normal range, it implies that some unusual changes have happened to the system and made the system deviate from the normal operating status. In this situation, we can adjust some system parameters to mitigate the impact of risks.

Different risk situations (slight or severe, long-term or short-term) could result in different impacts on system operating status, the monitor values will accordingly deviate in different manners. We therefore should select suitable parameters to change as the risk-response actions. In consideration of different influences on system performance, we set different monitor control limits for adjusting the 3-level parameters.

As shown in Figure 3.4, we have four pairs of control limits $(LCL_K, UCL_K), (LCL_{Ts}, UCL_{Ts}), (LCL_{Ns}, UCL_{Ns}), (LCL_{su}, UCL_{su})$ for judging the mi_rate value; and a set of control limits $(ss_{low}, ss, ss_{high})$ for judging the mi_inv value. LCL_K and UCL_K signify the lower and upper control limits for adjusting the operational-level parameter "Kanban number Kp_i, Kt_i"; LCL_{Ts}, UCL_{Ts} mean the lower and upper bounds for changing the tactical-level parameter "machine service time Ts_i"; LCL_{Ns}, UCL_{Ns} are the lower and upper limits for modifying the strategic-level parameter "number of servers Ns_i"; and LCL_{su}, UCL_{su} are the lower and upper control limits for changing the strategic-level parameter "supply proportion from the backup supplier pr_{backup}". In addition, ss_{low}, ss_{high} are defined as lower and upper bounds of the safety stock level of finished product, they define a normal range for judging mi_inv value. And ss indicates a target normal safety stock level, its value should be set within the normal range. To apply the risk-response mechanism, the control limits should be determined properly before starting the system operation. Here we assume that the control limits for mi_rate should have the following relationships:
$LCL_{Ns} < LCL_{Ts} < LCL_K < UCL_K < UCL_{Ts} < UCL_{Ns}$
and $LCL_{su} < LCL_K < UCL_K < UCL_{su}$.

It is reasonable to assume that the control limits obey such orders, because adjusting a higher-level parameter (here we mean the strategic level is the highest level, and operational level is the lowest level among the three decision levels) needs more efforts and cost than adjusting a lower-level parameter. So we define wider ranges for higher-level parameters. Within the wider ranges, the higher-level parameters should be kept unchanged, no adjustment is suggested. By contrast, we specify narrower ranges for lower-level parameters; within the narrower ranges, the current lower-level parameters should be held unchanged. Such setting makes the adjustment of higher-level parameters much more difficult than that of lower-level parameters. Only when serious risks occur will mi_rate indicate a higher-level adjusting decision, which is more expensive but more effective to deal with the risks. Similarly, we also have the relationship: $ss_{low} < ss < ss_{high}$.

The decision cases in Step 2 are categorized as follows (see Figure 3.5 for reference). In short, the decision making process (Step 2) in each case contains three parts: 1) compare mi_rate to its control limits; 2) compare mi_inv to its control limits; 3) compare the additional cost of adjusting system parameters $cost_{change}$ with the potential risk cost caused by keeping the current parameters unchanged $cost_{notchange}$.

Operational-level response: to adjust the parameter Number of Kanbans K

Case 0: when $mi\_rate \in (LCL_K, UCL_K)$

If $mi\_inv \in (ss_{low}, ss_{high})$, keep current parameters unchanged;

If $mi\_inv \leq ss_{low}$ and $cost_{change} \leq cost_{notchange}$, add a Kanban ($K = K+1$);

If $mi\_inv \geq ss_{high}$ and $cost_{change} \leq cost_{notchange}$, extract a Kanban ($K = K-1$);

Otherwise, keep current parameters unchanged.

Case 1: when $mi\_rate \in [UCL_K, UCL_{Ts}]$

If $mi\_inv \leq ss$ and $cost_{change} \leq cost_{notchange}$, add a Kanban ($K = K+1$);

Otherwise, keep current parameters unchanged.

Case 2: when $mi\_rate \in [LCL_{Ts}, LCL_K]$

If $mi\_inv \geq ss$ and $cost_{change} \leq cost_{notchange}$, extract a Kanban ($K=K$-1);

Otherwise, keep current parameters unchanged.

Tactical-level response: to adjust the parameter Single-machine service time Ts

Case 3: when bottleneck=process machine, $mi\_rate \in [UCL_{Ts}, UCL_{Ns}]$

If $mi\_inv \leq ss$ and $cost_{change} \leq cost_{notchange}$, decrease the service time ($Ts=Ts*90\%$);

Otherwise, keep current parameters unchanged.

Case 4: when bottleneck=process machine, $mi\_rate \in [LCL_{Ns}, LCL_{Ts}]$

If $mi\_inv \geq ss$ and $cost_{change} \leq cost_{notchange}$, increase the service time ($Ts=Ts/90\%$);

Otherwise, keep current parameters unchanged.

Strategic-level response: to adjust the parameters Number of servers Ns, Backup supplier material order proportion pr_{backup}

Case 5: when bottleneck=process stage, $mi\_rate \in [UCL_{Ns}, +\infty)$

If $mi\_inv \leq ss$ and $cost_{change} \leq cost_{notchange}$, increase the number of servers ($Ns=Ns+1$);

Otherwise, keep current parameters unchanged.

Case 6: when bottleneck=process stage, $mi\_rate \in (0, LCL_{Ns}]$

If $mi\_inv \geq ss$ and $cost_{change} \leq cost_{notchange}$, decrease the number of servers ($Ns=Ns$-1);

Otherwise, keep current parameters unchanged;

Case 7: when bottleneck=supplier stage, $mi\_rate \in [UCL_{su}, +\infty)$

If $mi\_inv \leq ss$ and $cost_{change} \leq cost_{notchange}$, increase the material order proportion from the backup supplier ($pr_{backup}=pr_{high}$);

Otherwise, keep current parameters unchanged.

Case 8: when bottleneck=supplier stage, $mi\_rate \in (0, LCL_{su}]$

If $mi\_inv \geq ss$ and $cost_{change} \leq cost_{notchange}$, decrease the material order proportion from the backup supplier

$(pr_{backup}=pr_{low})$;
Otherwise, keep current parameters unchanged.

Case others: keep current parameters unchanged.

When carrying out the response actions of each case, some exceptional situations are considered as well. For example in case 1, when the response action $K=K+1$ is selected whereas the cyclic Kanban number is already the maximum $(K = K_{max})$, which indicates the adding-Kanban action cannot be executed actually, then other action could be adopted instead in response to risks. In this situation, if the order backlog level is sufficiently high, then the formerly selected adding-Kanban action will be switched to a higher-level response action like to decrease the machine service time, $Ts= Ts*90\%$. It means, for the exceptional cases, an auto-upgrade mechanism (operational level→tactical level) will take effect to switch the response action from operational-level to tactical-level. Similarly, in cases 3 and 5, the auto-upgrade mechanisms are also used when exceptional situations take place. In case 3, a "tactical level →strategic level" auto-upgrade action can be used. When the decreasing-service time action (Ts=Ts*90%) is selected whereas the current service time is already minimum $(Ts = Ts_{min})$, then the selected response action will be upgraded to a higher-level action. A strategic-level response action, to increase the number of servers $(Ns=Ns+1)$, will be adopted in place of the current decreasing-service time action, providing that the current order backlog level is sufficiently high. For the exceptional situation in case 5, where the response action of increasing the number of servers $(Ns=Ns+1)$ is selected but the servers in use has already reached the maximum capacity $(Ns = Ns_{max})$, an auto-upgrade mechanism (strategic level→all levels) will take effect as well. Although in case 5, the strategic level action of increasing the number of servers cannot be switched to a higher-level action, we can still enhance the process speed slightly by setting all 3-level parameters at full power. Thus, the system can reach the maximum service capacity to deal with the risk occurrence.

Following the above decision criteria, the robust Kanban system will generate the final decision "how to change the 3-level adjustable parameters in response to risks". The values of the control limits parameters (LCL and UCL series, ss series) should be properly defined before applying the risk-response mechanism, because it will strongly affect the final decision. Here we just briefly introduce the definitions and functions of the control limits. The methods for deciding suitable values for them will be discussed in Chapter 4.

Compare $cost_{change}$ and $cost_{notchange}$

The items $cost_{change}$ and $cost_{notchange}$ refer to the cost resulting from changing or not changing the 3-level parameters. In each decision case, we not only compare the monitor values to their control limits, but also compare $cost_{change}$ with $cost_{notchange}$ which are estimated on average, to see whether the additional cost of changing (e.g. adding a new server) 3-level parameters is less than the potential risk cost (e.g. inventory or backlog cost) if keeping parameters unchanged. We compare $cost_{change}$ with $cost_{notchange}$, because if the cost of adding a new server ($cost_{change}$) is very high, then keeping the current parameters unchanged will be a more economical decision, even though some backlog order penalty cost ($cost_{notchange}$) may occur. With such comparison, the system can avoid unreasonable changing-parameter decisions. The calculation methods for $cost_{change}$ and $cost_{notchange}$ are interpreted as below.

In the robust Kanban system, we expect to keep the inventory of finished product, which is held in the customer input buffer, at a safe and economical level. With the safety stock, the system can cushion the conflict between supply and demand, and mitigate the impact of demand or supply variability. We denote the target normal safety stock level of finished product by ss. The parameter ss is a necessary item used to calculate $cost_{change}$ and $cost_{notchange}$, it can be seen consist of two parts, as shown in Formula 3.10:

$$ss = ss_{base} + ss_{\mathrm{var}} \qquad (3.10)$$

Formula 3.10 is developed based on the concept: safetystock=$\mu + z \cdot \sigma$, where μ and σ are respectively the mean value and stand deviation of the inventory level (including both positive inventory level and negative backlog level) observed in the customer input buffer, and z is the multiplier of σ. A high value of z can lead to a higher service level of filling customer orders without delay. In Formula 3.10, ss_{base} (corresponding to μ) refers to the basic inventory amount required to cover an average

61

demand rate for a period; and ss_{var} (similar to $z \cdot \sigma$) indicates the additional inventory amount required to cover the variation of demand or supply.

The item ss_{base} is calculated by Formula 3.11:

$$ss_{base} = (rate_{demand} - rate_{service})^+ \cdot t_{review} \qquad (3.11)$$

This formula implies when $rate_{service} \geq rate_{demand}$, we have ss_{base}=0; and when $rate_{service} < rate_{demand}$, $ss_{base} = (rate_{demand} - rate_{service}) \cdot t_{review}$. When $rate_{service} < rate_{demand}$, the service (including both process and supply) rate is not sufficient to meet the demand rate. If we want to avoid order backlog, enough inventory should be stored in advance. Hence we want to hold the safety stock level at least above $(rate_{demand} - rate_{service}) \cdot t_{review}$. Under this condition, even without increasing the current service rate, the Kanban system is still be able to cover the demand for the coming review period.

The second item ss_{var} is the extra inventory amount used to cover the variation of uncertain demand or supply (such as stochastic demand time or process time). Here, we develop two estimation methods for deciding the suitable value of ss_{var}, we use Formula 3.12 (a,b) to calculate the parameter ss_{var}.

$$ss_{\mathrm{var}} = z \cdot \sigma_{inv} \qquad (3.12a)$$

$$ss_{\mathrm{var}} = K_{optimal} - K_{mean} \qquad (3.12b)$$

In the first method (Formula 3.12a), σ_{inv} is the standard deviation of inventory level observed in the customer input buffer, it can reflect the data variability; and z is the multiplier of σ_{inv}. σ_{inv} value is estimated based on historical inventory data or simulation output data. z value means the width of the inventory variability range the system intends to cover with abundant inventory, so as to avoid backlog occurrences. It means how likely the system can avoid the backlog occurrence. We can define z value arbitrarily according to the required customer service level or the manager's opinion. Different z values correspond to different service level. If the inventory probability distribution is known, it is easy to calculate the corresponding z value for a given service level. For example, in a standard normal distribution, z=3 will lead to a probability $\Pr\{inventory \leq \mu + z \cdot \sigma_{inv}\}$ around 99%.

In the second method (Formula 3.12b), K_{mean} is the Kanban number required to cover the average demand rate, and $K_{optimal}$ is the Kanban number that can generate the optimal result (minimum cost or maximum Netprofit). The parameter K_{mean} is calculated by $K_{mean} = time_{Kanbancollection}/mean(t_d)$, and the parameter $K_{optimal}$ is obtained using simulation or mathematical methods (see Chapter 4). If the distribution of demand interarrival time and inventory level are known, the suitable value of ss_{var} can be easily calculated using Formula 3.12. But the parameter ss_{var} value obtained from Methods a) and b) could be different. Because Method a) aims at reaching the required service level, whereas Method b) aims at generating the minimum cost, different objectives may result in different parameter value decisions.

Using Formula 3.10-3.12, the control parameter ss value can be calculated accordingly. With these parameters, we can further calculate $cost_{change}$ and $cost_{notchange}$.

In cases 1, 3, 5, response actions are about enhancing the service capacity. When we change the 3-level parameters, additional cost will be caused for operating a new server, speeding up the machine process rate, or adding more Kanbans. Therefore, the cost function of changing the 3-level parameters is defined in Formula 3.13.

$$cost_{change} = c_{Kanban} \cdot \Delta K_i + c_{stime} \cdot \Delta \frac{1}{Ts_i}$$
$$+c_{server} \cdot \Delta Ns_i + \lambda_d \cdot \Delta pricein_{supplier} \tag{3.13}$$

To be noted, Formula 3.13 is just an approximation method to estimate $cost_{change}$. The total cost incurred during the review period includes also other cost items such as the inventory holding cost and slight order backlog cost. But usually in realistic situations (e.g.P&G(2011)), if the system operates stable with a sufficient service capacity, the inventory related cost is much lower than the cost of changing 3-level parameters (for equipment capacity). Therefore, here we use Formula 3.13, which only considers the changing 3-level parameters cost, to estimate $cost_{change}$.

In contrast to the changing-parameter decision, we wonder what the result could be if the response action is not taken. Imagine that if the system keeps the previous parameter setting unchanged, then the cost of enhancing service capacity as given in Formula 3.13 will not occur. However, on the other hand, the potential risk of order backlog is increased due to the unchanged limited service capacity. In short, not to change parameters may cause more order backlog penalty cost, even though the changing service equipment cost is saved. We suppose the order backlog will cause the loss of customer goodwill; and comparing with abundant inventory occurrences, we prefer to reduce or avoid product shortages for the Kanban system. So the backlog penalty cost rate at the customer stage (b_c) is assumed to be much higher than the inventory holding cost rate ($h_i, i = 1, 2, ..., I$) (generally we have $b_c \geq 50h_i$ in this work). Hence, the $cost_{notchange}$ is mainly composed of backlog penalty cost caused per time unit. Due to this reason, we use the backlog penalty cost to estimate $cost_{notchange}$ approximately. The calculation of $cost_{notchange}$ is as follows.

First, using the value of mi_inv obtained in Step 1, we examine the result of $mi\_inv - ss_{var}$. Define $ss_{base}' = mi\_inv - ss_{var}$, written in another form, it is $mi\_inv = ss_{base}' + ss_{var}$. Consider that in cases 1, 3, 5, the system is under the condition $mi\_inv < ss = ss_{base} + ss_{var}$, then we always have $ss_{base}' < ss_{base}$ for the three cases that are relevant to increasing service capacity. We denote the currently observed demand rate by λ_d, the service rate by λ_s, the review period length by t_{review}.

Secondly, we classify the calculation of $cost_{notchange}$ into three cases according to different value ranges of ss_{base}': a) $ss_{base}' < ss_{base} = 0$; b) $ss_{base}' < 0 < ss_{base}$; c) $0 < ss_{base}' < ss_{base}$. As illustrated in Figure 3.6, the area of the shaded part in each case refers to the total order backlog amount during the review period. Multiply the area by b_c (the backlog penalty cost per product unit per time unit), the result means the total backlog cost incurred during the entire review period. Then the total backlog cost divided by t_{review} is used as the approximation for $cost_{notchange}$.

The methods for calculating $cost_{notchange}$ each case are presented as below.

Case a: when $ss_{base}' < ss_{base} = 0$

In case a), we have $ss_{base} = (\lambda_d - \lambda_s)^+ \cdot t_{review} = 0$, it is inferred that $\lambda_d - \lambda_s \leq 0$. To calculate $cost_{notchange}$, we define a new item $t_1 = \frac{ss_{base}'}{\lambda_d - \lambda_s} > 0$ $(if \lambda_d - \lambda_s \neq 0)$, and $t_2 = t_{review} - t_1$. As demonstrated in Figure 3.6 a1) or a2), the area of shaded part in an entire review period divided by t_{review} corresponds to the value of $cost_{notchange}$. When

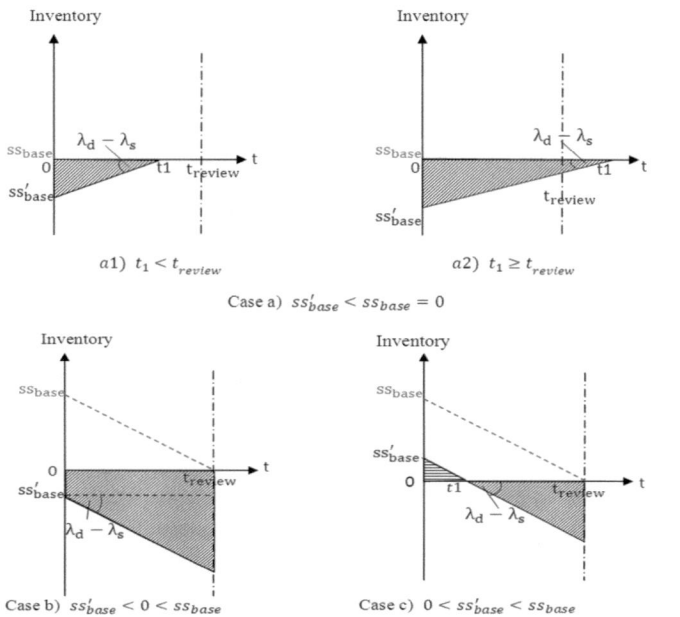

Figure 3.6: Three cases of calculating $cost_{notchange}$

$t_1 \leq t_{review}$ or $t_1 > t_{review}$, the calculation of $cost_{notchange}$ is of slight difference, as presented in Formula 3.14. Besides, when $\lambda_d - \lambda_s = 0$, the $cost_{notchange}$ is in a simpler form, it is also given in Formula 3.14.

$$
cost_{notchange} =
\begin{cases}
b_c \cdot |ss'_{base}|, & if\ \lambda_d - \lambda_s = 0 \\[2mm]
b_c \cdot \dfrac{|ss'_{base}|}{2} \cdot \dfrac{t_1}{t_{review}}, & if\ \lambda_d - \lambda_s < 0, t_1 \leq t_{review} \\[3mm]
b_c \cdot \dfrac{|ss'_{base}|}{2} \cdot \left(2 - \dfrac{t_{review}}{t_1}\right), & if\ \lambda_d - \lambda_s < 0, t_1 > t_{review}
\end{cases}
$$

$$(3.14)$$

Case b: when $ss'_{base} < 0 < ss_{base}$

In case b), since $ss_{base} = (\lambda_d - \lambda_s)^+ \cdot t_{review} > 0$, we infer that $\lambda_d - \lambda_s > 0$. Calculate the area of the shaded part in Figure 3.6b), then multiply it by the backlog penalty cost rate b_c, and then divide it by t_{review}, we can obtain the value of $cost_{notchange}$, as given in Formula 3.15.

$$cost_{notchange} = b_c[|ss'_{base}| + (\lambda_d - \lambda_s)\frac{t_{review}}{2}] \qquad (3.15)$$

Case c: when $0 < ss'_{base} < ss_{base}$

In case c), we can obtain the similar inference $\lambda_d - \lambda_s > 0$ based on the condition $0 < ss_{base} = (\lambda_d - \lambda_s)^+ \cdot t_{review}$. As shown in Figure 3.6c), the area of the left shaded triangle represents the total amount of abundant inventory during the review period, and the area of the right shaded triangle signifies the total amount order backlog during the same review period. Multiply the left area by inventory cost rate at the customer stage h_c, multiply the right area by backlog penalty cost rate b_c, then add the two results together; the sum we got is the total cost incurred during the review period. The total cost includes both inventory holding cost and backlog penalty cost; its value divided by t_{review} is used as the approximation for $cost_{notchange}$ in this case. We still define $t_1 = \frac{ss'_{base}}{\lambda_d - \lambda_s} > 0$, and $t_2 = t_{review} - t_1$. The calculation of $cost_{notchange}$ is shown in Formula 3.16.

$$cost_{notchange} = [h_c \cdot t_1 \frac{ss'_{base}}{2} + b_c \cdot t_2 \frac{(\lambda_d - \lambda_s)\, t_2}{2}]\frac{1}{t_{review}} \qquad (3.16)$$

So far, we have interpreted the calculation methods for $cost_{change}$ (Formula 3.13) and $cost_{notchange}$ (Formula 3.14 to Formula 3.16). After estimating the values of $cost_{change}$ and $cost_{notchange}$, we further compare them to find out which decision is cheaper. If the comparison result is $cost_{change} \leq cost_{notchange}$, which means that to change the parameters is a more economical choice, then we will perform the changing-parameter action. Otherwise, if $cost_{change} > cost_{notchange}$, which implies not to change the current parameters will cost less in the current review period, then we prefer to keep the old parameter settings unchanged until the next review period comes.

Different from the above cases, in cases 2,4,6 we have the condition $mi\_rate < LCL_K < 1$. Namely, the system service rate is faster than the demand rate. This implies that the current production or supply capacity is redundant for satisfying the current customer demand rate. In addition, if the condition $mi\_inv > ss$ is also reached in these cases, the parameter adjustment related to decreasing service capacity will be selected as risk response actions. The condition $mi\_inv > ss$ means the inventory stored in the customer input buffer is above the expected safe level; hence, redundant inventory may exist. Redundancy is also a type of waste for the system, because it could cause unnecessary cost of operating extra machines or keeping too much inventory. Therefore, we also need to reduce redundant service capacity, and make efforts to keep the service rate at an economical and sufficient level.

In cases 2,4,6, all the decisions are connected to decreasing the service capacity. The calculation of $cost_{change}$ and $cost_{notchange}$ here is slightly different compared with cases 1,3,5. When $mi\_rate < LCL_K$ (or $LCL_{Ts}, LCL_{Ns}, LCL_{su}$) and meanwhile $mi\_inv > ss$, a response action of decreasing the Kanban number, the machine process rate, the number of servers, or the supply proportion of the backup supplier will be selected to handle the risks. Whether to perform the response action will be decided after comparing $cost_{change}$ and $cost_{notchange}$, the decision with lower cost will be eventually selected and performed.

$$cost_{notchange} = 0 \qquad (3.17)$$

In cases 2,4,6, the monitor condition $mi\_rate < LCL_K < 1$ indicates $\lambda_d < \lambda_s$, then $ss_{base} = (\lambda_d - \lambda_s)^+ \cdot t_{review} = 0$. With this we have $ss = ss_{base} + ss_{var} = ss_{var}$. Thus the condition $mi\_inv > ss$ is actually $mi\_inv > ss_{var}$. This implies that only when the product stored in hand is more than the specified inventory variation ss_{var}, it is safe for the Kanban system to reduce the service capacity.

$$cost_{change} = cost_{save3level} + cost_{morebacklog} + cost_{saveinventory}$$
$$(3.18a)$$

$$cost_{save3level} = c_{Kanban} \cdot \Delta K_i + c_{stime} \cdot \Delta \frac{1}{Ts_i} + c_{server} \cdot \Delta Ns_i$$
$$+ \lambda_d \cdot \Delta pricein_{supplier} \quad (< 0) \qquad (3.18b)$$

$$cost_{morebacklog} = b_c \cdot \Delta B_{mean} \quad (> 0) \qquad (3.18c)$$

$$cost_{saveinventory} = h_c \cdot \Delta I_{mean} \quad (< 0) \qquad (3.18d)$$

For the sake of simplicity, we set $cost_{notchange} = 0$ (in Formula 3.17) as a baseline if none of the system parameters is changed in cases 2,4,6. In contrast, when a response action is performed, the additional cost incurred or saved by changing the system parameters is estimated on the basis of the baseline cost. Namely, $cost_{change}$ is defined as the value difference between the cost of changing parameters and the cost of keeping parameters unchanged (see Formula 3.18).

As presented in Formula 3.18, $cost_{change}$ is caused by three types of changes in the Kanban system. Firstly, the action of removing redundant service equipment will save some operating-equipment cost (named $cost_{save3level}$, with negative value). Secondly, the adjusted lower service rate will increase the risk of order backlog, so the backlog penalty cost is increased (named $cost_{morebacklog}$, with positive value). Lastly, due to the reduced service capacity, the amount of inventory in the buffer is decreased, hence related inventory holding cost is reduced (named $cost_{saveinventory}$, with negative value).

The calculation of $cost_{save3level}$ is similar to Formula 3.13. The calculation of $cost_{morebacklog}$ and $cost_{saveinventory}$ depend on the backlog level difference ΔB_{mean} and inventory level difference ΔI_{mean}, as shown in Formula 3.13c) and d). In practice, it is difficult to calculate the exact value of ΔB_{mean} or ΔI_{mean}; but based on historical data or simulation data, we can approximately estimate the value of ΔB_{mean} and ΔI_{mean} between different service capacity conditions. Moreover, when the system service capacity is sufficient or even redundant, the backlog level is quite low which makes the backlog cost become trivial. Thus, the item $cost_{morebacklog}$ can be estimated as 0. Another item $cost_{saveinventory}$ can be also estimated by

$$\Delta I_{mean} = mi_{inv}^{change} - mi_{inv}^{notchange} \approx ss - mi_{inv}^{notchange} \qquad (3.19)$$

Note that the value of $mi_{inv}^{notchange}$ can be observed during the system operation, and ss is a deterministic parameter. Thus with knowing their values, the estimation of ΔI_{mean} can be finally accomplished.

Step 3. Perform response actions

Step 3 is to perform the response actions selected in Step 2. The robust Kanban system will use the new parameter setting till the end of the current review period. Then at the beginning of the next period, the risk-response mechanism will repeat the three steps. The three steps will be regularly executed in each review period in the robust Kanban system. With the risk-response mechanism, a variety of risks can be detected quickly and suitable response actions can be selected to mitigate the impact of risks, thus the robust Kanban system can achieve a high performance level in the uncertain environment.

3.3 Simulation model construction

With the conceptual model of the robust Kanban system, we further study the operation of the robust Kanban system through building simulation models. In Section 3.3, we present the procedures of building the simulation model for the robust Kanban system.

3.3.1 Preliminary

Simulation is a very powerful modeling technique (Law 2007). It is widely used among researchers and practitioners, and becoming more and more popular as the computer power is growing fast in recent decades. Simulation is also a suitable approach to model and analyze complex systems, especially when uncertain factors are included in the environment and the system structure or working mechanism is complex. If we use analytical models to study the complex systems, many simplifying assumptions and restrictions are often required, which makes the model too different from the realistic situation, and the solutions could be consequently inadequate and inferior. Therefore, in realistic problems, using analytical models is often not able to generate sufficiently good results because of the complexity and uncertainty in realistic problems. In these situations, simulation could be a better approach for modeling and analyzing the complex systems.

The robust Kanban system model in this work is a relatively complex system. The system is supposed to be working in an uncertain environment with various uncertainties (risk factors); and the working mechanism is a risk-response mechanism with complex operation rules and flexible system structures. Therefore simulation is an appropriate approach for the robust Kanban model formulation.

In this study, we use the Matlab-Simulink (Mathworks 2012) software package to develop the simulation model of the robust Kanban system. Since it is known that the queueing system is a typical application example of discrete-event simulation (Law 2007), and the studied Kanban system is actually a complex queueing system, we choose the discrete-event simulation approach to construct the robust Kanban system simulation model.

Choosing Matlab-Simulink as the simulation language is driven mainly by two reasons. First, the studied robust Kanban system model is an abstract and general model. Detailed characteristics of system elements are not considered in the model, like the inner structure of the machine, forklift truck, and conveying belt. Therefore, a very professional logistics or manufacturing simulation tool is not necessary. The functions provided by the general engineering software Matlab-Simulink are already sufficient. Second, the working mechanism and control logic of the robust Kanban system are quite complex and flexible. When performing the risk-response mechanism, the complex control logic requires more flexibility in programming from the simulation software. Moreover, when assuming risk scenarios for the Kanban system, the stochastic input data series such as demand interarrival time, machine process time should be generated according to the predefined probability distribution types; this requires powerful mathematical functions from the simulation software. The Matlab module can provide both powerful mathematical functions and flexible programming techniques; and the Simulink module can offer many convenient simulation blocks. Due to the above reasons, we finally choose the Matlab-Simulink software as the simulation language to build the robust Kanban system model.

The rest of Section 3.3 is organized as follows. First, we give an overall description of the robust Kanban system simulation model. Then we sequentially discuss the model constructing procedures, including the design of the system structure, the specification of input and output data, and the realization of the risk-response mechanism in simulation environment. Lastly, the verification and validation of the Kanban simulation model are presented with numerical examples.

3.3.2 Model construction

As shown in Figure 3.7, we build a simulation model to implement the robust Kanban system. The simulation model is built based on the con-

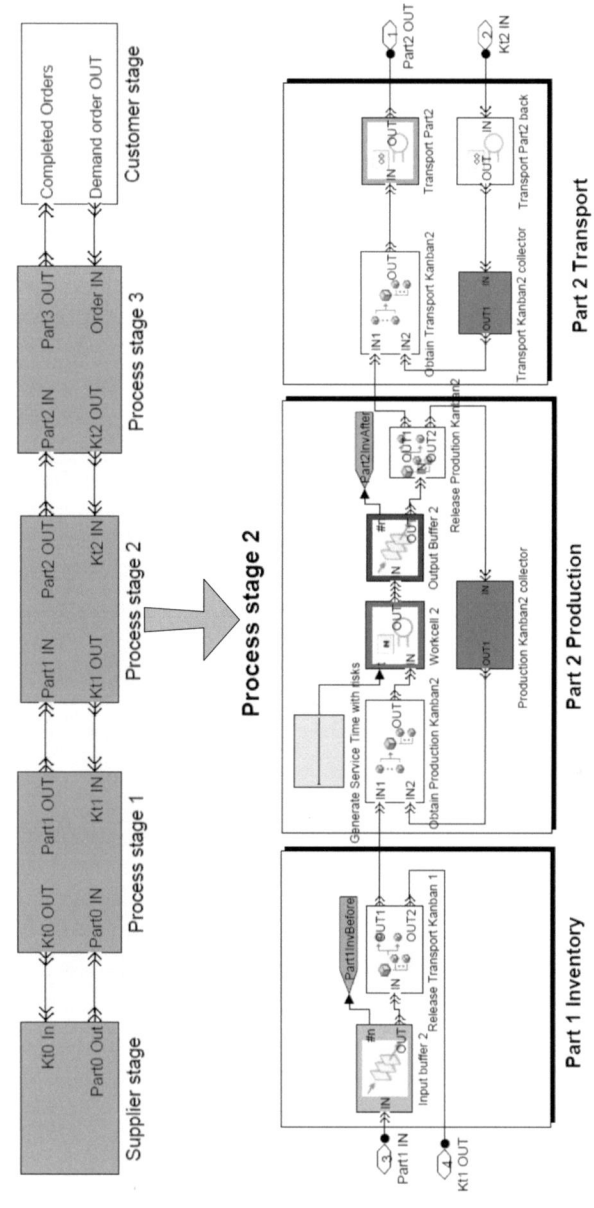

Figure 3.7: Simulation model of Robust Kanban System (dual-Kanban mechanism)

71

ceptual model framework shown in Figure 3.2. In Figure 3.7, the upper part presents the root layer of the simulation model; and the lower part is the second layer of Process-stage 2. The second layer depicts the detailed mechanism inside Process-stage 2, such as the system elements (servers, buffers) and operation details using Production Kanbans and Transport Kanbans. Here we just take Process-stage 2 as illustration, other stages have similar mechanisms.

Recall in the conceptual model of the robust Kanban system, some parameters are defined to characterize the system structure and the operating mechanism. Correspondingly, these system parameters can be specified in the simulation model as well. In each simulation element block (such as a server or a buffer block), some property parameters need to be input to define the element's structure or capacity. For example, in the N-server block "Workcell 2", the number of servers is a property parameter, and we can input its value directly in the element's property window. Similarly, the values of all the 3-level adjustable parameters $(Kp_i, Kt_i, Ts_i, Ns_i, pr_{backup})$ in the robust Kanban system can be defined by specifying property parameters in the simulation element blocks. But there are also some parameters in the robust Kanban system conceptual model, like the control limits parameters for mi_rate and mi_inv (LCL, UCL series, ss series), cannot be specified by using the property parameters of simulation elements. We need to define them in the simulation programming code that is running background.

Before we start the simulation, we should determine suitable values for all system parameters. It should be distinguished, in the robust Kanban system, the control limits parameters for mi_rate and mi_inv (LCL, UCL series, ss series) are not allowed to be changed during the simulation; whereas the values of the 3-level adjustable parameters can be adjusted dynamically during the simulation in response to risks.

Above is a general description of the simulation model. Nextly we will give a detailed introduction of the simulation components (such as simulation elements, input data, output data) and the control logic.

The simulation components include the simulation clock, events, entities, input data, output data, terminating conditions, and so on. As mentioned earlier, the robust Kanban system model is a discrete-event simulation model. The system is operated as a chronological sequence of events, and the simulation clock is event-driven. We suppose the simulation will be terminated arbitrarily when a planned time horizon (e.g. 4000 time units in simulation clock) is reached.

The entities in the simulation model can group into four types: the product entity (material), customer entity (demand order), Kanban entity (Production Kanban and Transport Kanban), and server entity (process server and transport server). The material flow in the Kanban system is essentially the product entity flow accompanied by Kanban entities (Only at the customer stage the product entity is accompanied by customer entity). And the server entity has two concrete types: the process server and the transport server.

The events in the simulation model include: customer order arrival, customer order departure with finished product, to attach a Kanban to product, to detach a Kanban from product, to generate product at the supplier stage, to process product in a workcell, to transport product between workcells.

The input data involves random variables and deterministic parameters. The input data information is summarized in Table 3.5 and Table 3.6. In Table 3.5, the variables are classified into three types depending on the risk sources: supply side, process side, or demand side. And in Table 3.6, the parameters are divided and introduced in a similar way.

Location	Random Variables	Indicated risks
Supply side	Supplier material supply time (given probability distribution)	material supply interruption or shortage. Related parameters: risk measure parameters and probability distribution parameters.
Process side	Machine service time (given probability distribution)	machine breakdown or service time variation. Related parameters: risk measure parameters and probability distribution parameters.
Demand side	Customer demand interarrival time (given probability distribution)	demand rate fluctuation. Related parameters: risk measure parameters and probability distribution parameters.

Table 3.5: Simulation model input data (part 1): random variables

	Parameters
Demand side	Demand interarrival time probability distribution type and parameters (e.g. μ, σ)
Process side	Number of Kanbans (adjustable) and its adjusting range. Probability distribution type and parameters of machine service time (e.g. μ, σ). Baseline machine service time (adjustable) and its adjusting range. Number of in-use servers (adjustable) and its adjusting range. Setup time($=0$), transport time. Inventory holding cost rate, backlog penalty cost rate, product sell price, product purchase price, cost coefficient of changing Kanban number, cost coefficient of changing machine service time, cost coefficient of changing server number, cost coefficient of changing supplier proportion cost
Supply side	Probability distribution type and parameters (e.g. μ, σ) of supplier material supply time, supply proportion from the backup supplier.
Risk-response mechanism related	$sf, sf_{dt}, sf_{st}, sf_{inv}, ss_{low}, ss, ss_{high}, \quad LCL_K, UCL_K, \\ LCL_{Ts}, UCL_{Ts}, LCL_{Ns}, UCL_{Ns}, \quad LCL_{su}, UCL_{su}.$ (see Notation List 4 in Section 3.2.2 for parameter specification)
Simulation setting	simulation terminating time, warm up time, risk measure parameters (location, extent, duration, probability) for different risk scenarios.

Table 3.6: Simulation model input data (part 2):
deterministic parameters

The output data in the simulation model refer to the observed status variables and summary statistics about the system operating status and performance. There are many status variables and statistics that can be recorded in simulation. The output data of interest are selected as performance measures of the robust Kanban system.

The system status variables that are directly observed include: the inventory and backlog level in each buffer (especially in the customer input buffer), waiting time of each customer order, recollection time of each Kanban, demand interarrival time, service completion time of each task, and so on. Every time the status variable value changes, the simulation model will record the new value and the occurrence time. Thus, in

	Performance measure	Status variable
Manufacturer view	Daily average net profit, Daily average operating cost, Daily average risk-response actions cost, Average inventory level at customer stage, Average backlog level at customer stage, Average Work-In-Process level at each workcell.	Real-time inventory and backlog level in each buffer data series, In-use Kanban number data series, Machine service time data series, Server number data series, Backup supplier proportion data series, Number of completed customer orders, Number of purchased material orders from the backup supplier, Number of purchased material orders from the main supplier.
Customer view	Average waiting time of customer orders, Customer service level (order fill rate without delay).	Waiting time of each customer order data series
Risk-response mechanism related		Recovery time after each risk event, Monitor value related data series (for monitor mi_rate, mi_inv, including: Real-time supply rate data series, Real-time process rate data series, Real-time demand rate data series, Real-time inventory and backlog level at customer stage data series).

Table 3.7: Simulation output data of robust Kanban system

the end of simulation, we can obtain the output data series of the status variables.

Except the directly observed status variables, another type of output data, the summary statistics, is also of interest in the simulation. Summary statistics cannot be observed directly, they have to be calculated using other output data and statistical methods. Take the mean waiting time of all the customer orders as an example, we cannot observe the mean value directly because it is a summary statistic. Instead, we have to calculate the mean value of waiting time after collecting every customer's waiting time data, which is a directly observed status variable. In this simulation model, the summary statistics are used as performance measures of the robust Kanban system. The statistics include such as the average waiting time of customer orders, the average inventory level and backlog level in the input buffers, the percentage of customer orders that are filled without delay (the customer service level), the net profit, and the total cost of operating the Kanban system.

The information about simulation output data is summarized in Table 3.7. The output data are classified into three classes according to their functions in the robust Kanban system. Some performance measures, such as the total net profit and average inventory level, are selected for the manufacturer's requirements. While other performance measures, such as the average waiting time of customer orders, are designed for the customer's requirements. In addition, we record a set of special output data used in the risk-response mechanism, to check whether the mechanism is applied correctly; they are also included in Table 3.7.

Recall Figure 3.3 and Figure 3.5, the control logic of the risk-response mechanism of the robust Kanban system has been described detailedly in these figures. Now we implement the control logic in the simulation model by programming in Matlab language. The 3 steps of applying the risk-response mechanism are executed periodically (in each review period) during the simulation, till the terminating time (e.g. 4000 time unit in simulation clock) is reached.

So far, the simulation model of the robust Kanban system with its risk-response mechanism has been completely established. Nextly, we want to check whether it is a useful and correct simulation model to represent the conceptual model, the model verification and validation work is then performed.

3.3.3 Model verification

Model verification is an important step of the simulation model development. It aims at answering the question: "Are we building the model right?" In this study, the verification of the Kanban simulation model is to find out whether the risk scenarios and the working mechanism of the robust Kanban system are correctly represented in the simulation model. Especially, it is of great concern whether the proposed risk-response mechanism is accurately implemented by the simulation model as designed in the conceptual model.

In order to observe the operation details of the simulation model, simulation animation is used to show the dynamic status changes of system elements during the system operation. Animation data include such as the data series of the inventory level and backlog level in the customer input buffer (see Figure 3.8), data series of monitor mi_rate and mi_inv values (see Figure 3.9a,b), and data series of 3-level adjustable parameters values (see Figure 3.9c,d). These data can provide very useful information for the model verification (and validation). With these data we can gain more insights into the system operation.

The verification work of the simulation model contains two parts. First, we examine whether the basic dual-Kanban control mechanism is operated correctly. Second, we verify whether the advanced risk-response mechanism, which can dynamically change 3-level system parameters, is implemented correctly.

Verification work part 1

We first set fixed values for all the parameters in the robust Kanban system, thus the robust Kanban system can be seen as a normal Toyota Kanban system. Then we run the simulation model and analyze output data, to check whether the dual-Kanban mechanism is working correctly. The plots in Figure 3.8 illustrate the dynamic changes of the important output data during simulation. The output data include not only status

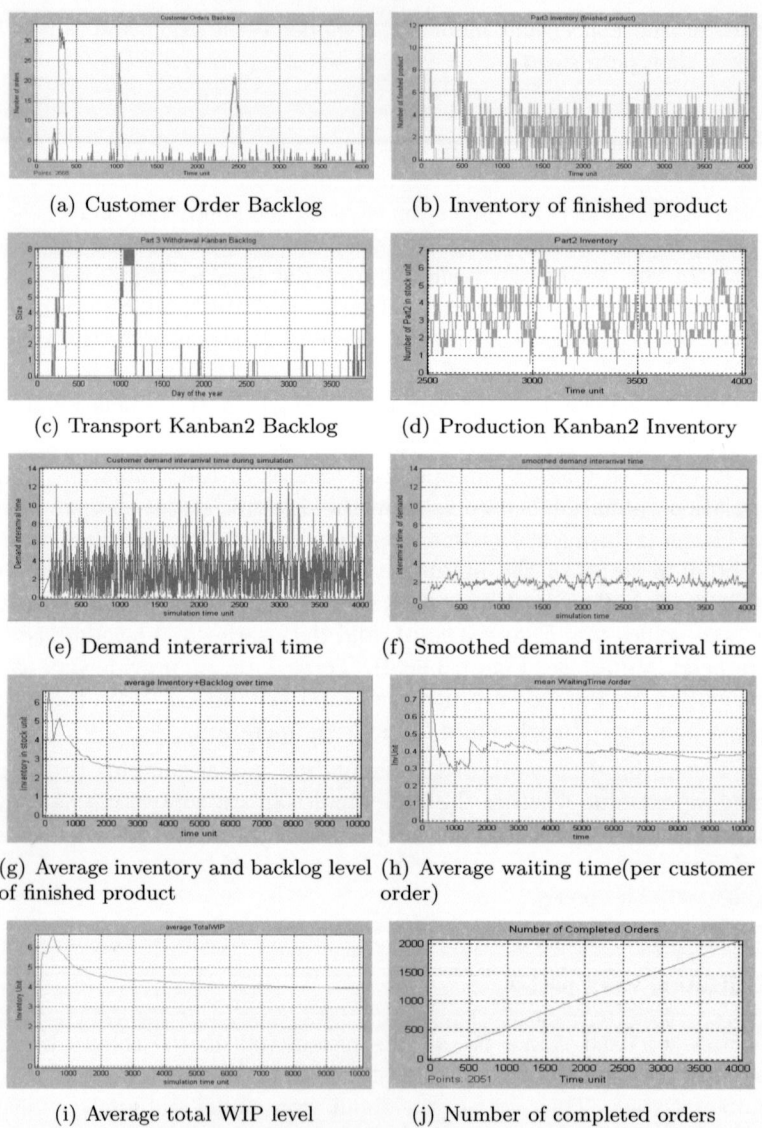

(a) Customer Order Backlog

(b) Inventory of finished product

(c) Transport Kanban2 Backlog

(d) Production Kanban2 Inventory

(e) Demand interarrival time

(f) Smoothed demand interarrival time

(g) Average inventory and backlog level of finished product

(h) Average waiting time(per customer order)

(i) Average total WIP level

(j) Number of completed orders

Figure 3.8: Typical simulation output data (system status and performance measures) vs. Time in Robust Kanban System, given fixed-value parameters

variables but also summary statistics (performance measures). For example, Plot a) and b) display the real-time inventory and backlog levels of finished product in the customer input buffer. Plot g) and h) show the average inventory backlog level over the past time, and the average waiting time of customer orders (as performance measures). The other plots in Figure 3.8 also provide useful information about the system behavior. With the output data plots, the system operating status can be visually represented. Every time a simulation event occurs, values of relevant variables and parameters can be recorded in the output data series. Then through analyzing the output data, we can know whether the dual- Kanban mechanism is implemented correctly in the simulation model. For instance, when a demand order arrives at the customer stage, we check the values of the status variable "inventory and backlog level" before and after the demand arrival. When a service completion event occurs at a workcell, we check whether the "inventory and backlog level" in the input or output buffer is changed correctly. When analyzing the simulation output data (as shown in Figure 3.8), we found that the observed behavior and results of the dual-Kanban mechanism in the simulation model is in line with the prediction given by the conceptual model. Hence, we conclude that the simulation model is operating the dual-Kanban mechanism correctly.

Verification work part 2

In the second part, we aim to verify whether the risk-response mechanism can correctly change the 3-level adjustable parameters (K, T_s, N_s, T_{su}) in response to risks, as the conceptual model designed.

Recall in Figure 3.5, we have listed all possible decision cases the robust Kanban system may face. Following the control logic, we examine the actual response actions taken by the simulation model when different risk events happen. If it is observed that the output responses of simulation models are in accordance with the responses generated by the conceptual model, we can then conclude that the risk-response mechanism of the robust Kanban system is implemented correctly by the simulation model.

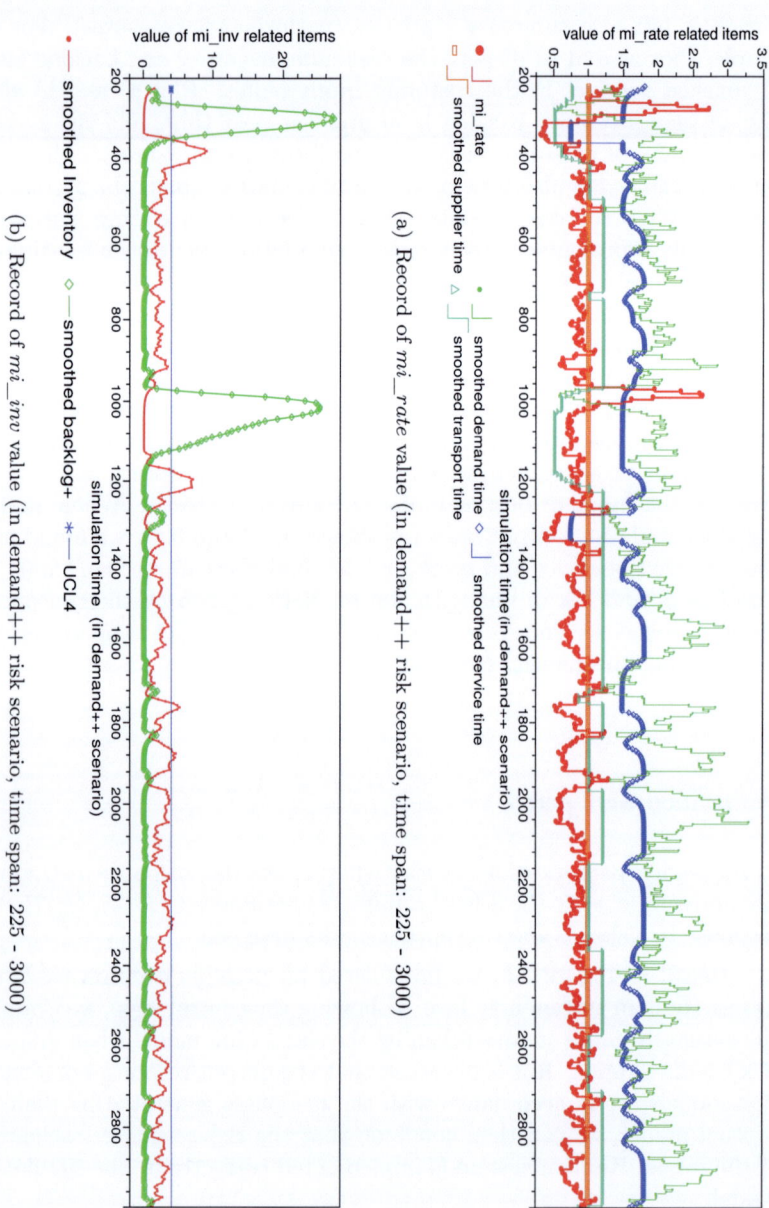

(a) Record of *mi_rate* value (in demand++ risk scenario, time span: 225 - 3000)

(b) Record of *mi_inv* value (in demand++ risk scenario, time span: 225 - 3000)

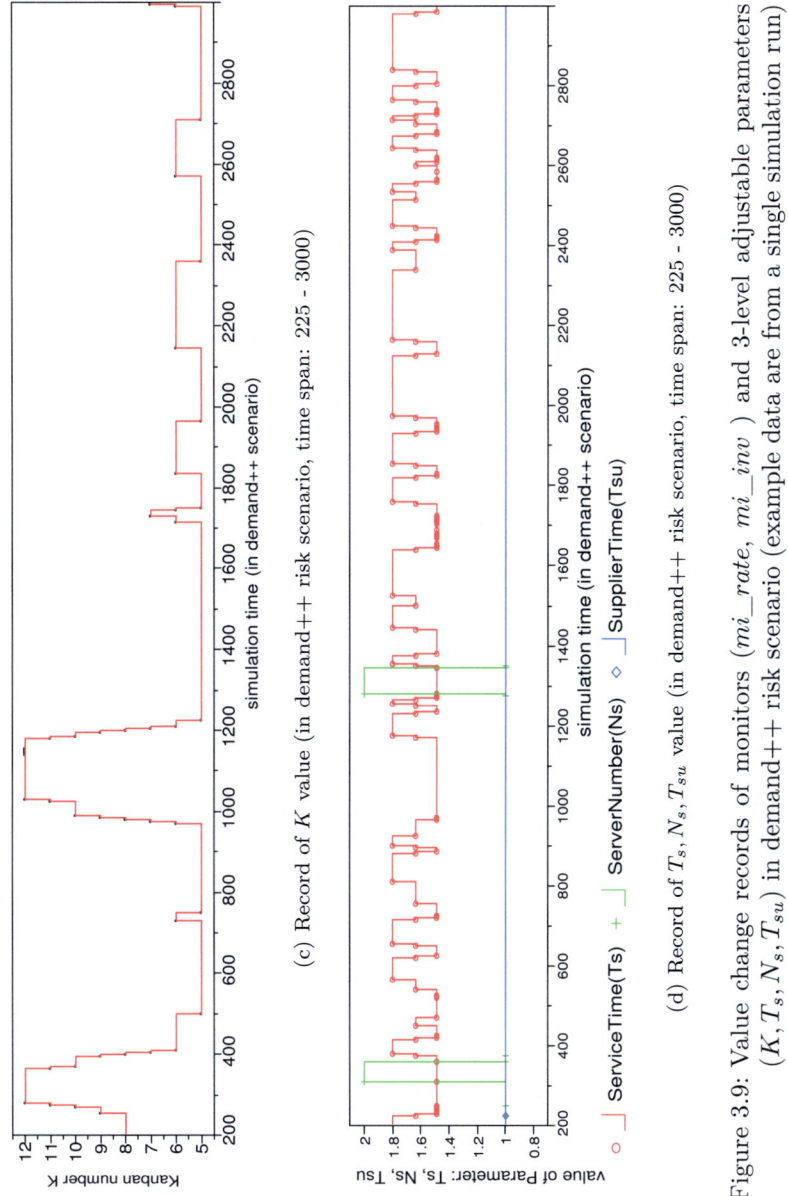

(c) Record of K value (in demand++ risk scenario, time span: 225 - 3000)

(d) Record of T_s, N_s, T_{su} value (in demand++ risk scenario, time span: 225 - 3000)

Figure 3.9: Value change records of monitors (mi_rate, mi_inv) and 3-level adjustable parameters (K, T_s, N_s, T_{su}) in demand++ risk scenario (example data are from a single simulation run)

The second-part verification work was performed through a series of simulation experiments. The output results and related analysis are presented as below.

We select some simulation output results as sample data to analyze. As an example, Figure 3.9 shows some value change records of the monitors (mi_rate and mi_inv) and the 3-level adjustable parameters (K, T_s, N_s, T_{su}). They are collected from a single simulation run of the robust Kanban system in a demand++ (severe demand increase) risk scenario. The time spans of all the data fragments are identical, from 225 to 3000 in simulation clock, and the total operating time is 5000 time units in simulation clock. Figure 3.9a) illustrates the value change of mi_rate as the simulation time passes. In addition to mi_rate, other items which account for the mi_rate value are also presented in Figure 3.9a), including the smoothed machine service time, smoothed demand interarrival time, and smoothed material supply time. And in Figure 3.9b), the smoothed inventory level and backlog level of finished product, which are contributing factors of mi_inv, are displayed in the same time span. As a supplement, the dashed line marks the inventory upper control limit (we set UCL=4 in this example) in the same plot for reference.

Besides recording the value changes of monitors, we also observe the value changes of the 3-level adjustable parameters during simulation. Figure 3.9c) presents the value records of Kanban number K and Figure 3.9d) is about other adjustable parameters (Machine service time T_s, Server number N_s, Material supply time T_{su}) in the same demand++ risk scenario.

By comparing the monitors' value changes with the 3-level parameters' value changes, we find that the 3-level parameters are adjusted reasonably according to the observed monitor values. For example, in Figure 3.9a) we observed that a sudden decrease of smoothed demand interarrival time (the green line) occurred around time 1000, which caused an increase in mi_rate value. Then the smoothed backlog level in Figure 3.9b) increased shortly after time 1000 due to the increased demand rate. To deal with the demand-increase risk, the risk-response mechanism decided to take the response actions of increasing the service capacity. The selected actions (the adjusted parameters) can be observed in Figure 3.9c) and d). From Figure 3.9c), we can see that the Kanban number gradually increased since the demand-increase risk occurred around time 1000. On the other hand, the machine service time (in Figure 3.9d)) accordingly declined at the same time. When the demand-increase risk was gone, the deviated monitor value gradually went back to the normal range, and the 3-level parameters were correspondingly adjusted back to the normal level too. Based on this observation, we can verify the risk-response mechanism control logic is correctly implemented by the simulation model.

In conclusion, it is reasonable to conclude that the simulation model of the robust Kanban system is a correct implementation of the conceptual model; the risk-response mechanism of the robust Kanban system is accurately executed in the simulation environment.

3.3.4 Model validation

Model validation is to find out whether the model is an accurate representation of the real world system. It intends to answer the question: "Are we building the right model?" In this study, the robust Kanban system is a newly developed model; no existing real system can be observed and compared with the simulation model. Therefore, the validation of the simulation model is mainly performed from two aspects: 1) analyze the simulation model based on common sense in real life; 2) compare the simulation model with other existing Kanban system models. The detailed validation work is presented in the following parts.

Validation work part 1

In Part 1 of the validation work, we conduct some simulation runs and collect their output data to examine whether the output results are in line with the common sense (including related theories and actual behaviors in real world). This is a basic and important step of the model validation. If the result is satisfactory, further validation work can be done. Otherwise, if the simulation results are inconsistent with reality, it can be inferred that the model is not an appropriate representation of the real system; more adjustments are required to improve the model formulation.

Here we did two common sense-based validation tests through running a series of simulation experiments. We assume a set of different input parameters, then analyze the output results to check whether the model behavior is in accordance with the real-life behavior or common sense.

The first test is to run the Kanban system under a stable scenario. The output results are shown in Figure 3.8. Take Figure 3.8g) and h) as an example to analyze. These results are obtained from a simulation run in a stable scenario, where the demand is stably distributed and the service rate is sufficient to cover the demand. From the plots we can observe that, as the operating time passes, both the mean inventory backlog level and the mean waiting time tend to remain at stable levels, which implies the system reached a stable operating status in the long run. This observation is consistent with the theoretical knowledge about the queueing system. And in real world, it is also common and reasonable for a production system with a sufficient service capacity and a stable demand type to achieve a stable state, if the operating time is sufficiently long. Thus, the first common sense-based validation test is passed.

The second test is to run the Kanban system in a series of different scenarios. Given a series of different parameter conditions, the simulation model is run respectively under each condition. We adjust the values of parameter K (Kanban number) and T_s (machine service time) in each simulation run, but keep other parameters unchanged. In a single simulation run, the values of parameters K and T_s are fixed over the entire operating time, thus the robust Kanban system is equal to a traditional Toyota Kanban system. But in different runs, the values of parameters are changed systematically as input conditions. After a series of simulation runs, we can collect output results of interest (such as mean net profit, mean inventory and backlog level) under each input condition (different combinations of K and T_s values). Through analyzing the output data, we judge whether the simulation model behavior is reasonable in real life.

Figure 3.10 illustrates the results of the second test. In this test, a series of simulation runs is performed with parameter K ranging from 4 to 14 (integers), and T_s ranging from 1.4 to 1.8 time units (discrete values: 1.4, 1.6, 1.8). Since the mean value of demand interarrival time is supposed to be 2 time units ($t_d^{mean}=2$), the average traffic intensity ρ

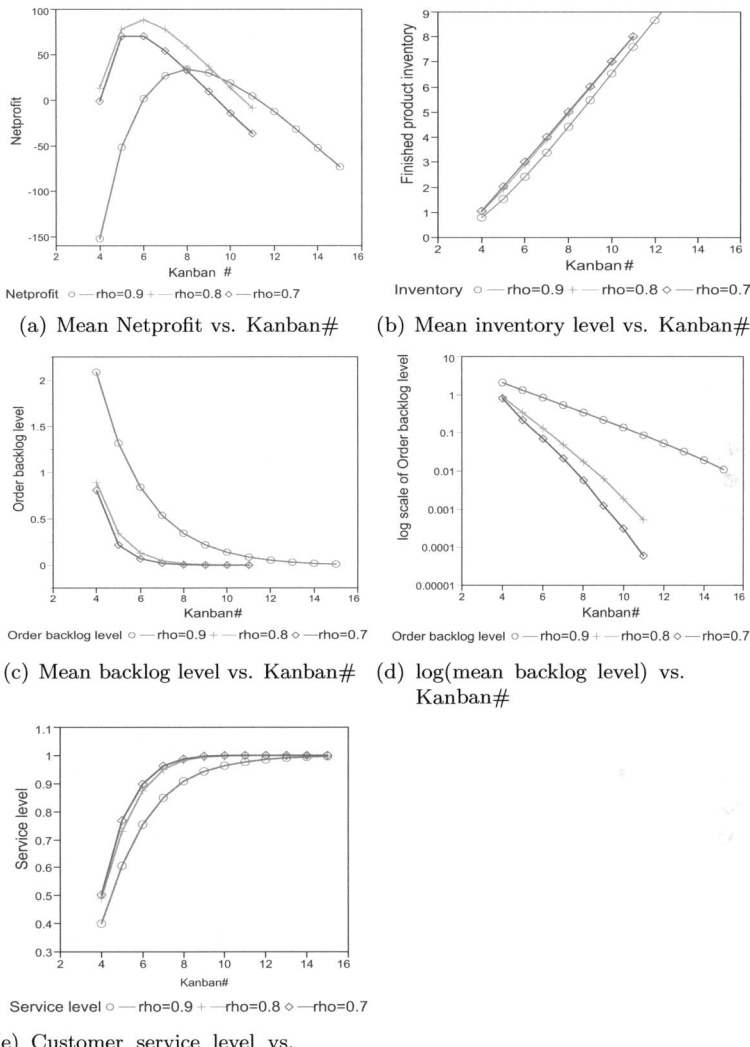

(a) Mean Netprofit vs. Kanban#

(b) Mean inventory level vs. Kanban#

(c) Mean backlog level vs. Kanban#

(d) log(mean backlog level) vs. Kanban#

(e) Customer service level vs. Kanban#

Figure 3.10: Simulation output results of validation test 2

$(\rho = \lambda/\mu = T_s/t_d^{mean})$ is consequently ranging from 0.7 to 0.9 (discrete values: $0.7, 0.8, 0.9$). The plots a)-e) in Figure 3.10 present the simulation results of related performance measure.

In Figure 3.10a), we can observe that for each ρ (or Ts) value (ρ=0.7,0.8,0.9, indicating T_s=1.4, 1.6, 1.8), the mean Netprofit data form an "arch" curve as parameter K (Kanban number) changes from 4 to 14. There exists a peak point in each curve, and the peak points are achieved with different K values under different ρ (or Ts) values. The "arch" form of the Netprofit curves is consistent with real world experience. Because when using a small Kanban number in the system, the production rate and machine utilization are limited at a low level; this could cause the risk of backlog orders and penalty cost. On the contrary, when a large Kanban number is adopted, additional cost could be incurred due to too much inventory stored in the buffers. Hence, there must be a better point between the two extreme points, which can generate the lowest cost or the highest Netprofit value. For example, as can be seen in Plot a), given ρ=0.8 (T_s=1.6), the maximum Netprofit value (around 95) is reached at K=6. Given ρ=0.9 (T_s=1.8), the optimal Netprofit value is 30 with K=8. And given ρ=0.7 (T_s=1.4), the optimal Netprofit value (around 75) is achieved at K=5. Comparing the three Netprofit curves under different ρ values, we can select the global optimal Netprofit value and its corresponding control parameters K and T_s among all input parameter combinations. In this example, the global optimal Netprofit value is around 95, which is reached at K=6 and T_s=1.8 (ρ=0.8). This numerical example also suggests a simulation-based method to find the optimal setting of the 3-level parameters.

In Figure 3.10b), we found that the mean inventory level has a linear relationship with Kanban number. This is also a reasonable phenomenon. The inventory level is limited by the Kanban number at that stage. The total number of Kanbans minus the transport-underway Kanban number is the number of Kanbans remaining in the buffer, which means the inventory level in that buffer. If the transport-underway Kanban number is relatively stable (given stable demand rate and transport time, the transport-underway Kanban is then stable), it is no surprise that the inventory level and Kanban number form a linear relationship.

Figure 3.10c) and d) show us the relationship between the mean order backlog level and the Kanban number. Plot c) is a normal plot, while

Plot d) is a semi-log plot (Y-axis is log(Backlog level value), X-axis is normal Kanban number value). The linear relationship observed in semi-log plot d) implies that an exponential function is a good approximation for the "Backlog level vs. Kanban number" relationship. In this example, the customer demand interarrival time is assumed to be exponentially distributed, and the machine service time is constant, this is a special input condition with the exponential feature. It is wondered whether the exponential-relationship conclusion obtained from this semi-log plot can be extended to other cases, such as the cases with a gamma, uniform or other general distribution of demand interarrival time and service time. Further investigation of this problem is carried out in the following study; it can be found in Section 4.1.3.

Lastly, Figure 3.10e) presents the changes of customer service level as the Kanban number increases. The observation is also parallel to common sense: the more Kanban cards we use (implying more inventory is stored in the buffer), the more probably the customer order is filled without delay. To be noted, the customer service level (order fill rate without delay) is increasing as the Kanban number increases, but the marginal increasing rate is becoming lower and lower. There seems to be a "saturation point" for the Kanban number, and there also exists an upper limit 1 for the service level, which can be never exactly achieved.

Validation work part 2

Since there is no existing robust Kanban system in real world, we cannot compare the simulation model with real systems. Therefore, we consider comparing the new simulation model with other existing Kanban models as part 2 of the validation work.

The robust Kanban system is a flexible system, if we define specific system structures and parameters for the system, some other Kanban systems can be built as special versions of the robust Kanban system. For example, if all 3-level adjustable parameters are kept constant, the robust Kanban system is identical to a traditional Toyota Kanban system (standard Kanban system). If only the Kanban number is allowed to change, the robust Kanban system can be seen as an adaptive Kanban system (Tardif and Maaseidvaag 2001). Therefore in this study, we select two Kanban system models presented in literature (DiMascolo, Frein and

Dallery 1996; Tardif and Maaseidvaag 2001) as comparison objects for the robust Kanban system model. We model the structures and working mechanisms of the two object models based on modifying the parameters of the robust Kanban system model. We set the same input data in the two object models as the data used in literature, then run the models in the simulation environment to see whether the output results are identical to the results given in literature. If the results are identical, it can be inferred that the robust Kanban system with the specified configuration is a correct representation of the Kanban models from literature. This can be seen as a kind of validation for the robust Kanban system simulation model.

Number of stages	Number of Kanbans	Demand rate λ	Backlog level(from *1)	Backlog level(this work)	Relative error $= (R_{sim} - R_{lit})/R_{lit}$
3	5	0.100	0	0	0
3	5	0.500	0.033	0.0325	-1.52%
3	5	0.625	0.230	0.2211	-3.91%
3	5	0.800	4.260	4.2650	0.12%

Table 3.8: Results comparison for traditional Kanban system: data from literature*1 vs. data from robust Kanban system simulation model (*1: DiMascolo, Frein et al. 1996)

KERC (Kanban Code in*2)	Total cost Z (from *2)	Total cost Z (this work)	Relative error $= (R_{sim} - R_{lit})/R_{lit}$
6000	6.3903	6.3905	0.00%
6100	6.2658	6.2663	0.01%
6200	6.2505	6.2553	0.08%
6300	6.2443	6.2455	0.02%
5134	6.1096	6.1144	0.08%
4634	5.6122	5.6302	0.32%

Table 3.9: Results comparison for adaptive Kanban system: data from literature*2 vs. data from robust Kanban system simulation model (*2: Tardif and Maaseidvaag 2001)

The two Kanban system models we selected from literature are typical Kanban models in the Kanban systems development history. The first model is the traditional Toyota Kanban system which uses a constant Kanban number (refer to DiMascolo(1996)). The second model is an inventory-based adaptive Kanban system model where the Kanban number can be dynamically changed (refer to Tardif (2001)). Based on modifying some parameters of the robust Kanban system simulation model, we rebuilt simulation models for the two object models, with following their configuration given in literature. The traditional Kanban system model is a 3-stage production system using only Production Kanban. And the inventory-based adaptive Kanban system model is a single-stage system using only Production Kanban. Accordingly, when rebuilding the two models, the Transport Kanban function in the robust Kanban system model is blocked, and the number of stages in the robust Kanban system model is modified. After specifying the system configuration, we conduct simulation experiments for the two rebuilt simulation models, and then compare the output results with the results from literature.

The output results of the two rebuilt simulation models and the original results from literature are summarized in Table 3.8 and Table 3.9. Comparing the simulation and literature results, we can see that the results of simulation models obtained by the modified robust Kanban system model are basically consistent with the results given in literature. The relative errors between simulation results and literature results are all within acceptable ranges. Hence, it is reasonable to conclude that the traditional Kanban system and the adaptive Kanban system can be modeled correctly by the robust Kanban system simulation model. The conclusion implies the robust Kanban system is comparing well with the two typical Kanban systems (although not real world systems). Thus the second part of the validation work is accomplished.

So far, the two parts of the validation work have been accomplished. From the validation results, some basic behavior rules of the robust Kanban system can be observed and summarized. This is helpful for our further study. Although there is no existing real world system for us to compare as validation, the comparison between the robust Kanban system simulation model and real world experience, or other Kanban models from literature, can still provide useful information as validation.

In this chapter, we have described a detailed conceptual model, and built the simulation model for the robust Kanban system. The parameters with respect to the system configuration or the risk-response mechanism implementation are introduced in this chapter with describing their functions, but the methods for determining their values are not discussed yet. The methods will be discussed in the next chapter.

4 Methodology of parameter setting

In order to apply the robust Kanban system, the values of two types of parameters need to be carefully determined. The first-type parameters are related to determining the configuration of the robust Kanban system. For instance, the 3-level adjustable parameters (Kanban number, machine service time, server number, and backup supplier proportion) are of the first type. The second-type parameters are related to the risk-response mechanism application. The smoothing weight factors used in monitor value calculation, and the control limit parameters involved in decision-making criteria, belong to the second type.

In Chapter 3 we have introduced the basic functions of the parameters. However, the methods about how to determine suitable values for them are not discussed yet. In this chapter, we aim to solve the parameter-setting problem. The remainder of this chapter is organized as follows. First, in Section 4.1, the methods for deciding the 3-level adjustable parameters (for system configuration) are introduced; the parameter setting is derived based on mathematical programming. Nextly in Section 4.2, the estimation methods for setting the control parameters used in the risk-response mechanism are explained.

4.1 Decision of 3-level adjustable parameters

When the environment is stable or repetitive, the traditional Kanban system can perform well with using a fixed Kanban number. Hence, in stable scenarios, we can use deterministic or simple stochastic models to determine a set of constant parameter settings for the Kanban system. It is more convenient and practical to obtain solutions in these models than in a complex stochastic model. Although some simplifying assumptions and restrictions are included in the deterministic or simple stochastic models, they can still provide useful information. In this study, it is supposed that the environment is uncertain, various risks may happen to the system. Hence, to investigate the behavior of the robust Kanban system in the uncertain environment, we select a series of typical risk scenarios to represent the uncertain environment. Each risk scenario can be seen as a stable scenario with some embedded risk events. Thus, we first study the parameter setting methods for the robust Kanban system in a stable scenario. Then, referring to the results, we further analyze the parameter-setting problem in risk scenarios.

In this work, if all the parameters and variables used in a scenario are known with certainty, we consider it as a "stable scenario". The parameters and variables could be either deterministic or stochastic but with certain distribution types and parameters. For example, a stable scenario can have an exponentially distributed customer demand interarrival time. Although the demand interarrival time is a random variable, the distribution type and scale parameter (mean demand rate) of demand interarrival time are constant. So it is seen as a stable scenario. Other scenarios with uncertain values or distributions of the parameters and variables are classified as risk scenarios, from which we select some typical risk scenarios to do further study.

The work in Section 4.1 is to find the suitable values for 3-level adjustable parameters (Kanban number, machine service time, server number, and backup supplier proportion), which characterize the basic structure of the robust Kanban system. We developed a mixed integer nonlinear programming (MINLP) model to help determine the 3-level parameters. The solutions obtained from the MINLP model can be thought of as the optimal parameter setting for the robust Kanban system in the stable scenario. Meanwhile, the MINLP model solutions can also provide useful reference for parameter-setting decisions in other risk scenarios. The MINLP-model solutions can be used as the baseline (and initial) parameter setting, when operating the robust Kanban system in other risk scenarios.

4.1.1 Introduction of decision model (MINLP)

In order to determine suitable values of the 3-level adjustable parameters, we formulate a mixed integer nonlinear programming (MINLP) model by using the AIMMS language package (Bisschop 2006).

Through implementing the MINLP model, the optimal solutions of the 3-level adjustable parameters setting can be obtained. Given a specific stable scenario, the MINLP model can help the robust Kanban system select an optimal parameter setting that generates minimum total cost. Then, in other risk scenarios (where risk events are added into the stable scenarios), the optimal solutions of the stable scenarios can be used as baseline-setting, which is important reference for the parameter-setting in other risk scenarios.

The objective of the MINLP model is to minimize the total cost of operating the robust Kanban system. The total cost consists of inventory holding cost, order backlog penalty cost, and the cost of changing 3-level parameters. Decision variables in the MINLP model are the 3-level adjustable parameters. To formulate the model, the relationships between model objective and decision variables need to be figured out. In reality, it is usually difficult to develop accurate functional relationships between the total cost and decision variables; hence approximation methods are adopted here to formulate the cost functions. Moreover, the constraints about system elements' relationships and the ranges of adjusting parameters are also contained in the MINLP model.

We do the following steps to build and apply the MINLP model. First step, the information about the system operation features should be collected as preliminary, in order to specify the input conditions of the model. The information includes such as the system structure, the adjusting ranges of machine service capacities, cost coefficients of operating service equipment, the probability distribution of demand interarrival time. Second step, the decision variables, and related parameters used in the MINLP model should be clearly defined; we should make the model simple but never too simple. Third step, the constraints should be well considered and formulated. Forth step, the formulas of calculating the inventory cost, backlog cost, changing and operating 3-level parameters cost, need to be identified to generate the objective cost function. Lastly, the MINLP model is then implemented and solved using AIMMS language package. The solution results can be conveniently obtained by running the AIMMS model in a computer.

A verbal statement of the MINLP model is summarized as follows:

Objective: *to minimize the total cost of operating the robust Kanban System*

$$Totalcost = cost_{inventory} + cost_{backlog} + cost_{change3levelparameters}$$

Subject to (constraints):

Rate constraints:

   supply rate>= demand rate

   process rate>=demand rate

   transport rate>= demand rate

Capacity constraints

Respective domains of 3-level decision variables

Service level constraints(optional):

   Probability {demand order waiting time is 0} ≥ target service level

The above verbal model is subsequently formulated as a mathematical model. The variables and parameters used in the MINLP model are summarized as below:

Indices:

i Index of stages $i \in \{0, 1, \ldots, I, c\}$

Variables:

Kp_i Number of Production Kanbans at stage i,
            $Kp_i \in [\min Kp_i, maxKp_i]$, integer

Kt_i Number of Transport Kanbans at stage i,
            $Kt_i \in [\min Kt_i, maxKt_i]$, integer

Ts_i Single-machine service time at stage i,
            e.g. $Ts_i \in [80\% \, Ts0_i, 120\% \, Ts0_i]$, where $Ts0_i$ is a baseline value (constant)

Ns_i Number of in-use servers at stage i, e.g. $Ns_i \in \{1, 2, 3\}$

T_{su} Material supply time required at the supplier stage, $T_{su} > 0$

pr_{backup} Material supply proportion from the backup supplier, e.g. $pr_{backup} \in [0, 0.5]$

Parameters:

sl	Target service level (order fill rate without delay), $0 < sl < 1$
t_d	Customer demand interarrival time (could be a stochastic parameter, e.g. $t_d \sim \exp(1/t_d^{mean})$)
t_d^{mean}	Mean value of t_d
t_d^{sl}	Critical value of demand time, which makes $\Pr\{t_d \leq t_d^{sl}\} = sl$
h_i	Inventory holding cost per product unit per time unit at stage i
b_i	Backlog penalty cost per product unit per time unit at stage i
cKp_i	Cost of operating a Production Kanban per time unit at stage i
cKt_i	Cost of operating a Transport Kanban per time unit at stage i
$cStime_i$	Cost coefficient of adopting the selected machine service time at stage i
$cServer_i$	Cost coefficient of operating a server per time unit at stage i
$cSupplier_i$	Cost coefficient of changing the supplier proportion contract each time
K_i^{mean}	Number of Kanbans required at stage i to cover the mean demand rate
sf	Safety factor which makes $\frac{demand\ rate}{service\ rate} \leq \frac{1}{sf} \leq 1$
Tc_i	Kanban collection time at stage i, $Tc_i = \max\{Tc_i^{production}, Tc_i^{transport}\}$
$Tc_i^{production}$	Time of collecting a Production Kanban at stage i
$Tc_i^{transport}$	Time of collecting a Transport Kanban at stage i
$\overline{I}_i$	Estimated mean inventory level at stage i, $\overline{I}_i = K_i - K_i^{mean}$
$\overline{B}_i$	Estimated mean order backlog level at stage i

To be noted, here we add a simplifying assumption in the Kanban system: we assume $Kp_i = Kt_i$ at stage i. Thus for the sake of simplicity, the decision variables Kanban number Kp_i, Kt_i can be rewritten by dropping the subscript as K_i. In the following text, the notation K_i will be used instead of Kp_i or Kt_i. Suppose a specific stage i is the bottleneck stage, then K_i signifies the number of Kanbans used at the bottleneck stage i.

4.1.2 Constraints

The constraints in the MINLP model can group into two types: rate constraints and capacity constraints. In addition, another optional service-level constraint can be also added into the model depending on the decision maker's requirement. The reasons and methods for formulating the constraints are explained as below.

Rate constraints

- *supply rate $\geq$ demand rate*
- *process rate $\geq$ demand rate*
- *Kanban collection rate (or called transport rate) $\geq$ demand rate*

The robust Kanban system model is essentially a complex queueing network. Therefore the stable condition in queueing theory ($\rho = \lambda/\mu < 1$) can be applied to the robust Kanban system model as well. The rate constraints in the MINLP model are designed based on the stable condition. In the condition formula $\rho = \lambda/\mu < 1$, λ means the average customer demand rate, μ signifies the average service rate of the bottleneck stage (the slowest stage), and ρ is the traffic intensity of the queueing system. The queue is stable only if $\rho < 1$, namely $\lambda < \mu$, which means the service completion rate is larger than the demand arrival rate. Otherwise $\rho \geq 1$, the waiting queue will grow indefinitely long, and the system cannot achieve a stable state. In the robust Kanban system model, the service rate μ could have different interpretations. The material supply rate at the supplier stage, the goods transporting rate between stages, and the processing rate in the workcell, all these rates could affect the final service rate of the Kanban system. Therefore, the stable condition is interpreted in the robust Kanban system using three rate constraints: supply rate$\geq$demand rate; process rate$\geq$demand rate; and Kanban collection rate (or transport rate)$\geq$demand rate.

Write the first constraint "Supply rate $\geq$ Demand rate" in another form, it is: "Supplier material supply time $\cdot sf \leq$ Demand interarrival time". Here we add a safety factor sf ($sf = 1+\varepsilon > 1$, ε is a small positive) in the constraint formula to ensure that supplier material supply time is strictly less than customer demand interarrival time, because $\rho = \lambda/\mu$ should be strictly less than 1 in the stable condition. It can be inferred that, higher sf values will lead to lower probability of order backlog. Usually the sf value is set slightly above 1. Here we set the safety factor sf=1.01 as an initial estimation. Then, we rewrite the verbal supply rate constraint in a mathematical form, as shown in Formula 4.1.

$$T_{su} \cdot sf \leq t_d^{mean} \qquad (4.1)$$

The second constraint "Process rate $\geq$ Demand rate" is interpreted as "Machine time/Server Number $\cdot sf \leq$ Demand interarrival time" in the robust Kanban system model. We estimate the average process time of the entire workcell by dividing the single-machine service time by the number of servers. The average process time of a workcell should be less than the mean demand interarrival time, if the system can reach a stable state. Formula 4.2 is the mathematical formula for the process rate constraint.

$$Ts_i \cdot sf \leq t_d^{mean} \cdot Ns_i \qquad (4.2)$$

The third constraint "Kanban collection rate $\geq$ demand rate" is related to the Kanban cycling rate; it is represented by "Kanban collection time/Kanban Number $\cdot sf \leq$ Demand interarrival time". The time consumed to recollect a Kanban into its buffer is called Kanban collection time. For a Transport Kanban, the time includes the transporting-underway time and the waiting time spent at the blocked output buffer. For a Production Kanban, the time includes machine process time and waiting time spent at the blocked input buffer. We consider the arrival of a Kanban card in the buffer as an arrival event; thus, the Kanban collection time divided by Kanban number can be seen as the mean Kanban interarrival time. The Kanban interarrival time is supposed to be less than the average demand interarrival time, because if the Kanban number is not sufficient to make the Kanban interarrival rate cover the demand rate, the customer waiting queue will grow infinitely long. This constraint is represented by Formula 4.3.

$$Tc_i \cdot sf \leq t_d^{mean} \cdot K_i \qquad \forall i \in \{1, 2, \ldots, I\} \qquad (4.3)$$

Capacity constraints

- Domain of Kanban number K_i
- Domain of single-machine service time Ts_i
- Domain of server number Ns_i
- Domain of supplier material supply time T_{su}

The capacity constraints refer to the domains of decision variables. Namely, which values (or ranges) are available for the decision variables to take. The domain constraints are considered because the capacity of machines or other service facilities is always bounded in practice. For example, if only two servers can be maximally located in a workcell due to the economic capacity, the domain of Ns_i is consequently $\{1,2\}$. If the process machine has only three optional speed levels (e.g. speed=1, 2, 3 product units/min) to work, the domain of Ts_i is then $\{1,1/2,1/3\}$. The capacity constraints are given arbitrarily depending on the practical situation of relevant service equipment.

Service level constraints (optional)

- Probability$\{$order waiting time=0$\} \geq$ target service level

The service level constraint is an optional constraint in the MINLP model, as a supplement to the above-mentioned constraints. The rate and capacity constraints are included with considering the average operation level. With the rate and capacity constraints, it can be ensured that the Kanban system can operate without indefinite congestion and reach a stable state in the long run. The model objective is to minimize the total cost. If we use only the rate and capacity constraints in the MINLP model, optimal solutions that generate the minimum cost can be already derived. However, if a specific service level is required by the customers (e.g. order fill rate is expected to be above 90%), only using the rate and capacity constraints is not sufficient. In this situation, the service level constraint should be taken into consideration, to guarantee the system can reach a 90% customer service level. The service level constraint in the MINLP model is a probabilistic constraint, it means "Probability$\{$customer order waiting time is 0$\} \geq$ service level" (denoted by Service Level Constraint-a).

In the model, the customer demand interarrival time t_d is supposed to be a stochastic parameter with a specified probability distribution. The cumulative distribution function (cdf) of t_d is roughly known for calculation in the probabilistic constraint. The probabilistic constraint is not easy to solve. Hence, to solve it, we first consider a stricter interpretation of Service Level Constraint-a): "Prob{Kanban interarrival time $\leq$ demand interarrival time} $\geq$ target service level" (denoted by Service Level Constraint-b). Write Constraint-b in a mathematical form, it is (see Formula 4.4):

$$Prob\{\frac{Tc_i}{K_i} \leq t_d\} \geq sl \qquad (4.4)$$

In Constraint-b, the probability that Kanban interarrival time is less than demand interarrival time, is supposed to be above the required service level sl. However, it should be noted that, Constraint-b is stricter than the original Service Level Constraint-a, because there is usually Kanban inventory remaining in the buffer. In the robust Kanban system, each stage has an output buffer. Usually some product stocks are stored in the buffer as inventory, waiting for demand arrivals. Imagine two extreme situations of the inventory level. If the inventory level is always maintained around 100 stock units in the buffer, then seldom will an unsatisfied demand order (order backlog) occur. By contrast, if the inventory level is controlled to be no more than 1 product unit, then the order backlog will happen much more frequently. From the two extreme situations, we can see the important functions of the buffer and inventory. The inventory can cushion the conflict between demand and supply, the smoothing effect is especially obvious when the demand or supply is with high variability. When holding sufficient inventory in the buffer, the customer service level can be significantly improved as a result. In the robust Kanban system, each stage holds an input buffer and an output buffer. Suppose the bottleneck stage of the system is stage i. Now we focus on stage i. On average, $K_i - K_i^{mean}$ product units (with Transport Kanbans i) are remaining in the input buffer of stage $i+1$, and waiting for demand order arrivals. It is not necessary to require that each Kanban interarrival time should be less than demand interarrival time as Constraint-b stated. Instead, a relaxed but still sufficient constraint interpretation of the original Constraint-a can be: Probability{time of recollecting $K_i - K_i^{mean}$

consecutive Kanbans $\leq$ time of consuming $K_i - K_i^{mean}$ consecutive Kanbans}(denoted by Service Level Constraint-c).

We write Constraint-c in a mathematical form, it is represented by Formulas 4.5.

$$\Pr\{\frac{Tc_i}{K_i} \cdot (K_i - K_i^{mean}) \leq \sum_{j=1}^{K_i - K_i^{mean}} t_d^j\} \geq sl \qquad (4.5a)$$

$$\text{i.e.} \quad \Pr\{\frac{Tc_i}{K_i} \leq \frac{\sum_{j=1}^{K_i - K_i^{mean}} t_d^j}{K_i - K_i^{mean}} = \frac{X}{K_i - K_i^{mean}}\} \geq sl \qquad (4.5b)$$

$$\text{Further,} \quad \frac{Tc_i}{K_i} \leq \frac{X_{sl}}{K_i - K_i^{mean}} = \frac{\left(\sum_{j=1}^{K_i - K_i^{mean}} t_d^j\right)_{sl}}{K_i - K_i^{mean}} \qquad (4.5c)$$

For the sake of simplicity, we introduce a symbol X in Formula 4.5b) to denote the sum of $K_i - K_i^{mean}$ consecutive t_d value ($X = \sum_{j=1}^{K_i - K_i^{mean}} t_d^j$). Suppose a specific situation, where the random variable t_d is exponentially distributed with mean value t_d^{mean}, i.e. $t_d \sim \exp(\frac{1}{t_d^{mean}})$. Then it can be reasoned that X is a random variable following the Erlang distribution: $X \sim Erlang\left(K_i - K_i^{mean}, \frac{1}{t_d^{mean}}\right)$. In order to solve Formula 4.5b), the probability distribution of t_d and X should be roughly known as preliminary. In this "exponential demand time distribution" example, we can obtain $t_d \sim \exp(\frac{1}{t_d^{mean}})$ and $X \sim Erlang\left(K_i - K_i^{mean}, \frac{1}{t_d^{mean}}\right)$ which is convenient for further calculation. Nevertheless, in other general cases, the probability distribution of t_d and X may be difficult to acquire. In these situations, we can collect a set of important quantile points of t_d distribution (e.g. 50%, 75%, 80%, 90% data points) to get a big picture of t_d distribution for further calculation.

The item X_{sl} in Formula 4.5c) means the critical value of X which leads to $\Pr\{X \leq X_{sl}\} = sl$. Like Formula 4.5b) and c), the constraint formula using an exact probability distribution is usually too complicated to calculate in practice. To overcome the limitation, an approximation method is used to calculate Formula 4.5c).

The right hand item $\frac{X_{sl}}{K_i - K_i^{mean}}$ is replaced by a simpler approximation item $\frac{X_{sl}}{K_{iapproximate} - K_i^{mean}}$. Here $K_{iapproximate}$ is a constant, hence the service level constraint using $\frac{X_{sl}}{K_{iapproximate} - K_i^{mean}}$ instead of $\frac{X_{sl}}{K_i - K_i^{mean}}$ is much simpler for the MINLP model to solve. The value of $K_{iapproximate}$ should be appropriately determined. For example, when we solve the MINLP model with considering only the rate and capacity constraints, the obtained optimal K_i solution is a good value for $K_{iapproximate}$. And the mean inventory level in the buffer is now estimated by $K_{iapproximate} - K_i^{mean}$. The distribution of X is simplified as: $X \sim Erlang\left(K_{iapproximate} - K_i^{mean}, \frac{1}{t_d^{mean}}\right)$, where the original shape parameter $K_i - K_i^{mean}$ is replaced by a constant parameter $K_{iapproximate} - K_i^{mean}$. After the simplifying procedures, now Formula 4.5c) can be approximately calculated in a simpler form as shown in Formula 4.6.

$$\frac{Tc_i}{K_i} \cdot sf \leq \frac{X_{sl}}{K_{iapproximate} - K_i^{mean}} \qquad (4.6)$$

Comparing the previous exact Formula 4.5a) with the simplified approximation Formula 4.6, we can find that only the variable K_i is included in Formula 4.6, all other items are constant parameters. The approximation makes the calculation of the service-level constraint much easier than using Formula 4.5a).

4.1.3 Objective function

The objective of MINLP model is to minimize the total cost. The total cost is composed of three cost items: inventory cost, backlog cost, and the cost of changing 3-level parameters.

Inventory cost is a function of inventory level, and it reflects the production efficiency. Backlog cost is a function of the order backlog level (the number of unfinished customer demand orders) or a function of customer waiting time, and it can indicate customer service quality. The probability of satisfying demand orders without delay (customer service level) is affected by how much inventory is stored in the buffer as safety stocks, when other service capacity parameters are fixed. The more inventory stocks the buffer stores, the more probably the demand order is satisfied without delay (no backlog order is incurred). However, the goal of decreasing the backlog level is achieved at the price of increasing the safety stock level. There is a trade-off relationship between inventory cost and backlog cost.

The third cost item is the cost caused by changing 3-level parameters, including the parameter K_i (Kanban number), Ts_i (machine service time), Ns_i (server number), and pr_{backup} (material supply proportion of the backup supplier). The 3-level parameters characterize the capacity of service equipment in the robust Kanban system. It is reasonable to assume that, working with small-capacity equipment will cause less operating cost. There is also a trade-off relationship between the change 3-level parameters cost and the backlog cost. Compared with using a sufficient machine capacity, to operate the Kanban system using a tight machine capacity will save more operating cost. Nevertheless, the potential risk of order backlog will increase at the same time; more backlog cost will be caused.

To sum up, the objective function of the MINLP model is to minimize "Total cost", the total cost function is shown in Formula 4.7, where $Cost_{inventory}, Cost_{backlog}, Cost_{change3level}$ represent respectively the inventory cost, backlog cost, and the cost of changing 3-level parameters.

$$Cost_{total} = Cost_{inventory} + Cost_{backlog} + Cost_{change3level} \qquad (4.7)$$

The calculation methods of the secondary cost items $Cost_{inventory}$, $Cost_{backlog}$, $Cost_{change3level}$ will be sequentially discussed in the following parts.

Inventory cost function

As mentioned earlier, the inventory cost is designed as a function of the inventory level $\overline{I}_i$. In a Kanban system, the inventory is controlled by the number of Kanbans at that stage, hence the mean inventory level can be approximately calculated by the function:

$$\overline{I}_i = f_{inventory}(\cdot) = K_i - K_i^{mean} \qquad (4.8)$$
$$K_i^{mean} = Tc_i / t_d^{mean} \qquad (4.9)$$

Here $\overline{I}_i$ represents the mean inventory level at stage i, K_i is the actual Kanban number working at stage i, and K_i^{mean} means the Kanban number required to satisfy a mean demand rate. K_i^{mean} also implies there are on average K_i^{mean} Kanbans that are not stored in the buffer but transported underway. Therefore, the total Kanban number K_i minus the underway Kanban number K_i^{mean} is equal to the average Kanban number suspended in the buffer as inventory, namely, $\overline{I}_i = K_i - K_i^{mean}$. Based on this analysis, the inventory cost is designed as a function of the inventory level. The total inventory cost is a sum of inventory cost caused at each stage, its calculation is presented by Formula 4.10. h_i is the inventory holding cost rate (the holding cost per product unit per time unit) at stage i.

$$Cost_{inventory}(\cdot) = \sum_{i=1}^{i=I} h_i \cdot \overline{I}_i = \sum_{i=1}^{i=I} h_i \cdot (K_i - K_i^{mean}) \qquad (4.10)$$

The inventory cost shown in Formula 4.10 is a function of a series of parameters K_i. To investigate the effects of Kanban number at the bottleneck stage, we add a simplifying assumption into the Kanban system model: the cyclic Kanban number at other stages is parallel to the Kanban number at the bottleneck stage, namely, all $K_i = K$. Thus $C_{inventory}(\cdot)$ can be simplified as a function of a single parameter K, instead of a series of parameters K_i. It is shown in Formula 4.11.

$$Cost_{inventory}(K) = \sum_{i=1}^{i=I} h_i \cdot (K - K_i^{mean}) \qquad (4.11)$$

Change 3-level parameters cost function

The cost of changing 3-level parameters is relevant to the cost of operating the service equipment controlled by the 3-level parameters. We assume that the relationship between the operating cost and 3-level parameters is linear. The cost function is presented in Formula 4.12.

$$Cost_{change3level}(\cdot) = Cost_{Kanban} + Cost_{stime} + Cost_{server} + Cost_{supplier}$$
$$= c_{Kanban} \cdot K + c_{stime} \cdot \frac{1}{T_s} + c_{server} \cdot N_s + c_{supplier} \cdot \frac{1}{T_{su}} \qquad (4.12)$$

The parameters $c_{Kanban}, c_{stime}, c_{server} and c_{supplier}$ are cost coefficients of related decision variables K, T_s, N_s, T_{su}. The cost coefficients should be specified according to the practical situation of the factory or the decision maker's opinion.

Backlog cost function

Backlog cost is designed as a function of the customer order backlog level $\overline{B}_i$. The order backlog level is the shortage of finished product in the input buffer of the customer stage; it is an important performance measure. In this model we just focus on the backlog level at the customer stage, the remaining stages' backlog orders are not included in the calculation of backlog cost. The backlog cost function is shown by Formula 4.13, where $\overline{B}_{final}$ is the mean order backlog level at the customer stage, and b_c is the backlog cost coefficient (the penalty cost per product unit per time unit).

$$Cost_{backlog}(\cdot) = b_c \cdot \overline{B}_{final} \qquad (4.13)$$

The calculation of $\overline{B}_{final}$ is not as simple as the calculation of $\overline{I}_i$, because the relationship between $\overline{B}_{final}$ and the 3-level parameters (the decision variables in the MINLP model, including K, T_s, N_s, T_{su}) is not explicit. It was difficult to find a direct analytical function to represent the relationship. In this study, the calculation of $\overline{B}_{final}$ is mainly based on approximation or simulation-based methods. Namely, we use the data from simulation experiments to determine the backlog cost function. Given a stable scenario, the value of $\overline{B}_{final}$ is dependent on the 3-level parameters that characterize the system service capacity. The values of parameters like Kanban number K, machine service time T_s, and server number N_s may affect the order backlog level. If we treat K as a variable, and keep T_s and N_s as fixed-value parameters, then the function of mean backlog level can be described as

$$\overline{B}_{final} = f_{backlog}^\rho (K) \qquad (4.14)$$

$$\text{where} \quad \rho = \frac{\lambda}{\mu} = \frac{T_s/N_s}{t_d^{mean}} \qquad (4.15)$$

Here the parameter ρ is the service traffic intensity, and the values of T_s, N_s and t_d^{mean} are known in advance as deterministic parameters. As can be seen in Formula 4.15, the value of ρ is determined by the demand parameter t_d^{mean} and other service-capacity parameters except Kanban number K. Therefore, when different ρ values are given, the Kanban system configuration (except Kanban number K) is already specified. Further, when the value of K is specified, the performance of the Kanban system is accordingly determined as a certain result.

To develop the $\overline{B}_{final}$ function, we consider two methods: analytical method and simulation-based method.

If the analytical function for the relationship between $\overline{B}_{final}$ and 3-level parameters can be developed, the application of it will be convenient, and the calculation results are accurate. Nevertheless the formulation of analytical functions is usually difficult. Generally, the application of analytical methods is limited, because these methods are only suitable for the simple or some specific Kanban system models with simplifying assumptions and restrictions, such as a single-stage system, or a multi-stage system with exponentially distributed service time.

By contrast, simulation-based methods are more practical, they can be applied to more Kanban systems which have general structures. For example, in the robust Kanban system model, we can do simulation experiments to find out the functional relationship $\overline{B}_{final} = f^{\rho}_{backlog}(K)$. By trying a set of different K values under a fixed ρ-value on the simulation model, we can obtain a set of sample data points $(K, \overline{B}_{final})$ for the given ρ-value. Then, based on the sample data points, the curve fitting can be taken to formulate the $\overline{B}_{final}$ function. However, the simulation method has also shortcomings. Simulation is often time-consuming; many simulation experiments need to be taken to generate enough output data.

Both methods have advantages and limitations. For different problems, we select appropriate methods according to the problem features and conditions. In the following parts, we will discuss the application of analytical and simulation methods sequentially for the robust Kanban system.

Backlog level function: 1) Analytical method

The analytical method for formulating the backlog level function is based on queueing theory.

In the Kanban system, the performance of the bottleneck stage has crucial influence on the final output service rate. All downstream stages will be affected by the bottleneck stage. If we focus on the behavior of the bottleneck stage, the final service rate of the entire system can be known roughly. Therefore, we employ a G/G/k queue model to study the behavior of the bottleneck stage; we treat the bottleneck stage as a single-stage queueing system. Although the single-stage G/G/k queue model is a simplified approximation for the real bottleneck stage, it can still help us draw some insights into the entire Kanban system, especially the relationship between the order backlog level and Kanban number.

To formulate the backlog level function of the G/G/k queue, we first analyze a simpler M/M/k queue as preliminary. In an M/M/k queue (Kleinrock 1976; Gross and Harris 1998), the mean waiting queue length L_q (the mean order backlog level) is calculated by:

$$L_q = \sum_{n=k+1}^{+\infty} (n-k)\, p_n = \sum_{n=k+1}^{+\infty} (n-k)\, \frac{(k\rho)^n}{k!\, k^{n-k}} p_0 = \frac{(k\rho)^k \rho}{k!\,(1-\rho)^2} p_0 \quad (4.16)$$

where $\rho = \lambda/k\mu < 1$ and p_n is the probability that there are n customers staying in the queue in the steady state. The parameter p_0 can be calculated by Formula 4.17 (Gross and Harris 1998):

$$p_0 = \left(\sum_{n=0}^{k-1} \frac{(k\rho)^n}{n!} + \frac{(k\rho)^k}{k!\,(1-\rho)} \right)^{-1} \quad (4.17)$$

Then by applying Little's law (Gross and Harris 1998), the mean waiting time of customer orders can be obtained by Formula 4.18:

$$W_q = L_q/\lambda \quad (4.18)$$

The calculation of L_q or W_q in a G/G/k queue is not as simple as in an M/M/k, no explicit analytical formula can be applied for calculating L_q. However, there is vast literature concerned with appximation methods for calculating L_q or W_q. In this work, we adopt a practical approximation method to estimate L_q or W_q of the G/G/k queue, it is provided by Allen (1990).

Allen (1990) suggested a simple approximation method for any G/G/k queue to estimate the mean waiting time W_q (or mean waiting queue length L_q). It is called the Allen-Cunneen (AC) approximation formula, as shown by Formula 4.19.

$$W_q \approx \frac{p_{cb}(k)}{k(1-\rho)} \cdot \left(\frac{C_D^2 + C_S^2}{2}\right) \cdot \frac{1}{\mu} \tag{4.19a}$$

$$L_q = W_q \cdot \lambda \tag{4.19b}$$

In Formula 4.19b), $C_D = \sigma(D)/E(D)$ is the coefficient of variation of demand interarrival time D, and $C_s = \sigma(S)/E(S)$ is the coefficient of variation of service time S. The item p_{cb} represents the probability that all k servers are busy in an M/M/k queueing system; in another word, p_{cb} is the probability that the customer waiting time is above zero. For the special case $k = 1$, we have $p_{cb} = \rho$; and for other general cases where $k > 1$,

$$p_{cb}(k) = \sum_{n=k+1}^{+\infty} p_n = \sum_{n=k+1}^{+\infty} \frac{(k\rho)^n}{k!k^{n-k}} p_0 = \frac{(k\rho)^k \rho}{k!(1-\rho)} p_0 \tag{4.20}$$

It should be noted, the Allen-Cunneen approximation formula is an exact calculation formula for M/G/1 and M/M/k queues, and for other general queues it is an approximation formula. Although the formula was developed from computer techniques without formal proof, AC formula often gives a good approximation to W_q and L_q (Tanner 1995). Tanner did an extensive testing in various situations, and stated that W_q and L_q values obtained by the AC formula were within 10% of their true values. Hence, in this work, we recommend the Allen-Cunneen approximation formula to estimate the mean waiting time W_q and mean backlog level L_q for a given G/G/k queue.

The above-mentioned analytical methods are suitable estimation tools when we study a single-stage queueing model. For multi-stage systems, like the 5-stage robust Kanban system model in this work, the results of the analytical methods are not accurate. However, we can still use the analytical methods to derive some basic performance results as reference for further study on complex systems.

Backlog level function: 2) Simulation-based method

The second method for developing the backlog level function is based on simulation experiments. Running the simulation model of the robust Kanban system (refer to Section 3.3 and Figure 3.2) under different input conditions, we can obtain a collection of output data. The output data provide useful reference for generating the backlog level function. For example, based on the data points, we can do curve fitting to find a good approximation function for the backlog level.

The steps of implementing the simulation-based method are as follows. First, we define a series of input conditions (giving different values to input parameters and variables). Then we conduct the simulation experiments under each condition, and record the output results. At last, we analyze the output results of interest, such as total cost, inventory level, and backlog level, to derive the functional relationship between the mean order backlog level and the decision variables (the 3-level parameters, e.g. Kanban number).

Using the simulation output data, the plot of data points $(K, \overline{B}_{final})$ can be drawn to depict the relationship between the mean order backlog level and Kanban number. For example, the backlog level curves under different ρ values are displayed in Figure 4.1. Figure 4.1a) presents the curves of $\overline{B}_{final}$ vs.K under different ρ values; and Figure 4.1b) shows the curves of $\log(\overline{B}_{final})$ vs. K under different ρ values. In all simulation runs, the input demand interarrival time is a random variable following an exponential distribution (The exponential distribution is denoted by M, the mean value is $1/\lambda$), and the single-machine service time is constant (The constant distribution is denoted by D, the mean value is $1/\mu$). The parameter ρ is set with different values in different simulation runs. We set ρ value by specifying λ, μ, k for the Kanban system ($\rho = \lambda/k\mu$, where k is the number of servers at the bottleneck stage).

The notation like M/D/085, M/D/09 shown in Figure 4.1 signify some characteristics of the robust Kanban system simulation model. The first letter means the distribution type of demand interarrival time, e.g. M corresponds to exponential distribution. The second letter means the distribution type of single-machine service time at the bottleneck stage, e.g. D indicates the constant (deterministic) distribution. The third number means the adopted ρ value; for example, 085 means ρ=0.85, 09 means ρ=0.9, and 06 means ρ=0.6.

From Figure 4.1b) we observe a coincidence: all the curves of "log(Backlog level) vs. Kanban number" follow approximately a straight line. This phenomenon implies an exponential relationship between the

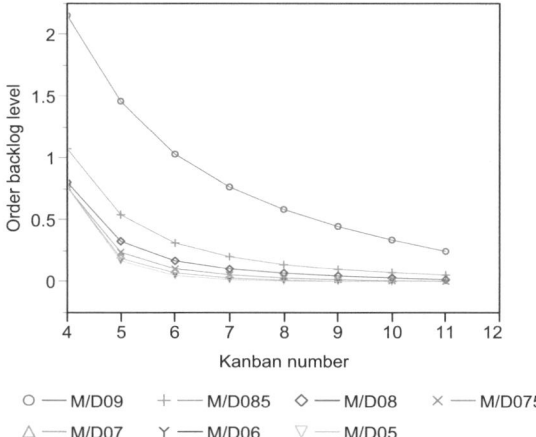

(a) Mean order backlog level vs. Kanban number, given different ρ values

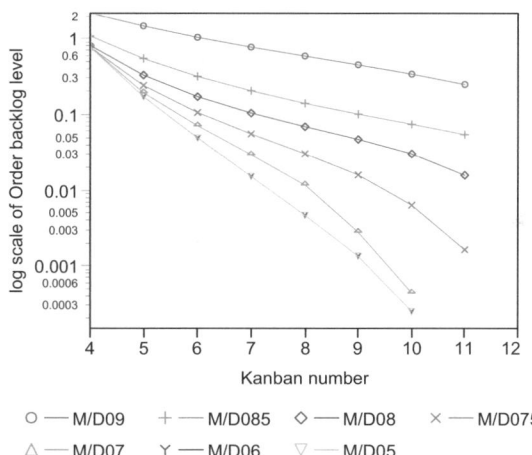

(b) log(Mean order backlog level) vs. Kanban number, given different ρ values

Figure 4.1: Relationship between the mean order backlog level and Kanban number (data points are obtained from M/D/k type robust Kanban system simulation)

Backlog level and Kanban number. In another word, the backlog level function should have an exponential form as shown in Formula 4.21.

$$\overline{B}_{final} = f^{\rho}_{backlog}(K) = a \cdot e^{b \cdot K} \tag{4.21}$$

Based on this inference, we use the exponential type to generate the fitting curve for the $\overline{B}_{final}$ function. We need to estimate the coefficients a and b in Formula 4.21. Using the data points $(K, \overline{B}_{final})$ shown in Figure 4.1, we do the curve fitting to determine coefficients a and b. The curve fitting is performed by using the Matlab Curve-Fitting toolbox; and the results (given $\rho=0.7,0.8,0.9$) are summarized in Table 4.1.

Now we analyze the results in Table 4.1. The "Goodness of fit" item is an indicator to describe how well the selected curve function (the Formula 4.21) is fitting the data points (shown in Figure 4.1). If SSE and RMSE are close to 0, R^2 and Adjusted-R^2 are close to 1, it can be inferred that the selected curve is fitting the data points well. Seeing that all the "Goodness of fit" results under conditions $\rho=0.7,0.8,0.9$ are close to 1, we conclude that the exponential curve (Formula 4.21) is a good approximation for the relationship between the mean backlog level and Kanban number for the studied "M/D/k"-type robust Kanban system.

Input ρ value	$\rho = 0.9$	$\rho = 0.8$	$\rho = 0.7$
Coefficients a,b (with 95% confidence bounds)	a = 12.78 (12.61, 12.95)	a = 40.92 (39.43, 42.41)	a = 139 (115, 163)
of the Backlog level function $y = a \cdot e^{b \cdot x}$	b = -0.4535 (-0.4562, -0.4507)	b = -0.9566 (-0.9653, -0.9479)	b =-1.287 (-1.329, -1.245)
Goodness-of-Fit test results:			
SSE	0.0001278	0.0000143	0.000112
R-square	1	1	0.9998
Adjusted R-square	1	1	0.9998
RMSE	0.003575	0.001544	0.004321

Table 4.1: Curve fitting results for the backlog level function (using data points of Figure 4.1)

From Figure 4.1, we observed an exponential-form coincidence of the curves "mean order backlog level vs. Kanban number". In this simulation experiment, the bottleneck stage of the robust Kanban system can be approximately modeled by an M/D/k queue, because the demand interarrival time follows an exponential distribution, and the single-machine service time at the bottleneck stage was constant. We wonder whether the exponential-form conclusion derived from the "M/D/k"-type Kanban system can be extended to other general Kanban systems, such as a "G/G/k" Kanban system. (The "G/G/k" Kanban system means the bottleneck stage of the multi-stage Kanban system has a "G/G/k" type, namely, the demand interarrival time and machine service time are both distributed generally, and server number at the bottleneck stage is k.)

To answer this question, we carried out the second simulation experiment with assuming more general demand time and service time distributions. Both the demand interarrival time and the machine service time are supposed to follow a variety of distribution types, including exponential, uniform, gamma, and constant. We run the robust Kanban system simulation model under different demand time and service time distribution types, then collect and analyze the output data to see whether there still exists the exponential-form in the backlog level curves. The results of the second experiment are demonstrated in Figure 4.2.

As Figure 4.2 demonstrated, in the second experiment for the "G/G/k"-type Kanban system (where more general distribution types of demand interarrival time and machine service time are included), the backlog curves "mean backlog level vs. Kanban number" still present a good exponential form. In most of the cases, we observed that the relationship between mean order backlog level and Kanban number approximated well to an exponential curve.

Based on this observation, we infer that the exponential-curve phenomenon is not just a coincidence; it must be incurred by some inherent features of the robust Kanban system. We reason that the bottleneck stage is the main contributing factor of the exponential-curve phenomenon. The final output service rate of the entire Kanban system is mainly influenced by the bottleneck stage that generates the slowest service rate. Hence, we focus on studying the bottleneck stage rather than modeling the entire Kanban system as a complex queueing network. Here we use a G/G/k queue model as approximation for the bottleneck stage,

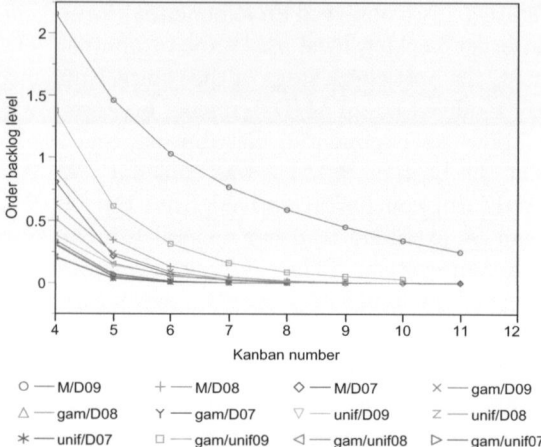

(a) Mean order backlog level vs. Kanban number, with constant/unif process time, exp/gamma/unif demand interarrival time

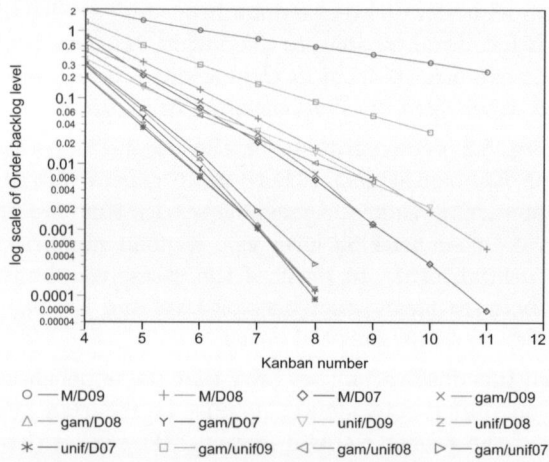

(b) log(Mean order backlog level) vs. Kanban number, with constant/unif process time, exp/gamma/unif demand interarrival time

Figure 4.2: Relationship between the mean order backlog level and Kanban number (data points are obtained from G/G/k type robust Kanban system simulation)

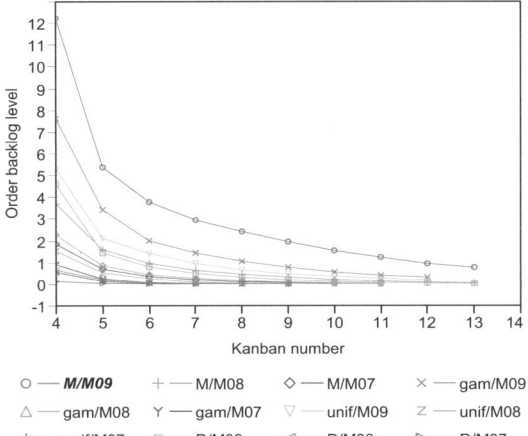

(c) Mean order backlog level vs. Kanban number, with exp
process time, exp/gamma/unif/constant demand interarrival
time

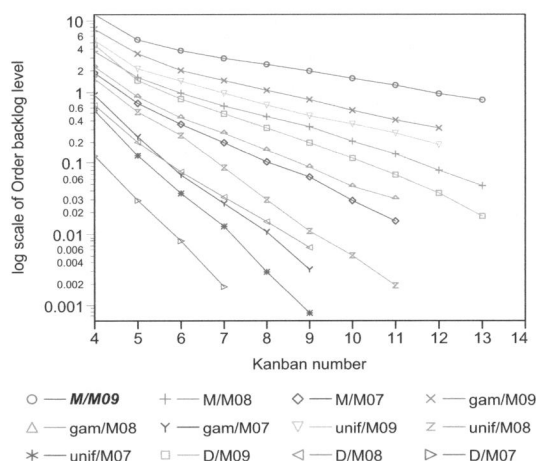

(d) log(Mean order backlog level) vs. Kanban number, with
exp process time, exp/gamma/unif/constant demand interarrival time

Figure 4.2: Relationship between the mean order backlog level and Kanban number (data points are obtained from G/G/k type robust Kanban system simulation)

because analyzing the behavior of the G/G/k queue is more convenient than studying the simulation model of the Kanban system.

As mentioned earlier, in the robust Kanban system, each stage includes two work modules: a production module and a transport module. For the bottleneck stage, if the slowest service rate is caused by the transport module, then adding a Transport Kanban is equal to adding a server to the Transport Kanban queue. Otherwise, if the slowest service rate is generated by the production module, then adding a production Kanban is equal to increasing the output buffer size by 1 product unit, while the server number in the production module remains the same. We individually model the transport module and production module as a G/G/k queue, then analyze their behaviors when a Transport Kanban or a Production Kanban is added into (or removed from) the Kanban system. Then, we can analyze the relationship between mean order backlog level and Kanban number, to examine whether it can form the exponential curve.

Thus, to investigate the causes of the exponential-curve phenomenon on the order backlog level, we discuss the problem in two cases: 1) The production module is the bottleneck; 2) The transport module is the bottleneck. In the following parts, we separately analyze the relationships between mean order backlog level and Kanban number for the two cases. The analysis is carried out based on related analytical models of the G/G/k queue.

Case 1: Production bottleneck

In Case 1, the production module of the bottleneck stage generates the slowest service rate. Namely the production module of the stage is the real bottleneck part. Given that all other parameters related to ρ-value are kept constant, only the Kanban number is adjustable; thus the change of Production Kanban number will significantly affect the final output service rate and other performance measures of the entire Kanban system. We use a G/G/k queue to model the production module approximately. Thus, the waiting queue length L_q of the G/G/k queue corresponds to the backlog level in the output buffer of the production module.

To investigate the change of L_q when Production Kanban number is changing in the G/G/k queue, we first study a simpler M/M/k queue as preparation.

Recall the definition of L_q in an M/M/k queue (see Formula 4.24, where p_n means the probability that n customers are staying in the system in the steady state). Since there are k parallel servers existing in the workcell, the waiting queue will appear only when there are more than k customers simultaneously existing in the system ($n=k+1,k+2,...$). Hence, the L_q is calculated by Formula 4.25:

$$L_q(k) = \sum_{n=k+1}^{+\infty} (n-k)\, p_n \tag{4.22}$$

$$L_q(k) = \sum_{n=k+1}^{+\infty} (n-k)\, p_n = \sum_{n=k+1}^{+\infty} (n-k)\, \frac{(k\rho)^n}{k!k^{n-k}} p_0 = \frac{(k\rho)^k \rho}{k!(1-\rho)^2} p_0 \tag{4.23}$$

In the production module, there exists an output buffer behind the service machines. Thus, the demand order from the succeeding stage will be unsatisfied and backlogged only when the output buffer is empty upon order arrivals. The existence of the output buffer makes the L_q calculation slightly different from that in a standard M/M/k queue, because there is no extra output buffer in the standard M/M/k queue. Hence we modify Formula 4.22 to calculate L_q (mean backlog level) in the production module. Comparing to the standard M/M/k queue, a new parameter, the output buffer size p, is introduced in the L_q calculation in the production module. Note that p is determined by the Production Kanban number Kp_i, we always have $p \le Kp_i$. In this robust Kanban system, we suppose that $p = Kp_i$.

Then, in an M/M/k queue, where an output buffer (with size p) is standing behind the k parallel servers, the mean waiting queue length

115

$L_q(k, p)$ can be calculated by

$$L_q(k, p) = \sum_{n=k+p+1}^{+\infty} (n - k - p) \, p_n = \sum_{n=k+p+1}^{+\infty} (n - k - p) \, \frac{(k\rho)^n}{k! k^{n-k}} p_0$$

$$= \frac{(k\rho)^{k+p} p_0}{k! k^p} \sum_{n=k+p+1}^{+\infty} (n - k - p) \, \rho^{n-k-p}$$

$$= \frac{\rho^p (k\rho)^k p_0}{k!} \sum_{m=1}^{+\infty} m \rho^m = \rho^p (k\rho)^k p_0 \frac{\rho}{k!(1-\rho)^2} \tag{4.24}$$

In short, we get

$$L_q(k, p) = \rho^p (k\rho)^k p_0 \frac{\rho}{k!(1-\rho)^2} \tag{4.25}$$

Furthermore, when we add a new Production Kanban to the production module (now the buffer size is $p+1$), the new mean backlog level $L_q(k, p+1)$ becomes (see Formula 4.26):

$$L_q(k, p+1) = \rho^{p+1} (k\rho)^k p_0 \frac{\rho}{k!(1-\rho)^2} \tag{4.26}$$

Comparing Formula 4.25 and Formula 4.26, we can get:

$$\frac{L_q(k, p+1)}{L_q(k, p)} = \rho \tag{4.27}$$

Formula 4.27 implies that, when fixing k and varying p, the $L_q(k, p)$ function should follow an exponential form, as shown in Formula 4.28, where a, b are constant coefficients:

$$L_q(k, p) = L_q^{base} \cdot \rho^p = a \cdot e^{b \cdot p} \tag{4.28}$$

Formula 4.28 implies that the relationship between the mean order backlog level and the number of Production Kanbans follows an exponential form, when k and other parameters are fixed.

So far, we have analyzed the backlog level in an M/M/k queue. The conclusion in Formula 4.28 can explain the exponential form of the backlog level curves. Nextly, we extend the analysis to a more general case: a G/G/k queue.

In a G/G/k queue, the calculation of L_q is not as simple as in the M/M/k queue. It is difficult or even impossible to derive an analytical formula for L_q calculation. Due to this reason, we adopt the Allen-Cunnen approximation formula (see Formula 4.19) to roughly calculate L_q in the G/G/k queue. We notice that the Allen-Cunnen approximation formula is applied based on the results of the M/M/k queue. The parameter p_{cb} employed in the AC Formula is the "demand order waiting time>0" probability obtained in the corresponding M/M/k queue; it is related to the output buffer size p $(p = Kp_i)$. The other parameters in the AC Formula are irrelevant to the output buffer size p, and they are kept constant when p value is changing. Hence, if we can show that the change of p_{cb} approximates well to an exponential curve as the buffer size p is varying, the L_q in a G/G/k queue will accordingly have a good approximation to the exponential curve, too.

In a standard M/M/k queue where no output buffer exists, the "demand order waiting time>0" probability $p_{cb}(k)$ is calculated by Formula 4.20.

By contrast, if an output buffer exists in the M/M/k queue, with buffer size=p, the calculation of $p_{cb}(k)$ is modified as follows (Formula 4.29):

$$p_{cb}(k,p) = \sum_{n=k+p+1}^{+\infty} p_n = \sum_{n=k+p+1}^{+\infty} \frac{(k\rho)^n}{k!k^{n-k}}p_0 = \frac{\rho^{p+1}(k\rho)^k}{k!\,(1-\rho)}p_0 = \rho^p p_{cb}(k)$$

(4.29)

Notice that $p_{cb}(k)$ (see Formula 4.20) is relevant to k, irrelevant to p. If we keep k constant, $p_{cb}(k)$ is then a constant. Thus in Formula 4.29, when fixing k value, the value of $p_{cb}(k,p)$ is only affected by p, and the relationship between them is exponential. Thus, the $p_{cb}(k,p)$ function of p can be written by Formula 4.32, which is also an exponential form function.

$$p_{cb}(k,p) = \rho^p p_{cb}(k) = a' \cdot e^{b' \cdot p}$$

(4.30)

Since we have $p = Kp_i$, the $p_{cb}(k,p)$ can be seen as an exponential function of Production Kanban number Kp_i. Combining Formula 4.30 and AC Formula 4.19, we can conclude that, in a G/G/k queue with an output buffer (size=p), the exponential curve is still a good approximation for the relationship between the mean backlog level L_q and the number of Production Kanbans Kp_i.

Recall the question "Can the exponential-form conclusion on the backlog level curves be extended to other general Kanban systems?" Now

117

we can answer the question in the first case. In a "G/G/k"-type Kanban system, if the production module is the bottleneck, the backlog level function approximates well to an exponential-form curve. The above analysis (from Formula 4.22 to Formula 4.30) explained why the exponential curve appears in this situation.

Nextly, we will discuss the question in case 2, when the transport module is the bottleneck.

Case 2: Transport bottleneck

When the transport module generates the slowest service rate among supply chain partners and becomes the bottleneck, it implies that there are not sufficient Transport Kanban cards to transport the product in time to meet the demand. Thus, the limited Transport Kanban capacity is the main contributing factor of the order backlog. If the Transport Kanban number is varying, the order backlog level will be directly influenced. Thus, through increasing the Transport Kanban number, we can increase the transport rate of the bottleneck stage, and mitigate the order backlog level. Similar to the production-bottleneck case, in the transport-bottleneck case, the relationship between the mean order backlog level and Transport Kanban number can be analyzed by building a G/G/k queue to model approximately the bottleneck transport module, too. The G/G/k queue model for the transport module of the bottleneck stage i is illustrated in Figure 4.3.

We still use the Allen-Cunneen approximation formula (Formula 4.19) to estimate the mean waiting queue length (indicating the mean order backlog level) of the G/G/k queue. In this case, the parameter k in the G/G/k queue signifies the Transport Kanban number of the bottleneck stage. The action of adding a Transport Kanban to the transport module corresponds to adding a server to the G/G/k queue (becoming G/G/k+1 queue). As can be seen in Figure 4.3, there is no output buffer existing in the transport module-based G/G/k queue. Therefore, we can directly calculate $L_q(k)$ and $L_q(k+1)$ using AC approximation formula (Formula 4.19). The results mean the estimated mean order backlog level of the G/G/k and G/G/k+1 queues.

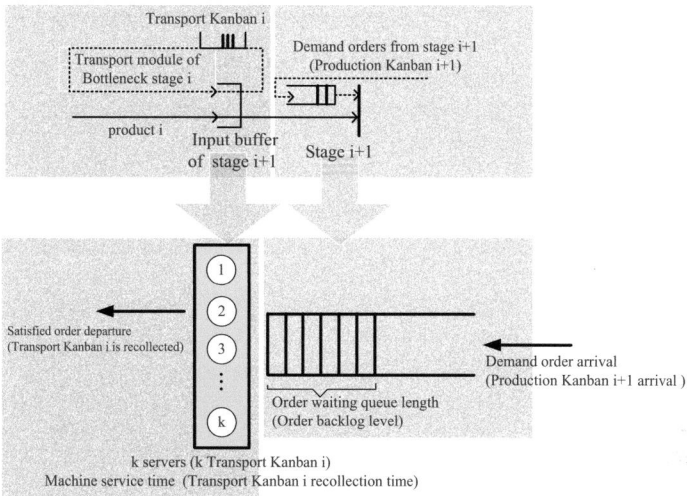

Figure 4.3: The G/G/k queue model for the transport module of bottleneck stage i

From the AC approximation formula, we can see that $L_q(k)$ is a function of k in the G/G/k queue (k corresponds to the Transport Kanban number Kt_i. However, $L_q(k)$ function is not of a simple exponential-form due to the complex calculation of $p_cb(k)$. It is not that possible to find the exponential-form backlog level function for the bottleneck transport module. But we can still use the exponential curve as a good approximation for the backlog level function $L_q(k)$; two reasons are given as follows.

First, generally in real-world problems, as we are increasing the number of Kanbans, it is much more probable that the bottleneck occurs in the production module than in the transport module. This is because adding a Transport Kanban makes the G/G/k queue become a G/G/k+1 queue; namely the server number is increased by 1. As a result the service rate can be markedly increased. On the other hand, adding a Production Kanban is just equal to increasing the output buffer size by 1 product unit. So we can imagine, the effect of adding the output buffer size by 1(adding a Production Kanban) is much weaker than adding the server number by

1 (adding a Transport Kanban). Therefore the bottleneck occurs in the production module more probably than in the transport module. And in the bottleneck production module, the relationship between the mean order backlog level and Kanban number can be well described using the exponential curve approximation.

Second, even if the transport module is the bottleneck, we can use a G/G/k queue to model the transport module and calculate L_q; the exponential curve is still an acceptable approximation for the backlog level function. The error that the real backlog level deviates from the exponential curve prediction is within a small and acceptable range. When giving different k values (e.g. k=3,4,5,...) to the G/G/k queue, we can observe that, although the L_q curve is not exactly following an exponential curve as k increases, the deviation from the exponential curve is not obvious. The mean backlog level still can be roughly described using the exponential curve.

Due to the two reasons, the exponential function can be used as a good approximation for the backlog level function in many cases.

k (Server number)	$L_q(k)$ (Mean waiting queue length)	Curve Fitting result (using function $y = a \cdot e^{b \cdot x}$):
4	1.528302	Coefficients a,b
5	0.354227	(with 95% confidence bounds):
6	0.099143	a = 483.7 (412, 555.4)
7	0.028234	b = -1.439 (-1.476, -1.403)
8	0.007769	**Goodness of Fit test results:**
9	0.002025	SSE: 0.0003113
10	0.000496	R-square: 0.9998
11	0.000114	Adjusted R-square: 0.9998
12	0.000025	RMSE:0.006238
13	0.000005	

Table 4.2: Curve fitting results of Mean waiting queue length $L_q(k)$ vs. Server Number k in an M/M/k queue

Table 4.1 shows a numerical example of the transport-bottleneck case. It lists the $L_q(k)$ value changes in an M/M/k queue, given that demand interarrival time $t_d \sim exp(1/2)$, single-machine service time $Ts_i \sim$

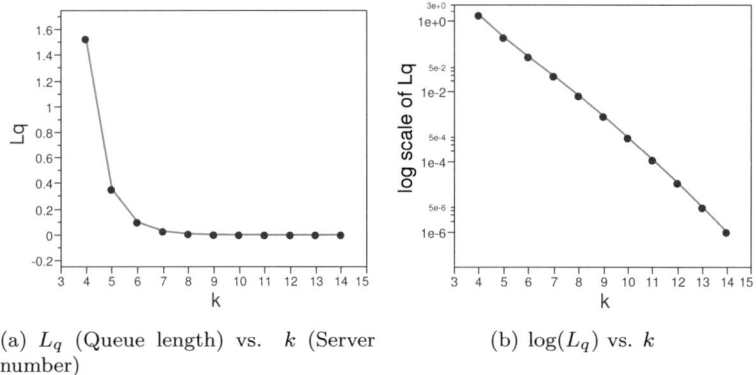

(a) L_q (Queue length) vs. k (Server number)

(b) $\log(L_q)$ vs. k

Figure 4.4: Queue length L_q vs. Server number k in an M/M/k queue

$exp(1/6)$. As k varies, corresponding $L_q(k)$ value is calculated. Then, the curve fitting for the $L_q(k)$ function ($L_q vs.k$) is performed using the exponential form. The fitting results are presented in Table 4.2. Referring to the "goodness of fit" results, we know that the exponential function is fitting the data points well. Thus, in the transport-bottleneck case, the exponential curve is also an appropriate approximation for the backlog level function. As a supplement, Figure 4.4 visually presents the data points of Table 4.2.

Summary of backlog cost function

When implementing the simulation-based methods to develop the backlog level function in the robust Kanban system, we found an exponential-curve coincidence phenomenon on the backlog level function (mean order backlog level vs. Kanban number). To explain the interesting phenomenon, the calculation of the mean order backlog level L_q is discussed in two cases separately: the production-bottleneck case and the transport-bottleneck case.

After intensive analysis, we can conclude that it is reasonable and appropriate to adopt the exponential curve as an approximation for the backlog level function. Now the problem "Can the exponential-curve conclusion for the backlog level function be extended to other general

121

Kanban systems?" can be solved with the answer "yes". The exponential-form function is a good approximation to describe the relationship between the mean order backlog level and Kanban number in many cases (general Kanban systems). The exponential-curve conclusion offers us a useful reference for developing the backlog level function with simulation models.

As introduced above, both the analytical and simulation-based methods have advantages and disadvantages for developing the backlog cost function. In the robust Kanban system model, we recommend to adopt the simulation-based methods. Because most analytical methods are only applicable to some simple or specific Kanban systems with simplifying assumptions and restrictions. Therefore its application is quite limited in real world problems due to the system complexity. For example, the characteristics of demand or service mechanism are stochastic, and the system structure or control logic is complex in real Kanban systems. Under such conditions, to adopt the simulation-based methods is a better choice. The simulation-based methods can be applied to general Kanban systems without considering many simplifying assumptions and restrictions; this makes the model closer to reality and more practical in application. Even if the Kanban system has complex mechanisms, the simulation model can still be built to represent the system characteristics in many cases. Then, the output results can be collected for further analysis. On the other hand, the disadvantages of simulation-based methods also exist. Compared to the analytical method, the simulation method is usually more time-consuming. Much time and work have to be spent on building a simulation model, collecting valid input data, and performing a large number of simulation runs under different conditions. Only with good preparation work can we derive useful statistical inferences. In this work, the studied robust Kanban system is a complex multi-stage queueing system. It is operated under the Production Kanban and Transport Kanban control. The system has input and out buffers located at each stage. And the demand time and machine service time are supposed to be uncertain and have general probability distributions. The working mechanism is the newly developed risk-response mechanism that has a complex control logic. Considering the above features, we consequently select the simulation-based methods to develop the backlog cost function.

So far, we have discussed the formulation of the inventory cost function, changing 3-level parameters function, and backlog cost function in Section 4.1.3. With figuring out all the subtotal cost items, the objective function $Cost_{total}$ in the MINLP model can be consequently established.

4.1.4 Model formulation summary

Having defined all model elements, the MINLP (Mixed Integer Nonlinear Programming) model is formulated. It is summarized as follows:

To minimize:

$$Cost_{total} = Cost_{inventory} + Cost_{backlog} + Cost_{change3level}$$

$$where$$

$$Cost_{inventory} = \sum_{i=1}^{i=I} h_i \cdot (K_i - K_i^{mean})$$

$$Cost_{backlog} = b_c \cdot f_{backlog}^{\rho}(K_i) \qquad i \in bottleneck\ stage$$

$$Cost_{change3level} = \sum_{j=1}^{j=I} c_{Kanban}K_j + c_{stime}\frac{1}{Ts_i} + c_{server}Ns_i + c_{supplier}\frac{1}{T_{su}}$$

Subject to:

$$T_{su} \cdot sf \leq t_d^{mean}$$

$$Ts_i \cdot sf \leq t_d^{mean} \cdot Ns_i \qquad i \in bottleneck\ stage$$

$$Tc_i \cdot sf \leq t_d^{mean} \cdot K_i \qquad \forall i \in \{1, 2, \ldots, I\}$$

$$(Tc_i \geq Tc_i^{production}, Tc_i \geq Tc_i^{transport})$$

$$Pr\left\{\frac{Tc_i}{K_i} \leq t_d\right\} \geq sl \qquad i \in bottleneck\ stage$$

$$original\ service\text{-}level\ constraint$$

$$\frac{Tc_i}{K_i} \cdot sf \leq \frac{X_{sl}}{K_{iapproximate} - K_i^{mean}} \qquad i \in bottleneck\ stage$$

$$simplified\ service\text{-}level\ constraint$$

$$K_i \in [K_{min}, K_{max}], integer \qquad \forall i \in \{1, 2, \ldots, I\}$$

$$Ts_i \in \{Ts_{minn}, Ts_{mid}, Ts_{max}\} \qquad i \in bottleneck\ stage$$

123

$$Ns_i \in [Ns_{\min}, Ns_{\max}], integer \qquad i \in bottleneck\ stage$$

$$T_{su} \in [Tsu_{\min}, Tsu_{\max}]$$

$$K_i^{mean} = Ttr_i/t_d^{mean} \qquad \forall i \in \{1, 2, \ldots, I\}$$

$$\rho = Ts_i/t_d^{mean} \qquad i \in bottleneck\ stage$$

The decision variables of the MINLP model are K_i, Ts_i, Ns_i of the bottleneck stage, and T_{su} (with respect to pr_{backup}) of the supplier stage. In addition, the Kanban number K_i of other stages can also be estimated using this model for reference.

The inventory cost $Cost_{inventory}$ and changing 3-level parameters cost $Cost_{change3level}$ are increasing functions of K_i ($i \in$ all stages, including the bottleneck stage). On the contrary, the backlog cost $Cost_{backlog}$ is a decreasing function of K_i ($i \in$ bottleneck stage). These function features make sense in real life. If we keep more Kanbans working in the system, the product inventory in the buffer will accordingly increase; as a result more cost of holding inventory and operating the Kanban equipment will be caused. On the other hand, more Kanbans and a high inventory level will reduce the risk of order backlog occurrences. The objective $Cost_{total}$ includes both increasing and decreasing functions of K_i ($i \in$ bottleneck stage). Due to the trade-off between the subtotal cost functions, it can be inferred that there must exist an optimal K_i value that leads to the minimum $Cost_{total}$. This conclusion ensures the existence of the optimal solution (optimal 3-level parameter setting) for the MINLP model.

4.1.5 Model implementation: a numerical example

The MINLP model can be built and solved using AIMMS software package. In this section, we present a numerical example to show how to apply the MINLP model to determine suitable values for the 3-level parameters.

It is a mixed integer nonlinear programming (MINLP) model because the decision variables K_i and Ns_i are integers, T_{su} are continuous, and Ts_i is supposed to be of specified discrete values; and the objective function $Cost_{total}$ includes nonlinear items, such as $Cost_{backlog}$. In order to solve the MINLP problem, an AOA solver in AIMMS package is adopted.

We first specify the values of input parameters in the MINLP model. The information of input parameters is summarized in Table 4.3. With the input parameter setting, the MINLP model is formulated and solved in AIMMS environment. Then, we can obtain the optimal solutions of the decision variables that generate the minimum $Cost_{total}$. The optimal solutions are presented in Table 4.4.

stage	0	1	2	3	4
index i	Supplier				Customer
h_i	1	2	3	4	
b_i	0	0	0	0	160
T_i^{pr}	1	1	1	1.8	
T_i^{pr}	4	2	4	6	

Distribution of Demand time t_d	$t_d\ exp(1/2), t_d^{mean} = 2$
Distribution of Service time ts_i at bottleneck stage	$ts_i = Ts_i$, where Ts_i is a constant $Ts_i \in \{1.80, 1.64, 1.48\}$ $= \{Ts_{low}, Ts_{mid}, Ts_{high}\}$
$\rho = ts_i/t_d^{mean}$	0.90, 0.82 or 0.74
Backlog level function $\overline{B_{final}} = f_{backlog}^{\rho}(K)$	$= \begin{cases} 12.78 \cdot e^{-0.4535K}, & \rho = 0.90 \\ 40.92 \cdot e^{-0.9566K} & \rho = 0.82 \\ 139 \cdot e^{-1.287K} & \rho = 0.74 \end{cases}$
Target service level (sl)	90%
Safety factor sf	1.01
$\min K_i, \max K_i$	3, 20
$Ts_{low}, Ts_{mid}, Ts_{high}$	1.80, 1.64, 1.48
$minNs_i, maxNs_i$	1, 3
Tsu_{low}, Tsu_{high}	0.5, 1
$cKanban_i$	2
$cStime_i$	400
$cServer_i$	120
$cSupplier_i$	200

Table 4.3: Input parameters of the MINLP numerical example

As reported in Table 4.4, we study the optimal setting of the 3-level parameters in two cases: without/with a service level constraint. When

Decision variables and related results	Optimal solutions (without service level constraint)	Optimal solutions(with service level =90% constraint)
Kanban number K_i	6	7
Service time Ts_i	1.64	1.64
Server number Ns_i	1	1
Supplier inter-time T_{su}	1	1
Inventory cost $Cost_{Inventory}$	35.233	45.223
Backlog cost $Cost_{Backlog}$	21.056	8.09
Cost of using 3-level parameters $Cost_{change}$	647.902	661.902
Cost of using K_i	84	98
Cost of using Ts_i	243.902	243.902
Cost of using Ns_i	120	120
Cost of using T_{su}	200	200
Total cost	704.182	715.215

Table 4.4: Output solutions of the MINLP numerical example

the service level constraint is not considered, the optimal solution of the 3-level parameter setting is: K_i=6, Ts_i=1.64 (Ts_{mid}), Ns_i=1 (Ns_{min}), T_{su}=1(Tsu_{min}), the minimum total cost is 704.182. When we add a service level (sl=90%) constraint to the MINLP model, the new optimal solution is: K_i=7, Ts_i=1.64 (Ts_{mid}), Ts_i=1 (Ns_{min}), T_{su}=1(Tsu_{min}), the minimum total cost is 715.215. Comparing the two cases, we can see that in the "90% service-level" case, the optimal Kanban number increased from 6 to 7. Accordingly, the inventory cost increased, backlog cost reduced, and operating Kanban cost increased. In all, the total cost of this case is slightly higher than the cost of the "without service-level" case. It can be inferred that the 90% service level cannot be achieved when the cyclic Kanban number is 6. Actually when given K=6, the caused service level is about 85% (when we use a 85%-service level constraint, the generated optimal Kanban number remains to be 6). On the other hand, when the Kanban system achieved the 90% service level by increasing the Kanban number, more operating Kanban cost and inventory cost were incurred at the same time. In real world problems, whether to consider the "service level constraint" depends on the impact of the service level. If the goods shortage will seriously affect the customer goodwill and the product market share, then to include the service level constraint is a better choice. In this example, we suppose that no serious impact will be caused by the customer order backlog, thus we use the "without service level constraint" MINLP model. This model was simpler to solve, and it generated a lower total-cost result.

In order to investigate further the effect of decision variables on the total cost, we set the variable Ts_i as a fixed parameter, then solve the MINLP model again with using different Ts_i values to see how the results will change. We fix the single-machine service time Ts_i at 1.8 (slow time), 1.64 (middle time), 1.48 (fast time) (ρ value is 0.90, 0.82, 0.74 correspondingly) to solve the MINLP model (without service level constraint). The obtained optimal results are summarized in Table 4.5.

We can see when ρ=0.90, 0.82, 0.74 (indicating Ts_i =1.80, 1.64, 1.48), the decided optimal Kanban number is 8, 6, 6, respectively. And the values of Ns_i or T_{su} are identical in three cases: Ns_i=1, T_{su}=1. Comparing the total cost results of three cases, we find that the minimum total cost 704.182 is obtained in the case ρ=0.82, namely Ts_i=1.64. The optimal results are consistent with the results given in Table 4.4. In the case ρ=0.90, the total cost 762.976 is much higher than the optimum 704.182, because the order backlog cost is higher when using the slow service time Ts_i=1.80. And in the case ρ=0.74, the total cost is 719.527; in this case the order backlog cost is lower than in the ρ=0.82 case, but the cost of operating the machine at high-speed (Ts_i related cost) is increased at the same time, therefore the final total cost is not better than in the ρ=0.82 case.

As a confirm test, we run the robust Kanban system simulation model using the same input conditions as the MINLP model used. Then we can compare the MINLP model results with the simulation model results, to examine whether the optimal solutions given by the MINLP model are correct in the realistic simulation environment.

The results of simulation experiment can be found in Figure 3.10. In Plot a), we can see that the optimal values of Kanban number at ρ=0.90,0.82,0.74 are respectively 8, 6, 6. Note that in the simulation model, we calculate the statistic Netprofit instead of Total cost with

Decision variables and related results	Optimal solutions $\rho = 0.9$	Optimal solutions $\rho = 0.82$	Optimal solutions $\rho = 0.74$
Kanban number K_i	8	6	6
Service time Ts_i	1.8(fixed)	1.64(fixed)	1.48(fixed)
Server number Ns_i	1	1	1
Supplier inter-time T_{su}	1	1	1
Inventory cost $Cost_{Inventory}$	54.425	35.233	35.405
Backlog cost $Cost_{Backlog}$	54.329	21.056	9.852
Cost of using 3-level parameters $Cost_{change}$	654.222	647.902	674.270
Cost of using K_i	112	84	84
Cost of using Ts_i	222.222	243.902	270.270
Cost of using Ns_i	120	120	120
Cost of using T_{su}	200	200	200
Total cost	762.976	704.182	719.527

Table 4.5: Optimal solutions of MINLP model when the service time is fixed (without service level constraint)

defining Netprofit=Income-Total cost. Thus, the maximum Netprofit is considered as the optimal result.

From Figure 3.10a) we observed that among all (K_i, ρ) combinations, the combination K_i=6,ρ=0.82 (green line) achieved the maximum Netprofit, and the optimal 3-level parameter setting is in agreement with the MINLP-model optimal result shown in Table 4.4. In Plot b), the straight lines of inventory level indicate a linear relationship between the inventory level (in the customer input buffer) and Kanban number; and it also validates the inventory cost function applied in the MINLP model. Plot c) and d) illustrate the curves of mean order backlog level vs. Kanban number. The order backlog level is a decreasing function of K_i; this also makes sense in real life. Lastly, the service level curves are demonstrated in Plot e). The service level is rising as the Kanban number increases, but the marginal increasing rate is gradually getting small. There exists theoretically an upper limit of Service level (100%) that cannot be reached with a finite Kanban number. Take the green curve (ρ=0.82) as an example, the 90% service level can be reached when Kanban number

$K_i > 6$. At $K_i = 6$, the corresponding service level is between 85% and 90%. This observation from Plot e) is consistent with the result given by the MINLP model. Therefore, through comparing the simulation results and MINLP-model results, we can confirm the usability of the MINLP model.

4.1.6 Define adjusting ranges of 3-level parameters

As mentioned earlier, given a specific stable scenario, the optimal solution of the 3-level parameters can be obtained using the MINLP model. Then, when risks are added into the stable scenario, we need to change the parameter values to mitigate the risk impact. The allowable adjusting ranges of the 3-level parameters need to be carefully specified in advance. To find proper adjusting ranges for the 3-level parameters, we consider the following factors: the potential risk situations, customer requirement, production capacity or financial capacity of the factory, and related results from the former analytical or simulation model. In this section, we still use the numerical example given in Section 4.1.5 to present the procedures of deciding adjusting ranges of the 3-level parameters.

Range of Kanban number K_i:
$K_i \in [K_{\min}, K_{\max}]$, integer

Kanban number is an operational-level adjustable parameter of the robust Kanban system. In Section 3.2.2, we have denoted the lower and upper bounds of Production (Transport) Kanban at stage i by $minKp_i$ and $maxKp_i$ ($minKt_i, maxKt_i$). Here we add a simplifying assumption into the model: all stages have the same lower/upper bounds of Production Kanbans and Transport Kanbans. We use two parameters K_{min}, K_{max} to denote the lower and upper bounds of Kanban number (K_i). The number of Kanbans working at each stage should be changed within the range $[K_{min}, K_{max}]$.

The value of K_{max} is determined depending on the simulation experiment results. As can be seen from Figure 3.10e), as the Kanban number becomes larger, the service level is rising more slowly. There seems to be a "saturation point". The curve tail after the saturation point becomes much flatter. When K_i is larger than the saturation point value, the increasing rate of service level becomes so small that we can approximately use a straight line to describe the tail part of the curve. For example, in the case ρ=0.90 (red curve in Figure 3.10e), the Kanban number K_i=12 which results in the service level=97% can be seen as a saturation point. The service-level curve rises much slower after K_i>12. This implies the marginal cost required for increasing 1% service level is growing rapidly after K_i=12. Also in Figure 3.10c), we can observe the similar saturation point phenomenon in the decreasing backlog level curves. In the case ρ=0.90, when K_i=12, the corresponding backlog level is 0.0525. This is a sufficiently low backlog level, and since K_i>12, the curve tail becomes almost flat. Hence, the K_i=12 is considered as "saturation point" too. Based on the above analysis, we define K_{max}=12 in this numerical example.

The value of K_{min} is derived from the constraint $Tc_i \cdot sf \leq t_d^{mean} \cdot K_i$. We define $K_{\min} = Tc_i/t_d^{mean}$, indicating the minimum Kanban number required for covering the mean demand rate. If K_i is set below K_{min}, it will cause "$rate_{demand}/rate_{service} > 1$" ($\rho = \lambda/\mu > 1$), namely the Kanban system cannot reach a stable state in the long run. In this numerical example, we have K_{min}=4.

Range of single-machine service time Ts_i:
$Ts_i \in \{Ts_{\min}, Ts_{mid}, Ts_{\max}\}]$, discrete value

Machine service time is a tactical-level adjustable parameter of the robust Kanban system. The single-machine service time at the bottleneck stage is allowed to be changed within a specific range or at several discrete values. In this example, we assume discrete values of service time Ts_i to describe this feature. Suppose there are three processing rate level for the machine to choose: slow (Ts_{max}), middle (Ts_{mid}), fast (Ts_{min}). Usually the single-machine service time is an inherent characteristic of the service equipment, its value is dependent on the process nature other than the manager's opinion.

Hence, the allowable adjusting range should be properly defined depending on the machine capacity or other realistic conditions. We first collect information about the machine properties and other conditions.

Then, referring to the information, we can specify a normal service time (middle level Ts_{mid}), an enhanced service time (fast level Ts_{min}) and a relaxed service time (slow level Ts_{max}). In the presented numerical example, Ts_i is assumed arbitrarily to have three discrete levels: 1) $Ts_i=1.8$ (slow level, Ts_i is slightly less than $t_d^{mean}=2$); 2) $Ts_i=1.64$ (=1.8/110%, middle level); 3) $Ts_i=1.48$ (=1.64/110%, fast level). The parameter Ts_i is supposed to change its value between the three levels as the response action against risk.

Range of server number Ns_i:
$Ns_i \in [Ns_{\min}, Ns_{\max}]$, integer

Server number Ns_i is a strategic-level adjustable parameter of the robust Kanban system. It means the number of in-use servers (service equipment). To define an appropriate adjusting range of Ns_i, we first estimate a normal level of Ns_i as baseline, then change the Ns_i value around the baseline as the adjusting range. The baseline Ns_i value is decided with considering the single-machine service time Ts_i. For example, given the mean demand time $t_d^{mean}=2$ and the standard machine service time $Ts_i=6$, then the baseline value of Ns_i can be estimated by $Ts_i/Ns_i \leq t_d^{mean}$, which indicates "mean service time $\leq$ mean demand time". As a result, we get $Ns_i \geq 3$. Thus $Ns_i=3$ is set as the baseline, based on this result we further define the upper and lower bounds of Ns_i around 3.

To be noted, the adjusting range of Ns_i should be decided carefully with considering also the realistic situations, such as the financial or space capacity of the factory, or the potential risks from the uncertain environment. For example, when deciding Ns_i, we ask "Is it economical or affordable for the factory to setup a new machine? Is there enough space to locate a new server? Are there enough workers to operate it? Do they need to work overtime?" In the numerical example in Section 4.1.5, the baseline value of $Ns_i(i=3$ is the bottleneck stage) is calculated by $\lceil Ts_0/t_d^{mean} \rceil = \lceil 1.64/2 \rceil = 1$, hence we suppose the lower bound $Ns_{min}=1$. And the upper bound of Ns_i is determined with considering the financial and space capacity, and the potential risk extent. Suppose the demand variability is high, 20% of demand time data are below $t_d^{20\%}=0.44$, and we want to satisfy the rest 80% demand orders in time, then $Ns_{\max} = \lceil Ts_{\min}/t_d^{20\%} \rceil = \lceil 1.48/0.44 \rceil = 4$. But considering the financial and space capacity can afford maximally 3 servers, so we finally set $Ns_{max}=3$.

Range of backup supplier proportion pr_{backup}:

$pr_{backup} \in [pr_{low}, pr_{high}]$, continuous value

The backup supplier proportion pr_{backup} is also a strategic-level adjustable parameter used in the robust Kanban system, it refers to the proportion of material supplied by the backup supplier. We assume that a main supplier exists constantly at the origin of the supply chain, it can supply material to downstream stages. When risks happen to the supply chain, a backup supplier can be selected to supply material, too. Compared to the main supplier, the backup supplier can supply material with a higher rate and a higher material purchase price. In short, the backup supplier is more expensive and faster. Suppose the material supply proportion from the backup supplier is pr_{backup}; and the rest material is supplied by the main supplier with the proportion $1 - pr_{backup}$. Thus the value of pr_{backup} should follow: $0 \le pr_{low} \le pr_{backup} \le pr_{high} \le 1$. In real world problems, the proportion parameters pr_{low}, pr_{high} should be specified with considering the realistic risk situation like the supplier capacity, supply proportion contracts, demand and production status. In this numerical example, we suppose $pr_{low}=0(0\%$ material from the backup supplier), and $pr_{high}=0.5$ (50% material from the backup supplier) as the adjusting range of pr_{backup}. Accordingly, the mixed material supply time at the supplier stage can be calculated by $Tsu = pr_{backup}Tsu_{backup} + (1 - pr_{backup})Tsu_{main}$, where $Tsu_{backup} \le Tsu \le Tsu_{main}$.

Conclusively, the adjusting ranges of 3-level parameters determined in the numerical example (shown in Section 4.1.5) are summarized in Table 4.6. The optimal setting of the 3-level parameters obtained from the MINLP model is marked with "initial value" in the table, because these values are used as the initial setting of the 3-level parameters in the simulation model of the robust Kanban system.

3-level parameters	Adjusting Range		
	Low (min)	**Middle**	**High (max)**
Kanban number	4	7*	12
Machine service time	1.8	1.64*	1.48
Server number	1*	2	3
Backup supplier proportion	0*	Continuous [0,0.5]	0.5

Table 4.6: Summary of adjusting ranges of 3-level parameters (*:used as initial value)

4.2 Estimation of control parameters in the risk-response mechanism

As introduced in Section 3.2.3, the implementation of the risk-response mechanism contains three steps: 1) calculate monitor values; 2) make decisions on adjusting 3-level parameters; 3) perform response actions. Many control parameters are used by the mechanism, such as the smoothing weight factor for calculating mi_inv, and the lower and upper control limits for judging the mi_rate value. To implement the risk-response mechanism successfully, the values of control parameters need to be determined appropriately.

In this section, we introduce the methods for determining suitable values of the control parameters. It can be inferred that there must exist an optimal setting of the control parameters resulting in the best system performance. However, to find the accurate optimal setting out of numerous combinations of parameter values is difficult and time-consuming. It is impractical to spend much time searching for an accurate optimal solution. Hence, our goal is to find a suboptimal but still sufficiently good solution of the control parameter setting. The solving method should be simple to execute, and the result should be adequate to satisfy the management goal: to improve the Kanban system performance significantly in the uncertain environment. Therefore, we adopt a series of simply-implemented estimation methods to decide values of the control parameters. Although these methods just offer roughly-estimated parameter values, the effects in application are adequately good (the effects will be discussed in Chapter 5).

The remainder of Section 4.2 is organized as follows. First, we explain the estimation methods for deciding control limits parameters of mi_inv. Then the methods for estimating the control limits of mi_rate are introduced. At last, the smoothing weight factors and safety factor, which are included in the monitor value calculation, are estimated as well. Having decided suitable values for the above control parameters, the risk-response mechanism can be then implemented smoothly in the robust Kanban system.

4.2.1 Control limits for monitor mi_inv

Recall Figure 3.5 that illustrated three steps of applying the risk-response mechanism. In the second step, the mi_inv value is compared to its control limits ss_{low}, ss_{high} and ss, as a part of the judging work. The values of the control limits parameters have crucial influences on the final adjusting-parameters decision. Therefore, to decide suitable values for the control limits is of great importance.

mi_inv is used for monitoring the inventory and backlog level of finished product in the customer input buffer. The control limit ss functions actually as a baseline-safety stock level; and ss_{low}, ss_{high} are the lower, upper bounds of the allowable safety stock level.

The system aims to maintain mi_inv value within the range $[ss_{low}, ss_{high}]$ during system operation. When $mi\_inv < ss_{low}$, it is inferred that the order backlog will occur more probably. Accordingly, the parameter adjustment of enhancing the service capacity will be taken as response actions, such as to add a new Kanban to the system, to reduce machine service time, to start a new server, or to allocate more orders on the faster supplier. When $mi\_inv > ss_{high}$, which indicates the inventory is abundant, then the system parameters should be adjusted in the opposite direction to reduce the service capacity and save unnecessary inventory cost. The ss value is supposed to be between ss_{low} and ss_{high}, it refers to the expected stock level or the most frequently caused stock level in the customer input buffer.

We decide the values of ss_{low}, ss_{high} based on the optimal Kanban number solved by the MINLP model. Again we take the numerical example in Section 4.1.5 as an example. We have known that to keep K_i=6 (for $mi\_rate = 0.74$ or 0.82) or K_i=8 (for ρ=0.90) is optimal in the given stable scenario. Knowing optimal K_i value, the corresponding average inventory level can be calculated by the formula $\overline{I}_i = K_i - K_i^{mean}$. Thus we have $\overline{I}_i$=6-3=3 for $mi\_rate = 0.74$ or 0.82, $\overline{I}_i$=8-4=4 for mi_rate =0.90. With these results, we can estimate a suitable value for ss_{high}: ss_{high}=max{3,4}=4. The estimation can be explained like this. To keep $\overline{I}_i$=4 is already sufficient in the case where the service rate is the slowest (mi_rate =0.90) and the Kanban number is fixed at 8. Then in other cases where the Kanban system can serve faster (for $mi\_rate = 0.74$ or 0.82) or the 3-level parameters are adjustable in response to risks, the required $\overline{I}_i$ level should be accordingly less than 4. Hence, based on this inference, we set ss_{high}=4.

Nextly, we decide the value of ss_{low}. In the given example, the penalty cost for a backlog order b_c is much higher than the inventory holding cost rate (h_i=1,2,3,4 at stage i). So we prefer to keep more inventory to increase the service level and reduce order backlog. At least the lower bound of safety stock level, ss_{low}, should not be below 0, otherwise the expensive order backlog will be incurred. Therefore, we set ss_{low}=0 as an initial estimation.

The value of the baseline safety stock level ss should be set within $[ss_{low}, ss_{high}]$. Depending on the inventory level data obtained from the numerical example, the most frequently caused stock level is 3, hence we set ss=3 as the initial estimation.

In summary, the control limit parameters for mi_inv are set as follows:

Baseline safety stock level ss= 3;

Lower control limit ss_{low}= 0;

Upper control limit ss_{high}= 4.

4.2.2 Control limits for monitor mi_rate

Besides *mi_inv*, the "rate-balance" monitor *mi_rate* should be also compared with its control limits, to judge whether the system operating status is in normal range. The monitor *mi_rate* is calculated as the ratio of demand rate to service rate, and its control limits include: $LCL_K, UCL_K, LCL_{Ts}, UCL_{Ts}, LCL_{Ns}, UCL_{Ns}, LCL_{su}$, and UCL_{su}.

The ideal operating status of the Kanban system should be both sufficient and economical. Namely, the Kanban system can operate efficiently without causing much waste; meanwhile the system performance is maintained at a high level. To achieve or get close to the ideal status, the service utilization should be kept less than 1, but not too far below 1. Therefore, we introduce the rate-balance monitor *mi_rate* to monitor the service utilization. When we change any of the 3-level parameters, the value of *mi_rate* will change correspondingly. For instance, we add a new server to the Kanban system, the value *mi_rate* will change as below:

Before the change: $mi\_rate_{before} = \frac{servicetime_0}{demandtime_0}$

After the change ($N_s = N_s + 1$): $mi\_rate_{after} = \frac{servicetime_0}{demandtime_0} \cdot \frac{N_s}{N_s+1}$.

Thus, we have $mi\_rate_{after} = mi\_rate_{before} \cdot \frac{Ns}{Ns+1}$. Only when $mi\_rate_{before} \geq \frac{1}{sf} \cdot \frac{Ns+1}{Ns}$, should the action of adding a server be taken. Because in this situation, after increasing the server number, we still have $mi\_rate_{after} = \frac{servicetime_0}{demandtime_0} \cdot \frac{Ns}{Ns+1} \approx \frac{1}{sf}$. Thus, when the condition $\frac{servicetime_0}{demandtime_0} \geq \frac{1}{sf} \cdot \frac{Ns+1}{Ns}$ is reached, we will accordingly increase the parameter server number from N_s to N_s+1 as the risk response action.

Based on the above analysis, we define the control limit:

$$UCL_{Ns} = \max_{Ns} \left\{ \frac{1}{sf} \cdot \frac{Ns+1}{Ns} \right\} = \frac{1}{sf} \cdot \frac{Ns_{\min}+1}{Ns_{\min}}$$

The remaining control limits of *mi_rate* are calculated in a similar way the UCL_{Ns} is derived. First, we write down the calculation formulas for mi_rate_{before} and mi_rate_{after}. Subsequently, with considering the condition $mi\_rate_{after} = \frac{servicetime_{new}}{demandtime_{new}} \approx \frac{1}{sf}$, we can find the suitable values for the control limit parameters.

Conclusively, the setting of the control limits parameters used for *mi_rate* is summarized in Table 4.7. Recall the numerical example given in Section 4.1.5, the actual control limit values in the example are calculated using the given estimation methods and also presented in Table 4.7.

Control limits for mi_{rate}	Corresponding risk-response actions	Calculation methods	Example values
UCL_{Ns}	$Ns = Ns + 1$ (add a server)	$\max\limits_{Ns}\left\{\frac{1}{sf} \cdot \frac{Ns+1}{Ns}\right\}$	$\frac{1}{sf} \cdot \frac{2}{1}$
UCL_{Ts}	$Ts = Ts/110\%$ or $Ts = Ts/120\%$ (reduce service time)	$\max\limits_{Ts}\{\frac{1}{sf} \cdot \frac{Ts}{Ts/110\%}, \frac{1}{sf} \cdot \frac{Ts}{Ts/120\%}\}$ or 1 (Select the lower value between them)	$\min\left\{\frac{1.2}{sf}, 1\right\}$
UCL_K	$K = K + 1$ (increase Kanban#)	$\frac{1}{sf}$	$\frac{1}{sf}$
	Keep current parameters unchanged	N/A	
LCL_K	$K = K - 1$ (reduce Kanban#)	Arbitrarily defined, the value should be slightly below 1/sf	$\frac{1}{sf} \cdot 0.85$
LCL_{Ts}	$Ts = Ts \cdot 110\%$ or $Ts = Ts \cdot 120\%$ (increase service time)	$\min\limits_{Ts}\{\frac{1}{sf} \cdot \frac{Ts}{Ts\cdot110\%}, \frac{1}{sf} \cdot \frac{Ts}{Ts\cdot120\%}\}$	$\frac{1}{sf\cdot1.2}$
LCL_{Ns}	$Ns = Ns - 1$ (stop a server)	$\min\limits_{Ns}\left\{\frac{1}{sf} \cdot \frac{Ns-1}{Ns}\right\}$	$\frac{1}{sf} \cdot \frac{1}{2}$
UCL_{su}	$pr_{backup} = pr_{high}$ (add the backup supplier)	Arbitrarily defined, the value should be below 1/sf	$\frac{1}{sf} \cdot 85\%$
LCL_{su}	$pr_{backup} = pr_{low}$ (stop the backup supplier)	$\frac{1}{sf} \cdot \frac{t_{su}^{mixed}}{t_{su}^{main}}$, where $t_{su}^{mixed} = pr_{backup}tsu_{backup} + (1 - pr_{backup})tsu_{main}$	$\frac{1}{sf} \cdot 50\%$

Table 4.7: Specification of control limit parameters for *mi_rate*

4.2.3 Smoothing weight factors and safety factor

Besides the control limit parameters mentioned in Section 4.2.1 and 4.2.2, the risk-response mechanism contains also other types of control parameters, such as the safety factor and smoothing weight factors. In this section, we will discuss the setting of the remaining control parameters.

When implementing the risk-response mechanism, we need to first calculate the values of monitor mi_rate and mi_inv. This is the fundamental of other procedures and will have important influence on the further actions. The monitors are expected to be able to reflect the system operating status timely and accurately. Hence the calculation of monitor values should be properly taken. As mentioned earlier, we adopt the exponential smoothing method in monitor calculation; smoothing weight factors are used in calculation formulas. For example, the factor sf_{dt} is employed to calculate $\widetilde{T}_{demand}(n)$ (see Formula 3.3); factor sf_{su} is employed to calculate $\widetilde{T}_{supplier}(n)$ (see Formula 3.4); factor sf_{pr} is employed to calculate $\widetilde{T}s_i(t)$ (see Formula 3.5); and factor sf_{inv} is included in Formula 3.8 and 3.9 to calculate $\widetilde{I}(t)$ and $\widetilde{B}(t)$. To implement the risk-response mechanism successfully, the values of smoothing weight factors should be appropriately determined.

It is very difficult to determine the optimal setting of the smoothing factors based on analytical methods. Therefore, we use simulation-based methods to find suitable (suboptimal but still effective) values of the factors. We do simulation experiments with different factor settings, then analyze the output results and eventually select a good setting of the factors.

In order to know the system operating status and performance, various simulation output data of the robust Kanban system model are collected. The output data include customer demand interarrival time series, supplier material supply time series, server process time series, inventory and backlog level data series, and so on. Based on the output data series, we subsequently use exponential smoothing methods to calculate $\widetilde{T}_{demand}(n)$, $\widetilde{T}_{supplier}(n)$, $\widetilde{T}s_i(t)$, $\widetilde{I}(t)$ and $\widetilde{B}(t)$ (see Section 3.2.2). All these items are used in Formula 3.1 when calculating mi_rate.

When we set different values for the smoothing weight factors $sf_{dt}, sf_{su}, sf_{pr}, sf_{inv}$, the obtained smoothed data series $\widetilde{T}_{demand}(n)$,

$\widetilde{T}_{supplier}(n)$, $\widetilde{Ts}_i(t)$, $\widetilde{I}(t)$ and $\widetilde{B}(t)$ will vary correspondingly (refer to Formula 3.3-3.9). Actually, when using the exponential smoothing method, the variance of the smoothed data series can be estimated depending on the variance of original data series and the smoothing weight factor. Take the demand interarrival time series $\widetilde{T}_{demand}(n)$ as an example. Suppose the original demand time data series $t_d(n)$ is identically independently distributed $i.i.d$, its variance is σ_{dt}^2. The smoothed data series variance is denoted by σ_{dt}^2. Then, we have the following result (Lucas and Saccucci 1990)

$$\widetilde{\sigma}_{dt} \approx \sqrt{\frac{1 - sf_{dt}}{1 + sf_{dt}}} \sigma_{dt} \qquad (4.31)$$

Note that Formula 4.31 is applicable when the data series are $i.i.d$. Although in this simulation example, most of the output data series are not $i.i.d$, we can still use the formula result as an approximation and reference to help determine suitable factor values. To observe better the effect of smoothing weight factors on the data series, we plot out two types of data series that are collected from simulation examples. Figure 4.5 illustrates the data series of demand interarrival time $\widetilde{T}_{demand}(n)$ with different sf_{dt} values. And Figure 4.6 shows the data series of inventory and backlog level $\widetilde{I}(t) - \widetilde{B}(t)$ in the customer input buffer with different sf_{inv} values. From the figures, we can observe that curves are smoothed to different extents when sf_{dt} or sf_{inv} value is changed. Higher sf_{dt} or sf_{inv} value will generate smoother curves. This observation is in agreement with the inference given in Formula 4.31. Because σ_{dt} is a decreasing function of sf_{dt}. A higher sf_{dt} value will lead to a lower σ_{dt} value; and the smaller variance indicates a smoother curve.

The parameter sf_{dt} is a constant used in the calculation of the smoothed demand interarrival time series (see Formula 3.3); it indicates the weight of historical data. When $sf_{dt}=0$, it implies the smoothed data is exactly current data. In practice, the value of sf_{dt} is usually set between 0.7 and 0.9 in exponential smoothing formulas. In this example, referring to the simulation results, we arbitrarily select $sf_{dt}=0.8$ as the initial estimation. Similarly, the rest smoothing weight factors $sf_{su}, sf_{pr}, sf_{inv}$ are estimated depending on practical experience and simulation results as well.

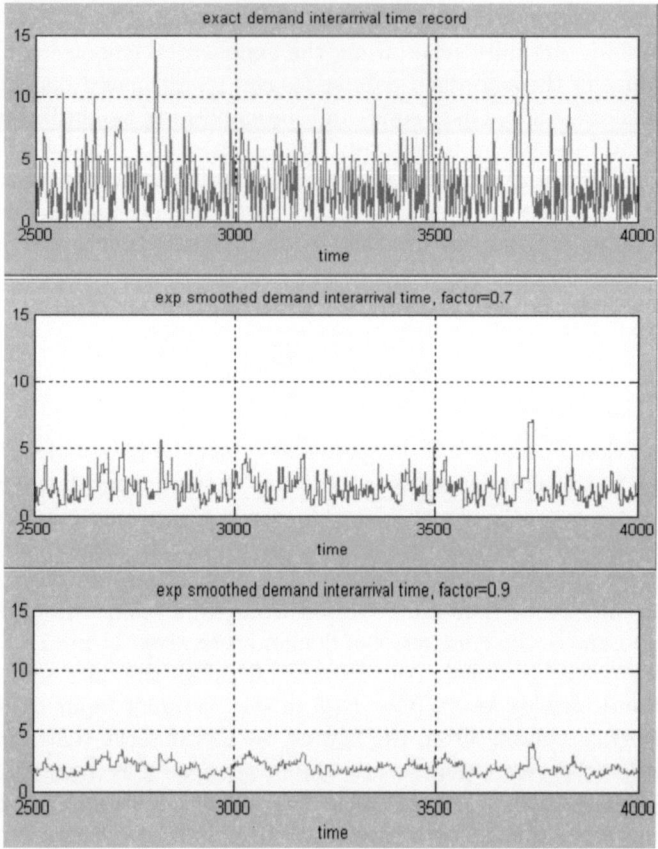

Figure 4.5: Smoothed demand interarrival time (sf_{dt}=0, 0.7, 0.9)

In summary, we set sf_{dt}=0.8,sf_{su}=0.8,sf_{pr}=0.8,sf_{inv}=0.9 as the initial estimation. Although the factor values are arbitrarily decided, the effects of using these factor values in the robust Kanban system is found quite good in the simulation-based comparative experiment (they will be discussed in Chapter 5).

The safety factor sf should also be specified with a suitable value when implementing the risk-response mechanism. The safety factor sf is used in the comparison between mi_rate and its control limits (see Table

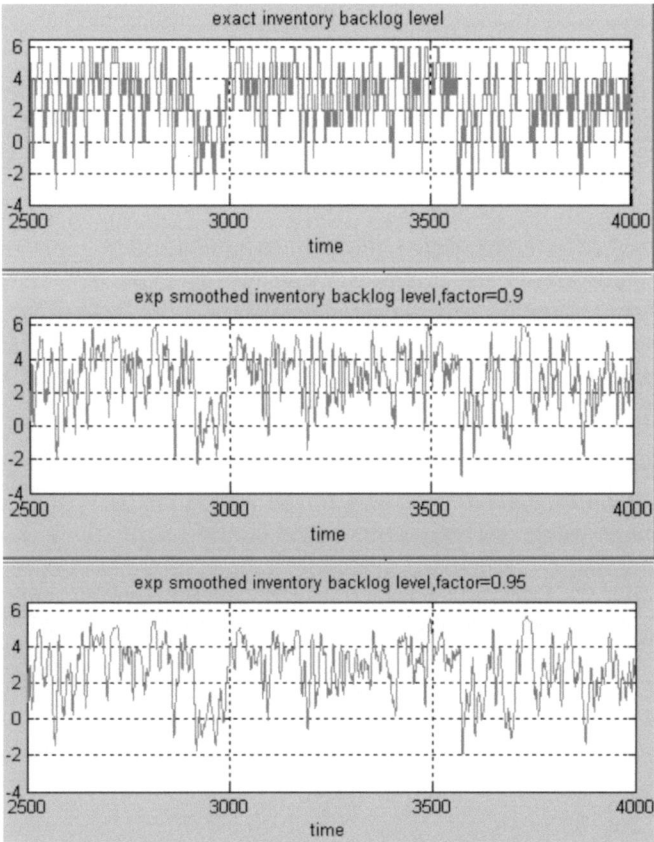

Figure 4.6: Smoothed inventory and backlog level in customer input buffer $(sf_{inv}=0,\ 0.9,\ 0.95)$

4.7 for the control limit parameters specification). Recall the original rate balance constraint: $mi\_rate = \frac{demand\ rate}{service\ rate} \leq \frac{1}{sf}$. In the right hand side of the inequality, sf is the safety factor used to specify the upper bound of normal mi_rate value. We define $sf=1+\varepsilon$, where ε is a small positive value. Thus, the value of sf is kept slightly above 1. We should keep sf not too far above 1. Otherwise, when sf is set too large, the required service capacity may be overqualified to cover the demand, which is a

141

kind of waste for the production. For example, we set $sf{=}2$ (resulting in $mi\_rate{=}0.5$), then we have $mi\_rate < \frac{1}{sf} = \frac{1}{2}$. The redundant service capacity may cause unnecessary operating cost. Therefore, the reasonable setting of sf should be slightly above 1. In this example, we set $sf{=}1.01$ as the initial estimation, then mi_rate is expected to be kept less than $\frac{1}{sf}{=}0.99$.

So far we have introduced the estimation methods for specifying the control parameters used in the risk-response mechanism. The control parameters (including the smoothing weight factors, safety factor, and monitor control limits) have important influence on the final response decision and performance of the robust Kanban system. Therefore, their values should be determined appropriately. Although the control parameter values are just determined using the above estimation methods, the effect of the estimation is satisfying. In the following study, we will show the robust Kanban system can generate adequately good performance when using this estimation-based factor setting. This conclusion is drawn based on the output results of a simulation-based comparative experiment. In the next chapter, we will present how the comparative experiment is designed and performed.

5 Simulation experiment 1: compare Robust Kanban System with others

In Figure 5.1, we use a general model to describe the operation process of a Kanban system. The system transforms input material into finished product; meanwhile a series of output data can be generated as performance measures. The process can be seen as a combination of operations, facilities, control methods, and other resources (such as risk factors) from the environment. During the process, some factors are controllable, whereas others are uncertain. As listed in Figure 5.1, the controllable factors include such as the service equipment capacity (3-level adjustable parameters), the control mechanism (different Kanban control policies). If the risk-response mechanism of the robust Kanban system is selected, related monitor control parameters will be included in the controllable factors as well (see the risk-response mechanism control parameters in Figure 5.1). The uncontrollable factors of the Kanban system are related to the risks from the uncertain environment. The risks group into three types: demand-side, process-side, and supplier-side risks. In the Kanban system model, we assume that the risks are the demand interarrival time variability, the machine process time variability, and the material supply time variability.

In this chapter, we aim to examine whether the robust Kanban system can perform robustly in the uncertain environment as the conceptual model expected. We compare the performance of the robust Kanban systems with the performance of two other Kanban systems (a traditional Toyota Kanban system, and an inventory-based adaptive Kanban system), to see whether the robust Kanban system can give better performance. We design and perform a series of comparative experiments

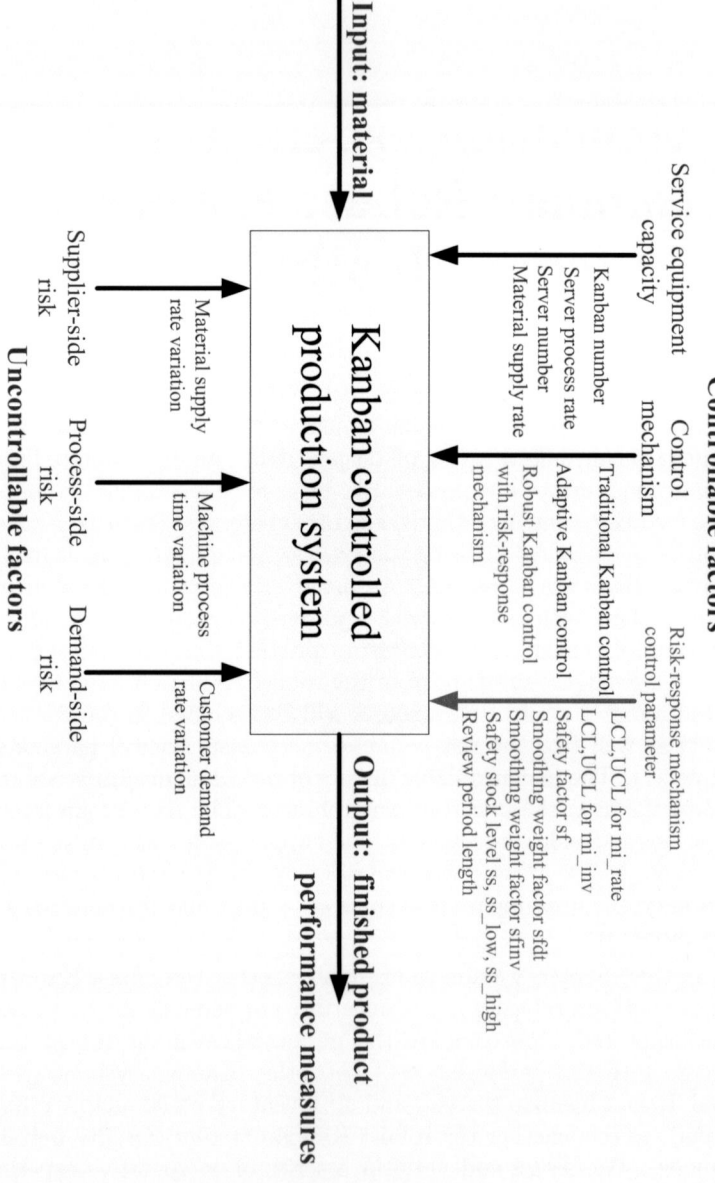

Figure 5.1: General model of the robust Kanban system operation process

(Montgomery 2007) based on simulation models of three Kanban systems. The controllable factor "control mechanism" is designed to have three levels in the experiment: traditional Kanban control, adaptive Kanban control, and the proposed robust Kanban control. And the uncontrollable factor "environment risk" is also assumed to have several typical types, we call them typical risk scenarios in the following text.

The rest of this chapter is organized as follows. In Section 5.1, we present the design details of the comparative experiment. In Section 5.2, after conducting the experiment, we analyze the output results using statistical techniques. At last, an intensive discussion about the experiment results is given in Section 5.3, and the comparison conclusion is drawn eventually.

5.1 Design of experiment

5.1.1 Problem statement

As introduced in Chapter 2, although the literature on Kanban systems contains a wide range of Kanban model variations, only a few models addressed how the system could dynamically change the Kanban number or other parameters during system operation to handle risks. Takahashi's inventory-based reactive Kanban model (Takahashi and Nakamura 1999; Takahashi 2003) and Tardif's adaptive Kanban model (Tardif and Maaseidvaag 2001) are two representative models with dynamical parameter design. Although they adopted flexible system parameters such as Kanban number to mitigate the risk impact, the shortcomings of these models are also noticeable. A brief comparison about three Kanban system variations is made and summarized in Table 5.1: 1) the traditional Toyota Kanban system (Monden 1983); 2) the reactive and adaptive Kanban systems from literature (Takahashi and Nakamura 1999; Takahashi 2003; Tardif and Maaseidvaag 2001); 3) the proposed robust Kanban system (this study).

The control techniques, advantages, and disadvantages of the three selected Kanban systems are summarized in Table 5.1. The traditional Toyota Kanban system keeps the Kanban number constant during system operation; no robust approach is adopted by the system to handle

	System status monitor	Robust approach	Advantages and disadvantages
Traditional Toyota Kanban system	None	None	No risk response measures can be taken, the system is only suitable in a stable environment.
Previous reactive, adaptive Kanban system	Demand time; Inventory and backlog level.	Change Kanban number	It can detect risks, change Kanban number as response actions. However response actions could be not effective (only changing Kanban number), and slow (only when inventory or backlog level is found significantly beyond the control limits). Enormous simulation experiment work is required to apply the models.
Robust Kanban system	mi_rate, mi_inv	Change 3-level parameters: Kanban number; Machine service time; Number of servers; Backup supplier supply proportion.	It can detect risks from supply, process, and demand sides. Response actions are quick and effective (can change 3-level parameters including Kanban number; can quickly change higher-level parameters according to monitor indication, even when inventory or backlog level is not significant yet). Required experiment work is not enormous; The model is practical and convenient in application.

Table 5.1: Comparison of three Kanban system models

risks. The traditional Kanban system works well in the stable environment; nevertheless in an uncertain environment, its performance is not good. Actually the assumption "certain or repetitive environment" is quite restrictive in real life. Most Kanban systems in real life are subject to various uncertainties. This fact leads to the application limitation of the traditional Kanban system.

In the second type, the reactive and adaptive Kanban systems can dynamically adjust the in-use Kanban number during system operation as response against risks. For example, Tardif (2001) proposed an inventory-based adaptive Kanban model aiming to cushion the demand variability. With monitoring the inventory level upon each demand arrival, the adaptive Kanban system can then decide how to change the Kanban number. Compared to the traditional Kanban system, the adaptive model improved the system performance in the uncertain environment. Nevertheless, there is still much room for improvement about the adaptive Kanban model, because it can only deal with slight-extent risks from the demand side. For example, when the risk situation is severe, the demand rate has far exceeded the service rate, thus only adjusting the Kanban number is not an effective approach to cover the inventory shortage. At this moment, to add a new server or speed up the current machine processing rate could be a better method. Another limitation is from the monitor items. When only observing the inventory and backlog level to detect risks, the response action may be not taken quickly enough. Suppose a supplier has to slow down its supply rate due to the heavy snow. If we monitor the supplier supply rate as well, this supply shortage risk can be detected immediately and the backup-supplier can be started soon to cover the material shortage. By contrast, if we only monitor the inventory level (like in the adaptive Kanban model), the supply shortage risk will be detected only after the inventory level goes far below the normal level. At this moment the inventory shortage is already too obvious where much backlog penalty cost has been caused. Thus, the response action could be taken too late if we only monitor the inventory level. Thirdly, before applying the reactive and adaptive Kanban models, enormous experiments are required as preparation work, we have to collect reference information and determine related control parameters. This could be quite time-consuming, and makes the model application impractical in realistic problems.

147

Seeing these limitations, we therefore propose the robust Kanban system model to improve the performance of a Kanban system in the uncertain environment. The brief information of the robust Kanban system is also listed in Table 5.1. In order to confirm the improvement made by the robust Kanban system, we plan to compare the performance measures of the three Kanban systems in simulation environment.

The comparative experiment is carried out based on the simulation models of three Kanban systems. The goal of the experiment is to find out whether the robust Kanban system can perform better than the other two systems when facing an uncertain environment. We assume a variety of risk scenarios, then run the simulation models of three Kanban systems to compare their response performance. Finally, we analyze the simulation output results using statistic methods, to find out whether the robust Kanban system can generate better performance.

5.1.2 Control factors

The first step of the experiment design is to define input conditions. The input control factors and each factor's levels should be appropriately selected with considering the experiment target as well as the realistic situation of the Kanban system.

Two factors are of interest in the comparative experiment: 1) Kanban control mechanism type; 2) risk scenario. As introduced in Table 5.1, we have three types of Kanban control mechanism in comparison: 1) traditional Toyota Kanban system; 2) inventory-based adaptive Kanban system; 3) robust Kanban system. And the risk situation is assumed to contain 7 typical scenarios. In each risk scenario, three Kanban system models are simulated respectively using identical input conditions. Then we collect the output data of each model to do further analysis and comparison.

For the sake of simplicity, we use short notation to mention the above three Kanban systems: 1) Old_Kanban (means the traditional Toyota Kanban system); 2) Inv_Kanban (means the inventory-based adaptive Kanban system); 3) Robust_Kanban (means the robust Kanban system). And seven risk scenarios are denoted by: 1) stable; 2) demand++; 3) demand+; 4) demand−−; 5) demand−; 6) process−; 7) supply−. Detailed

Risk Scenario	Risk description	Extent	Duration /time unit	Frequency /count#
stable	Baseline normal scenario, without risks. Only t_d is uncertain, exponential distribution.	Demand interarrival time: $t_d \sim exp(0.5)$, Total simulation time: 4000		
Demand++	Large increase in demand rate	$50\% t_d^{mean}$	250	2
Demand+	Small increase in demand rate	$90\% t_d$	500	2
Demand--	Large decrease in demand rate	$500\% t_d^{mean}$	250	2
Demand-	Small decrease in demand rate	$120\% t_d$	500	2
Process-	Longer machine service time	$200\% Ts_i$	100	2
Supply-	Longer supplier material generate time	$400\% t_{su}$	100	2

a) Specification of seven risk scenarios

Factor	Level	Predicted comparison results
Kanban control mechanism type	Old_Kanban, Inv_Kanban, Robust_Kanban.	Performance measure Netprofit: Old_Kanban < Inv_Kanban < Robust_Kanban
Risk scenario	Stable, demand++, demand+, demand--, demand-, process-, supply-	

b) Input factors and predicted comparison results

Table 5.2: Input factor design in the comparative experiment

description of the seven risk scenarios is given in Table 5.2a). The stable scenario is considered as the "baseline" normal environment for operating the Kanban system, no special risks will occur in the stable scenario. And the remaining 6 risk scenarios are designed by embedding specific risk events in the stable scenario.

In conclusion, the input factors and each factor's levels in the comparative experiment are summarized in Table 5.2b). The predicted comparison results are also given in the same table. In sum, we expect that the robust Kanban system can give better performance than the other systems in the uncertain environment. The predicted comparison results will be tested after doing the experiment and analyzing the simulation output data of three Kanban systems.

5.1.3 Response variables

It is natural to assume that the target of operating the Kanban system is to maximize the profit or minimize the cost. In this experiment, we select the time-averaged net profit "Netprofit" (also called $Netprofit_{mean}$, see Section 3.2.2 Notation list 3 for definition) as the main response variable.

Netprofit is an integrated performance measure that consists of several subtotal cost items, such as inventory holding cost and backlog cost. We divide the total Netprofit generated during the entire operation time by the time length, then the obtained result is the time-averaged Netprofit. The total Netprofit is calculated by:

$$
\begin{aligned}
Netprofit_{total} = Income &- cost_{purchase} - cost_{inventory} \\
&- cost_{backlog} - cost_{change3level}
\end{aligned}
\tag{5.1}
$$

As can be seen from this formula, the inventory cost (related to inventory level), backlog cost (related to order backlog level), and changing 3-level parameters cost (related to Kanban number, machine service time, server number, and backup supplier supply proportion), the income gained from completed demand orders, and the material purchasing cost, are all contributing factors of $Netprofit_{total}$. The detailed calculation methods for the subtotal cost items can be found in Section 3.2.2.

We have selected Netprofit as the main response variable in the comparative experiment. Besides, other performance measures, such as the inventory and backlog level of finished product at the customer stage, the cost of operating or changing the 3-level parameters, are also considered as supplementary response variables. They can provide more details about the robust Kanban system operation and performance.

Response variable	Notation	Measure unit	Relationship with Netprofit
Daily mean Netprofit (main response)	$Netprofit_{mean}$	Currency unit/time	Is the Netprofit
Mean inventory level	$I_{mean}(t)$	Product unit/time	Inventory↓, Netprofit↑
Mean order backlog level	$B_{mean}(t)$	Product unit/time	Backlog↓, Netprofit↑
Changing 3-level parameters cost	$cost_{change3level}$	Currency unit/time	Changing 3-level parameters cost ↓, Netprofit ↑

Table 5.3: Response variables used in the comparative experiment

Conclusively, we summarize the information of the response variables used in the comparative experiment in Table 5.3. The information includes the response variable name, notation, measure unit, and its relationship with the main response Netprofit. When running the Kanban system simulation models, all the response variables are recorded or calculated. The definition and calculation methods for each response variable can be found in Section 3.2.2.

5.1.4 Choice of design and conducting details

The design framework of the comparative experiment is illustrated in Figure 5.2. We take three types of Kanban control mechanism into comparison, and examine their performance measures (response variables) respectively in seven risk scenarios. In each risk scenario, three Kanban systems are simulated in several replications. In each replication, we sequentially run three Kanban system models using identical input data (including the data series of the customer demand interarrival time, supplier material supply time, and the single-machine service time). Nevertheless, in different replications of a given scenario, the realizations of

151

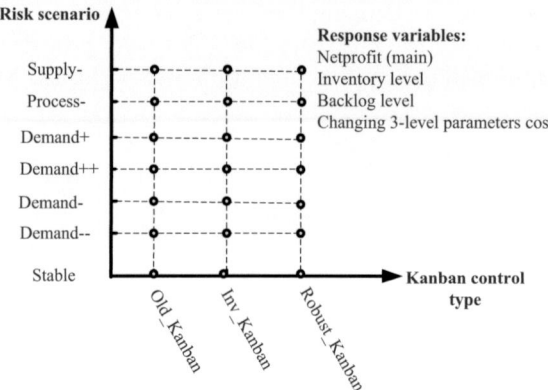

Figure 5.2: Comparison of 3 Kanban systems in 7 risk scenarios

random input data (e.g. exponentially distributed demand interarrival time series) are different. We conduct the experiments following the above design, and the simulation output data "Netprofit" are collected as the response variable. In each scenario, the Netprofit between any two of three Kanban systems are first combined as paired data for each replication, then further comparative analysis will be taken.

Here we select the paired difference test as the comparison method. It is because the paired difference test has more statistic power than the unpaired difference test, if the variability of the noise factor is significant compared to the group difference. In this experiment, the group difference means the data difference between three Kanban systems (the 40 replications data of each Kanban system are seen as a data group); and the noise factors refer to the factors that cause data variability within a group. Using the paired difference test can help us eliminate the variability caused by noise factors, thus we can focus on the effect caused by the factor of interest: the Kanban control mechanism types.

It should be noted that, we first arbitrarily select a sample size (number of replications) 40 for the paired difference test. Later, after performing the experiment, we will examine whether the selected sample size is sufficiently large through analyzing the output data. If the current sample size 40 is too small to generate good statistical inferences for the

152

paired difference test, we will increase the sample size and then redo the experiment. Otherwise, when the sample size 40 is large enough, the test results can be thought of as useful statistical inference.

The post test for the sample size is performed as follows. Suppose the current in-use sample size is n. We put n value into the test formula

$$n \geq \frac{(t_{n-1,\alpha/2} + t_{n-1,\beta})^2}{(\frac{\mu_1 - \mu_2}{S_d})^2} \quad\quad (5.2)$$

(Dupont and Plummer Jr 1990), to check whether the inequality is satisfied. $\mu_1 - \mu_2$ is the difference of two population means, S_d is the estimated standard deviation of paired response differences, and $t_{n-1,\alpha/2}$ and $t_{n-1,\beta}$ are Student t-distribution quantiles with n-1 degrees of freedom and with probability $\alpha/2$ and β. Here α is the probability of detecting a false effect, its usual value is 5%. And 1-β means the probability of detecting a true effect (the power), usually 1-β is supposed to be 90%, 85%,80%. If the given n can satisfy the inequality, then n can be considered as a suitable (sufficiently large) sample size. Otherwise, we have to increase the sample size n. In this comparative experiment, after collecting output data, we have done a series of post-tests using n=40 (40 replications in each Kanban system group) and the inequality is satisfied in each test; so in this experiment we run 40 replications for each Kanban system in each scenario.

As can be seen in Figure 5.2, the control factor "Kanban control mechanism type" has 3 levels; and the factor "risk scenario" has 7 levels. In all, we have 3*7=21 combinations for the input factor setting. Under each control factor setting, we run three Kanban systems in 40 replications. Overall, 7 (scenarios) *3 (Kanban control mechanism types) *40 (replications) =840 simulation runs need to be carried out for the whole comparative experiment.

In each risk scenario, each Kanban system can generate a sample of Netprofit data with size 40. Thus, we finally get three samples of Netprofit data: Netprofit_Old (traditional Kanban system), Netprofit_Inv (adaptive Kanban system), Netprofit_Robust (robust Kanban system), to do the comparison. We do the paired difference test between any two Kanban systems. As given in Table 5.2, the predicted comparison results are: Netprofit_Old < Netprofit_Inv < Netprofit_Robust. We denote

	Supplier	Stage1	Stage2	Stage3	Customer
Inventory Cost (per product unit per time unit)	1	2	3	4	N/A
Backlog Cost (per product unit per time unit)	N/A	N/A	N/A	160	N/A
Sell Price (per product unit)	N/A	N/A	N/A	N/A	200
Purchase Price of main supplier (per product unit)	5	N/A	N/A	N/A	N/A
Purchase Price of backup supplier (per product unit)	20	N/A	N/A	N/A	N/A
Operating Kanban Cost /time unit	2*Kanban number(at the bottleneck stage)*7 work modules				
Control service time cost /time unit	400/machine service time				
Control server number cost / time unit	120* server number				
Change supplier cost /count	1000				

Table 5.4: Input cost coefficient parameters for three Kanban systems in simulation

the mean value of Netprofit generated by three Kanban systems respectively by μ_{old}, μ_{inv}, μ_{robust}. Then, the hypotheses for paired difference tests are stated as below:

- Paired difference test between Traditional Toyota Kanban system (Old_Kanban) and Robust Kanban system (Robust_Kanban)

$$H_0 : \mu_{old} < \mu_{robust}$$

$$H_1 : \mu_{old} \geq \mu_{robust}$$

- Paired difference test between Inventory-based adaptive Kanban system (Inv_Kanban) and Robust Kanban system (Robust_Kanban)

$$H_0 : \mu_{inv} < \mu_{robust}$$

$$H_1 : \mu_{inv} \geq \mu_{robust}$$

	Robust_ Kanban	Inv_ Kanban	Old_ Kanban
Initial Kanban number (K)	6	6	6
K adjusting range $(K_{\min}, K_{\max})$	5,12	5,12	6
Control limits of inventory level (ss_{low}, ss_{high})	(0,4)	(3,4)	N/A
Initial machine service time (T_s)	1.64	1.64	1.64
T_s adjusting range $(Ts_{\max}, Ts_0, Ts_{\min})$	1.8,1.64,1.48	1.64	1.64
Initial server number (N_s)	1	1	1
N_s adjusting range $(Ns_{\min}, Ns_{\max})$	1, 3	1	1
Initial backup supplier proportion (pr_{backup})	0	1	1
pr_{backup} adjusting range (pr_{low}, pr_{high})	0, 0.5	1	1

Table 5.5: Input 3-level parameters of three Kanban systems in simulation

- Paired difference test between Traditional Toyota Kanban system (Old_Kanban) and Inventory-based adaptive Kanban system (Inv_Kanban)

$$H_0 : \mu_{old} < \mu_{inv}$$

$$H_1 : \mu_{old} \geq \mu_{inv}$$

To analyze the output results of paired difference tests, several statistical methods are taken into account. Paired Z-test and paired t-test can be used for data with normality; and Wilcoxon signed-rank test is suitable for non-normal data analysis. In the comparative experiment, the output data obtained from each Kanban system in each risk scenario is just a sample (with size 40) of possible output results. We can know the variance of the data sample but not the variance of the overall data population. Therefore, paired Z-test is excluded due to the required data population variance. If the paired sample data follow a normal distribution, we can apply the paired t-test for the analysis; otherwise, Wilcoxon signed-rank test will be selected for analyzing the non-normal data.

155

	Robust_Kanban	Inv_Kanban	Old_Kanban
Simulation length /simu time unit	4000	4000	4000
Replication per risk scenario	40	40	40
Warm up period /simu time unit	100	100	100
Review period /simu time unit	5	upon demand arrival; or 5 (with $sf_{dt}=0.8$)	N/A
Input random variables for 7 risk scenarios	Stable scenario: demand interarrival time $t_d \sim exp(1/2)$, $t_d^{mean} = 2$, Risk demand++: 50% t_d^{mean} for 250*2 orders, Risk demand+: 90% t_d for 500*2 orders, Risk demand−−: 500% t_d^{mean} for 250*2 orders, Risk demand−: 120% t_d for 250*2 orders, Risk process−: 200% Ts_i for 100*2 service tasks, Risk supply−: 400% T_{su} for 100*2 material orders		
Output data group 1: Real-time data series record	Inventory level at each stage, Order backlog level at customer stage, Waiting time of each demand order, Kanban collection time record, Changing-Kanban number record, Changing-service time record, Changing-server number record, Changing-backup supplier proportion record, Monitor mi_{rate} value record, Monitor mi_{inv} value record.		
Output data group 2: summary statistics	Mean Netprofit (main response), Mean inventory level of each stage, Mean backlog level, Mean customer service level, Mean change Kanban number cost, Mean control service time cost, Mean control server number cost, Mean change supplier cost, Mean total income, Mean total cost.		
Simulation software	Matlab-Simulink 2010a		

Table 5.6: Input scenarios and output performance measures of three Kanban systems in simulation

Control factor	Estimation value
Safety factor sf	1.1, 1.05,1.2
Smoothing weight factor sf_{dt}	0.96
Smoothing weight factor sf_{inv}	0.8
Safety stock level $ss(ss_{low}, ss_{high})$	2 (0,4)
UCL_K	$1/(1+ sf)$
LCL_K	$1/(1+ sf)*0.85$
UCL_{Ts}	1
LCL_{Ts}	$1/(1+ sf)*0.82$
UCL_{Ns}	$1/(1+ sf)*2$
LCL_{Ns}	$1/(1+ sf)*0.5$
UCL_{su}	$1/(1+ sf)*0.85$
LCL_{su}	$1/(1+ sf)*0.5$

Table 5.7: Input risk-response mechanism parameters for the robust Kanban system simulation model

So far, the design of the comparative experiment is accomplished. Nextly, to conduct the experiment, the input parameters with respect to the system configuration and simulation control techniques should be specified. The specification is presented from Table 5.4 to Table 5.7. They are respectively about cost coefficients parameters, 3-level system structure parameters, simulation model parameters, and risk-response mechanism parameters. To be noted, the simulation run length for each Kanban model is set identically as 4000 time units (in simulation clock). It is because when the simulation run length is around 4000, the operating status of each Kanban system can already show a stationary trend. Before doing the experiment, we tried many values of simulation run length from 500 to 10^7 time units, and found that 4000 is a useful and economical value. And the methods or reasons for other parameters settings can be found in related sections of Chapter 4.

5.2 Result analysis

As mentioned earlier, we need to carry out 7 (scenarios) *3 (Kanban system types) *40 (replications) =840 simulation runs in the comparative experiment. Thus, for each Kanban system in each risk scenario, we can obtain an output data sample with size 40. The output data of three Kanban systems in the same risk scenario will be compared together using paired difference tests.

Before doing statistical analysis on the data samples, we first plot out descriptive graphs to get a big picture of the output results. For example, we draw distribution graphs (histogram, outlier box plot) and scatter plots of Netprofit data. Subsequently, we take paired difference tests to analyze the sample data from each risk scenario to derive statistical conclusions. The statistical analysis software used in this study is JMP 8.0 package. In Section 5.2.1, we first present a brief summary of the statistical results. More analysis and implication of the results will be discussed in the following sections.

5.2.1 Result overview

Having collected the output data from the simulation experiment, we first draw scatter plots and box plots for each data sample to get a big picture of the results.

As shown in Figure 5.3, the sample data obtained from three Kanban systems in the stable scenario are illustrated by scatter and box plots. And the corresponding summary statistics of the data are listed in Table 5.8. From Figure 5.3, we can observe that the mean values of Netprofit data from three Kanban systems are quite close; all of them remain at a high level. However, the data scatter situations of three Kanban systems are of noticeable difference: Old_Kanban data points are more scattered, whereas Inv_Kanban and Robust_Kanban data points are distributed more densely. Looking into the statistical summary given in Table 5.8, we can find that: mean Netprofit value of Robust_Kanban>Inv_Kanban>Old_Kanban; and the standard deviation (or variance) of Robust_Kanban<Inv_Kanban<Old_Kanban. The comparison result is in good agreement with the predicted results given in Table 5.2b). The mean value of Netprofit data from Robust Kanban system is higher than the mean value from other two Kanban systems; and the inventory-based adaptive Kanban system performed also better than the Traditional Kanban system.

Nevertheless, the mean value-based comparison results are not very powerful, because the differences between three Kanban systems are not so significant compared with the sample data variation of each Kanban system. For example, mean Netprofit of Robust_Kanban sample is 85.36, of Inv_Kanban sample is 78.19, the difference between them is 85.36-78.19=7.17; whereas the standard deviation of the two samples are 28.68 and 23.41 respectively. The standard deviations are larger than the mean value difference, which implies that the inherent sample data variation within each Kanban system is larger than the effect of different Kanban control mechanisms. In this situation, we cannot simply conclude that the robust Kanban system can perform better than the other two Kanban systems. Further investigation has to be taken to confirm the conclusion. Since the within-group data variation is relatively significant, we think the paired difference test is a more suitable approach for the comparison than the unpaired difference test. Hence, we select the paired difference test to compare statistically the Netprofit data from three Kanban systems. The results of the paired comparison test in the stable scenario will be discussed in Section 5.2.2.

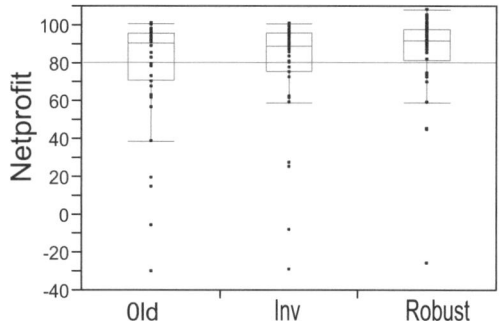

Figure 5.3: Scatter and box plots of mean Netprofit for three Kanban systems (in stable scenario)

Nextly, we look at the descriptive results of Netprofit from the remaining 6 risk scenarios. The scatter and box plots of three Kanban systems in the remaining 6 risk scenarios are displayed in Figure 5.4; and corresponding statistical summary results are given in Table 5.9.

Stable Scenario	Sample size	Mean	Std	CI*(95% lower)	CI(95% upper)
Old_Kanban	40	76.9532	30.2888	67.2664	86.6400
Inv_Kanban	40	78.1904	28.6817	69.0175	87.3632
Robust_Kanban	40	85.3638	23.4122	77.8762	92.8514

Table 5.8: Netprofit summary statistics of three Kanban systems in stable scenario (*: CI, Confidence Interval)

Similar to the stable scenario, in the majority of the remaining 6 risk scenarios, the mean Netprofit values of three Kanban systems obey the same order: mean Netprofit of Old_Kanban < Inv_Kanban < Robust_Kanban. The only exception is the demand$--$ risk scenario. In this scenario we observe that: mean Netprofit value of Inv_Kanban < Old_Kanban < Robust_Kanban.

Different from the stable scenario, the mean Netprofit value differences between 3 Kanban systems are much more significant in the remaining 6 risk scenarios. For instance, as can be seen in Figure 5.4a) and Table 5.9a), the differences of mean Netprofit in the demand++ scenario are: Robust-Old=93.60713, Robust-Inv=78.1979, and Inv-Old=15.40923; whereas in the stable scenario, the differences are smaller: Robust-Old=8.410652, Robust-Inv=7.173446 and Inv-Old =1.237206.

Furthermore, comparing the results of demand++ scenario and demand+ scenario, we find that in the demand++ (severe demand increase) risk scenario, the performance improvement made by the robust Kanban system is more obvious than in the demand+ (slight demand increase) risk scenario. When the environment is uncertain, the traditional Kanban system and the inventory-based adaptive Kanban system cannot perform so well. The more risks the environment has, the worse performance they will generate. By contrast, the robust Kanban system can still remain at an adequately good performance level due to the robustly designed risk-response mechanism.

Similar performance improvement made by the robust Kanban system can be also clearly observed in other 4 risk scenarios. In sum, in all the risk scenarios except the stable scenario, the Netprofit gained by the robust Kanban system is obviously higher than the other two Kanban systems. The risk-response mechanism of the robust Kanban system can significantly improve the Kanban system performance when facing a variety of risks in the uncertain environment. Especially when the risk is severe, the performance differences between robust Kanban system and other systems become much more distinct. In addition, comparing Inv_Kanban system with Old_Kanban system results, smaller but still obvious improvement can also be seen in the Inv_Kanban system in most of the cases. Thus, the observation in these risk scenarios confirms our predicted comparison result, namely, mean Netprofit value of Robust_Kanban system > Inv_Kanban system > Old_Kanban system.

We also notice that there is an exceptional case, the demand−− scenario. In this scenario, the comparison result is different from the others: mean Netprofit value of Inv_Kanban< Old_Kanban < Robust_Kanban. Namely, the traditional Kanban system gained more Netprofit than the inventory-based adaptive Kanban system. Although it deviated from our prediction "Netprofit of Old_Kanban<Inv_Kanban", the Netprofit difference between Inv_Kanban and Old_Kanban is quite small, as shown in Figure 5.4c) and Table 5.9c). We think the exceptional comparison result is caused by the trade-off relationship between the high order backlog cost and the low inventory holding cost. In the demand−− scenario, the customer demand rate decreased largely for some periods. In this situation, the Inv_Kanban system reduced its cyclic Kanban number to reduce the inventory level in response to the large demand-decrease risk. In contrast, the Old_Kanban system still kept a constant Kanban number in the demand−− risk scenario; hence the number of finished product stored in the customer input buffer became larger, which caused a higher inventory holding cost. Once the demand-decrease disruption was gone, the customer demand rate went back immediately to the normal level. But at this moment, the Inv_Kanban system was still using a lower-level Kanban number. Not until the demand rate change was detected in later periods, would the Inv_Kanban system increase its Kanban number. The delay of increasing Kanban number could result in more backlogged orders, consequently more backlog cost was incurred. In this experiment, we assume that the order backlog cost is much higher than the inventory cost, hence the saving from inventory cost might be balanced out by the increased order backlog cost in the Inv_Kanban system. If the inventory cost saved from reducing Kanban number is less

161

than the extra order backlog cost caused by the response-action delay, the Netprofit of Inv_Kanban system will be consequently lower than the Old_Kanban system. This can explain why the exceptional result "Netprofit of Old_Kanban > Inv_Kanban" occurred in the demand−− risk scenario. Actually in the demand−− scenario, the Netprofit difference between the two Kanban systems is not obvious.

To sum up, in most of the risk scenarios, the adaptive Kanban system achieved a higher performance level than the traditional Kanban system, and the robust Kanban system presented a significantly better performance than the other two Kanban systems.

So far, we have constructed descriptive graphs and tables of summary statistics to get a general understanding of the results of the comparative experiment. In the following parts, we will present and discuss the comparison results in each risk scenario with more details.

5.2.2 In a stable scenario

In the stable scenario, compared with the mean value difference between different groups, the variation of Netprofit data within the group (each Kanban system type is a group) is considerably large. Hence, we cannot evidently conclude that the robust Kanban system can outperform the other two systems, if only judging the mean value of Netprofit data. To mitigate the impact of within-group data variation, we use the paired difference test to compare the effects (on the response variable Netprofit) of different Kanban control mechanisms. In a given scenario, the input conditions of three Kanban system simulation models are set identically in each same-ordered replication, so that paired difference test is applicable in data analysis.

Two types of paired difference test are taken into consideration as option: paired t-test and Wilcoxon signed-rank test. The paired t-test is a very powerful quantitive tool for comparison. But doing paired t-test requires a precondition: the sample data should have normality; while doing Wilcoxon signed-rank test requires no normality for data.

Hence we first observe the distribution of Netprofit data. As demonstrated by histograms in Appendix A, the Netprofit data of "Robust-Old", "Robust-Inv" and "Robus" approximate to a normal distribution. The

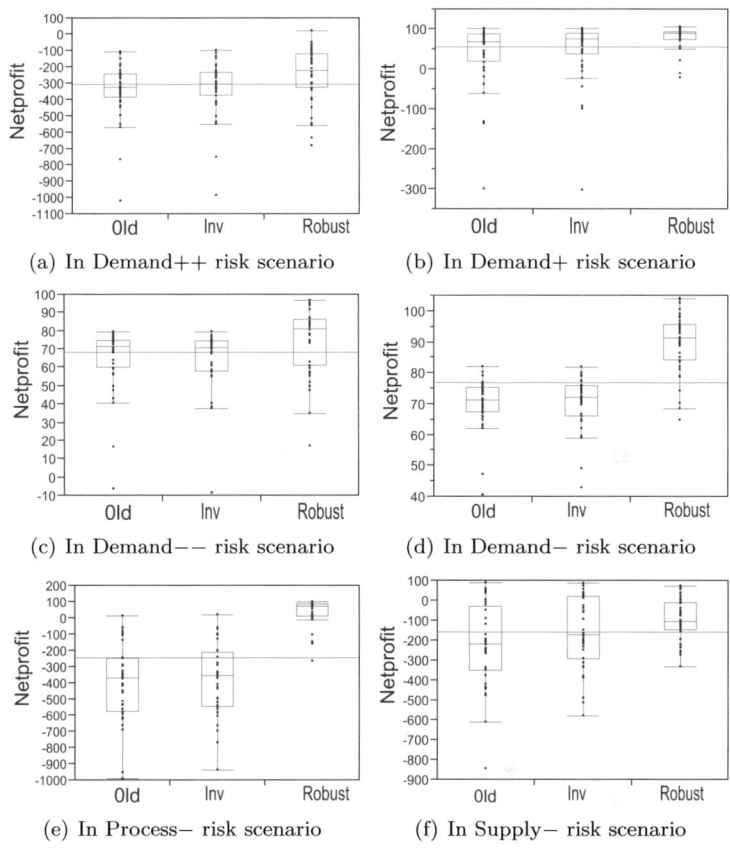

(a) In Demand++ risk scenario

(b) In Demand+ risk scenario

(c) In Demand-- risk scenario

(d) In Demand- risk scenario

(e) In Process- risk scenario

(f) In Supply- risk scenario

Figure 5.4: Scatter and box plots of meanNetprofit of 3 Kanban systems (in the remaining 6 risk scenarios)

observed normal distribution of Netprofit data can be explained by the central limit theorem. Recall the central limit theorem(see Law (2007) p.499). Given a series of *i.i.d* random variables $X_1, X_2, X_3, ..., X_n$ with finite mean μ and finite variance σ^2, if the sample size n is sufficiently large, then the sample mean $\bar{X}(n)$ is distributed approximately as a normal random variable with mean μ and variance σ^2/n . Even for some certain types of correlated data, we denote them by $Y_1, Y_2, Y_3, ..., Y_n$,

Demand++ Scenario	Sample size	Mean	Std	CI*(95% lower)	CI(95% upper)
Old_Kanban	40	-344.4317	167.8515	-398.1132	-290.7502
Inv_Kanban	40	-329.0224	165.9589	-382.0987	-275.9462
Robust_Kanban	40	-250.8245	167.0999	-304.2657	-197.3834

Demand+ Scenario	Sample size	Mean	Std	CI*(95% lower)	CI(95% upper)
Old_Kanban	40	38.3777	79.7236	12.8809	63.8746
Inv_Kanban	40	45.9516	75.4760	21.8132	70.0901
Robust_Kanban	40	78.4515	27.6596	69.6055	87.2975

Demand-- Scenario	Sample size	Mean	Std	CI*(95% lower)	CI(95% upper)
Old_Kanban	40	64.9669	17.3400	59.4212	70.5125
Inv_Kanban	40	64.7613	16.1070	59.6100	69.9126
Robust_Kanban	40	74.4997	17.6281	68.8620	80.1374

Demand- Scenario	Sample size	Mean	Std	CI*(95% lower)	CI(95% upper)
Old_Kanban	40	70.098	7.7521	67.6187	72.5772
Inv_Kanban	40	70.5328	8.0632	67.9540	73.1115
Robust_Kanban	40	89.6012	9.3200	86.6205	92.5819

Process- Scenario	Sample size	Mean	Std	CI*(95% lower)	CI(95% upper)
Old_Kanban	40	-398.906	236.0437	-474.3964	-323.4155
Inv_Kanban	40	-376.5615	221.3652	-447.3576	-305.7655
Robust_Kanban	40	34.4454	80.2497	8.7803	60.1105

Supply- Scenario	Sample size	Mean	Std	CI*(95% lower)	CI(95% upper)
Old_Kanban	40	-221.5351	205.1441	-287.1434	-155.9268
Inv_Kanban	40	-160.3998	179.7192	-217.8768	-102.9228
Robust_Kanban	40	-97.0472	104.5856	-130.4953	-63.5991

Table 5.9: Netprofit summary statistics of three Kanban systems in other 6 riks scenarios (*: CI, Confidence Interval)

the normal distribution is also a good approximation. The Y_i series are not *i.i.d* data, such as the waiting time of each customer in an M/M/1 queue. However, as the number of customers n is getting larger, the mean waiting time $\bar{Y}(n)$ will approximately follow a normal distribution as well. The conclusion is drawn referring to some variations of the central limit theorem (see Law (2007) p.499). In our Kanban simulation models, the output data Netprofit (mean Netprofit value) from each simulation run is such a $\bar{Y}(n)$ summary statistic. The response variable Netprofit is actually the time-averaged Netprofit value that is calculated by $\sum\limits_{n=1}^{n=RL} Netprofit_n/RL$, where RL is the simulation run length in simulation clock (we have $RL=4000$ time units in the presented experiment). The output data series $Netprofit_n$ from a simulation run is a correlated data series. However, when RL is sufficiently large, the distribution of mean Netprofit can approximate well to a normal distribution too.

Furthermore, it can be reasoned that the paired differences of Netprofit value between each two Kanban system samples should approximate to normal distributions (see Figure A.1 in Appendix). According to the above theorem, when RL is sufficiently large, we believe that all the Netprofit data should approximate to the normal distribution

But from Figure A.1, we observed that only the Robust-related Netprofit data ("Robust-Old", "Robust-Inv" and "Robust") show the normality, while the other data (from "Inv-Old", "Inv" and "Old") present non-normal shapes. This can be explained as follows. In the stable scenario, the demand variability (exponential distribution of demand interarrival time) is relatively large for the Old_Kanban and Inv_Kanban systems. Once the demand rate changes, the system operating status (such as inventory level) will be affected by the risk for a longer time than in the robust Kanban system. Thus, the $Netprofit_n$ data series in Old_Kanban and Inv_Kanban systems are more correlated than in the Robust_Kanban system. Therefore, with the current simulation run length ($RL=4000$), the Netprofit data from the two systems cannot present as good normality as the data from the Robust Kanban System. Since our study focuses on the effects of the robust Kanban system, we still use the paired t-test as the main tool to do the comparative analysis and generate statistical inferences. As a supplement, the Wilcoxon Sign-Rank test for non-normal data is also taken for reference.

165

Using the sample data, we did the paired t-test for any two of Robust_Kanban, Inv_Kanban and Old_Kanban systems. The statistical analysis software JMP 8.0 is used to perform the tests. The test results are also presented in Figure A.1.

To be noted, the statistical tests adopted in the comparative experiment are one-sided tests with 95% confidence interval (α=0.05). The null hypothesis $H_0 : \mu_{old} < \mu_{robust}$ indicates the robust Kanban system is supposed to perform better than the traditional Kanban system in the view of Netprofit. We calculate the p-value of "Prob>t" other than "Prob>|t|" to estimate the risk of wrongly rejecting hypothesis H_0. The smaller the "Prob>t" p-value is, the more confident it is to accept the hypothesis H_0. As can be seen in Figure A.1, the "Prob>t" p-values in tests $H_0 : \mu_{old} < \mu_{robust}$ and $H_0 : \mu_{inv} < \mu_{robust}$ are 0.0155 and 0.0102, respectively; both values are far below α=0.05. This means it is powerful to accept the null hypotheses. Namely, it is reasonable to conclude that Robust_Kanban performs better than Old_Kanban and Inv_Kanban systems in the stable scenario.

On the other hand, in the test $H_0 : \mu_{old} < \mu_{inv}$, we find that "Prob>t" p-value is 0.2966, which is much larger than 0.05. Hence, we cannot state that the Inv_Kanban system outperforms the Old_Kanban system at a statistically significant level, even though the mean Netprofit value of Inv_Kanban (78.19084) is larger than that of Old_Kanban (76.9532). Actually all the three Kanban systems performed quite well in the stable environment, the difference between their performance is not obvious.

As a post test, we want to know whether the sample size 40 is suitable for the paired t-test. Therefore, we use Formula 5.2 to check the result. Take the data of paired t-test μ_{old} vs. μ_{robust} as an example. In this example, we have obtained μ_{old}=76.9532, μ_{robust}=85.3638, we use the difference of sample means to estimate the difference of population means, they are $\mu_{robust} - \mu_{old}$=8.41065. The current sample size n=40. From Figure A.1 we can get S_d=19.6907, and we also have $t_{n-1,\alpha/2} = t_{39,5\%}$=1.684, $t_{n-1,\beta} = t_{39,20\%}$=0.888, then the value of $\frac{(t_{n-1,\alpha/2}+t_{n-1,\beta})^2}{(\frac{\mu_1-\mu_2}{S_d})^2}$ is 36.26, which is less than 40. Namely, Formula 5.2 is satisfied by n=40. Then we can conclude that the sample size 40 is a sufficiently large value for the paired t-test μ_{old} vs. μ_{robust}.

In other cases, we can also use Formula 5.2 to examine whether the sample size 40 is suitable. In general, except the paired t-test between Old_Kanban and Inv_Kanban systems in the stable scenario, in all other comparison cases (the other 2 comparisons in the stable scenario, and all the comparisons in the remaining 6 scenarios), the sample size 40 is sufficiently large for the paired t-test to generate useful statistical inferences.

5.2.3 In a demand++ scenario

In the demand++ risk scenario, we add a large demand-increase risk into the "baseline" stable scenario. The assumed risk situation is that the demand rate suddenly increases to a much higher level for a time length, and then falls down to the previous normal level. The risk situation is realized through setting unusual values for the demand interarrival time data series in simulation. After running simulation models of three Kanban systems under the same demand++ scenario, we can obtain three output data samples respectively from Robust_Kanban, Inv_Kanban, and Old_Kanban systems. Similarly, in the demand++ scenario we set data sample size=40, namely each Kanban system simulation is run in 40 replications. And the simulation input conditions of three Kanban systems are set identically in each same-ordered replication, which guarantees the precondition of applying the paired difference test.

As shown in Figure A.2, we first constructed distribution histograms and outlier box plots of the response Netprofit data in the demand++ scenario. With the graphs, we can examine the normality of sample data, which is fundamental to further statistical analysis.

Similar to the results of the stable scenario, in Figure A.2, good normal distribution shapes can be observed in Robust Kanban related graphs in the demand++ risk scenario. Hence, we choose the paired t-test as the statistical tool to compare the data.

In Figure A.2, we list the Netprofit paired t-test results for each pair from Robust_Kanban, Inv_Kanban, and Old_Kanban system in the demand++ risk scenario. All the statistics and parameters have the same meaning as in the former stable-scenario paired t-test. In the demand++ risk scenario, we observe that the "Prob>t" p-values are quite small for all comparison pairs when comparing to the "Prob>t" p-values in the stable scenario. This implies that the risk of wrongly rejecting the hypothesis H_0 is very small in the demand++ case. Besides, in this case, the differences in Netprofit data sample means (see the parameter Mean Difference) become much larger than in the stable scenario. This also implies that the performance improvement made by robust Kanban system is more significant in the more uncertain demand++ risk scenario. Based on the paired t-test results, we conclude that the Netprofit value of Robust_Kanban>Inv_Kanban>Old_Kanban. Namely, the robust Kanban system can outperform the other two systems; and the inventory-based adaptive Kanban system can also perform better than the traditional Kanban system in the demand++ scenario. Furthermore, comparing the paired t-test results from the stable scenario and demand++ scenario, we can find that the performance improvement made by the robust Kanban system becomes more significant when the environment variability is larger.

5.2.4 In other scenarios

Doing the comparative experiment in the remaining 5 risk scenarios, similar results can also be obtained as shown in the stable and demand++ scenarios.

Suppose we can accept the null hypothesis H_0 in the paired test when "Prob>t" p-value<0.05. According to the p-value results, we get the same comparison result for the 7 risk scenarios: Netprofit value of Robust_Kanban > Inv_Kanban > Old_Kanban (the only exception is: Inv_Kanban<Old_Kanban in the stable scenario). The value of difference between groups may vary in different risk situations, but the order of the response Netprofit of three Kanban systems is always the same. The detailed results of all the 7 scenarios can be found in Appendix A.

In sum, based on the paired t-test results, it is reasonable to conclude that the robust Kanban system can achieve a better performance than the traditional and adaptive Kanban systems when facing a wide range of risks in the environment. Especially when the risk situation is severe, the performance improvement gained by the robust Kanban system will become more significant.

5.3 Result discussion

In Section 5.2, we have discussed the comparison results referring to the main response variable Netprofit. The Netprofit is an integrated performance measure that consists of many subtotal cost items (such as inventory cost, order backlog cost). To know more details about the system operating status and performance, we investigate the subtotal cost items of Netprofit in the following work.

Besides the integrated performance measure Netprofit, other specific performance measures can be also obtained from simulation. The output results include not only the real-time system operating status information but also summary statistics. Recall the Netprofit calculation formula (Formula 5.1). The values of the subtotal cost item like inventory cost, order backlog cost, and changing 3-level parameters cost are determined by related performance measures: the inventory level, order backlog level, and in-use service equipment capacity.

In Figure 5.5, we illustrate the detailed performance measure results of three Kanban systems in seven typical risk scenarios. The information includes the integrated performance measure Netprofit and detailed performance measures inventory level, backlog level, changing 3-level parameters cost. The data points in the graphs are collected from the comparative experiment in Section 5.2. The histograms represent the mean values of selected performance measures; they are calculated based on the sample data (with size 40) of each Kanban system in the given scenario.

In Figure 5.5a), we present the comparison result of Netprofit, the final integrated performance measure of the robust Kanban system model. When comparing the Netprofit of three Kanban systems in a specific scenario, we can observe that Robust_Kanban system always generates a higher Netprofit value than the other two systems. Moreover, comparing the Netprofit results across different scenarios, we can see the tendency that the performance improvement made by the robust Kanban system will become more obvious in the severer risk situation. Actually in these risk scenarios, the Netprofit results of Old_Kanban and Inv_Kanban system vary a lot, the results depend on the risk impact in that sce-

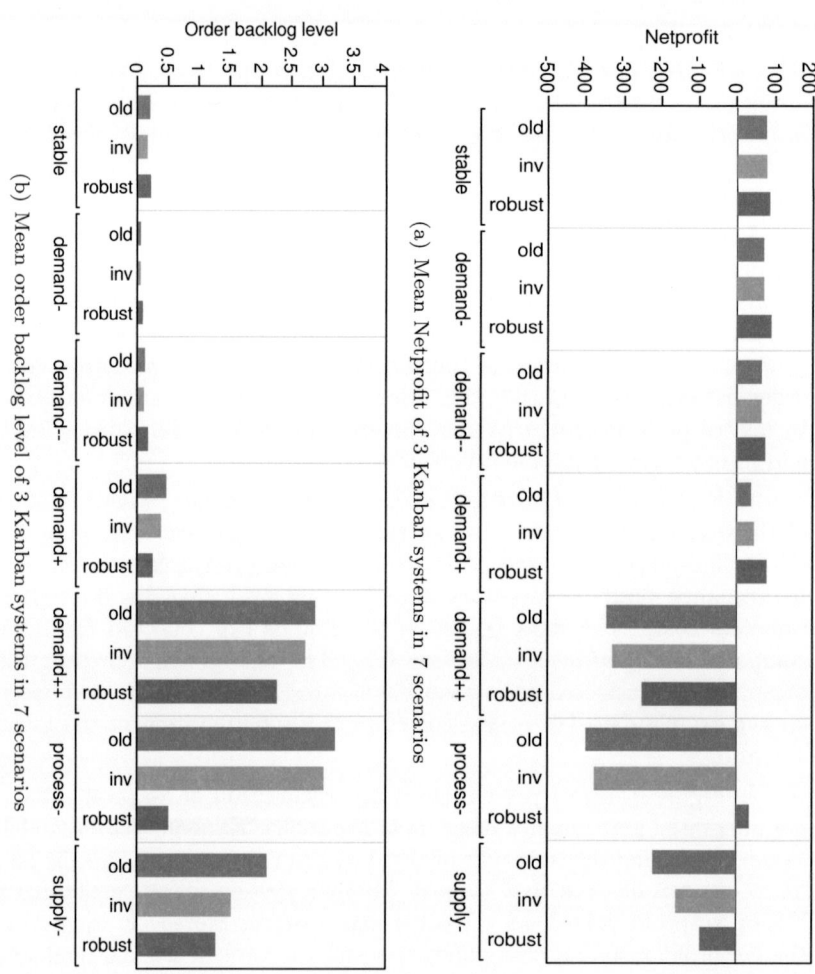

(a) Mean Netprofit of 3 Kanban systems in 7 scenarios

(b) Mean order backlog level of 3 Kanban systems in 7 scenarios

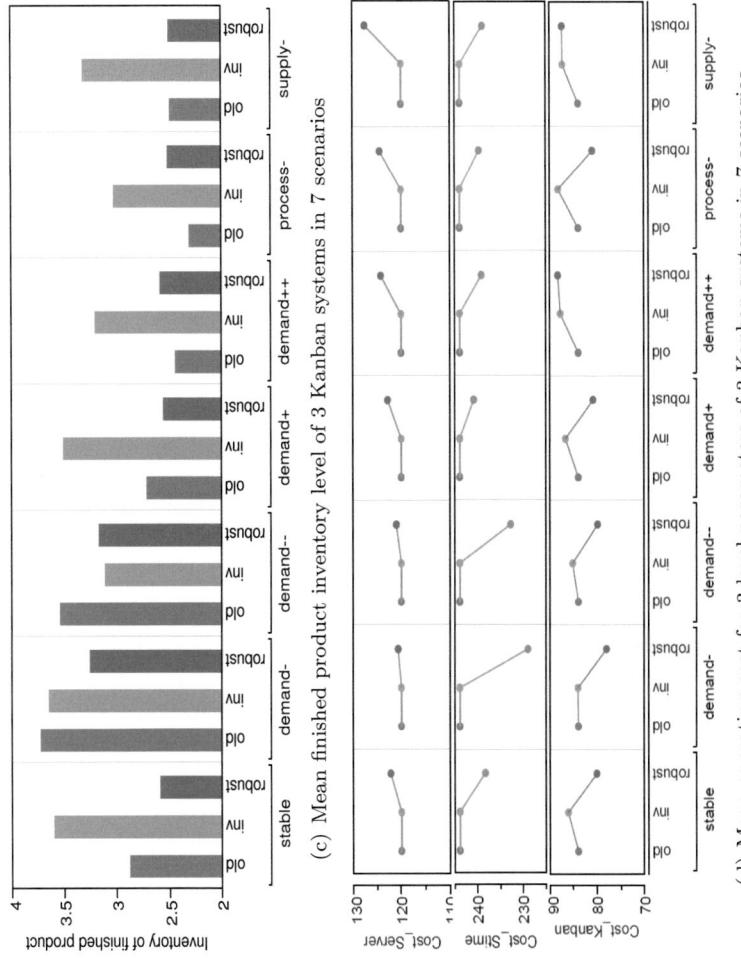

(c) Mean finished product inventory level of 3 Kanban systems in 7 scenarios

(d) Mean operating cost for 3-level parameters of 3 Kanban systems in 7 scenarios

Figure 5.5: Performance measure results of 3 Kanban systems in 7 risk scenarios

nario. By contrast, the robust Kanban system can retain a more stable performance level in different risk scenarios.

Figure 5.5b) illustrates the order backlog levels of three Kanban systems in different scenarios. The order backlog level is a performance measure considered from the customer view, and is used to reflect the system service quality. In these Kanban system models, the order backlog level is virtually the customer waiting queue length. Hence, a lower backlog level indicates the shorter waiting time and better customer service quality; while a higher backlog level means long waiting time that may cause loss of customer goodwill. If we intend to maintain a high customer service level, we should set a high penalty cost rate for backlogged orders. For example, in the comparative example, the order backlog cost is assumed to be160 per product unit per time unit. Compared to the inventory holding cost 4 per product unit per time unit, the order backlog cost is quite high. This makes the backlog cost become an important contributing factor to the final performance Netprofit.

Given the backlog penalty cost rate and inventory holding cost rate, suitable inventory and backlog levels can be consequently decided for generating the optimal Netprofit result. Since in this experiment, we assume that the order backlog cost rate is much higher than the inventory holding cost rate, then the Kanban systems tend to keep the order backlog level at a very low level (less than 1 product unit). When various risks occur in the environment, the Old_Kanban and Inv_Kanban systems cannot keep the order backlog at a low level as before; thus a considerable amount of order backlog penalty cost will be incurred. By contrast, the robust Kanban system can still retain a relatively low backlog level; thus the better Netprofit result gained by the robust Kanban system is mainly attributed to the saved backlog penalty cost. In general, the result of comparing the "order backlog level" between three Kanban systems is: order backlog level of Robust_Kanban < Inv_Kanban < Old_Kanban. The comparison orders of three Kanban systems are the same in all the seven risk scenarios, just the value difference of backlog levels between Kanban systems will vary in different risk scenarios.

The inventory information of three Kanban systems in 7 risk scenarios is demonstrated in Figure 5.5c). We can observe that, in all risk scenarios except the demand- and demand- scenarios, the Inv_Kanban system holds the highest inventory level, whereas Old_Kanban and Robust_Kanban systems keep relatively low and stable inventory levels. The observation reflects the features of different Kanban control mechanisms. For example, in the demand— and demand—— scenarios, the customer demand rate is supposed to decline slightly (demand—) or markedly (demand——) for a time length as the risk event. When risk occurs, Inv_Kanban system will reduce cyclic Kanban number as the response action. The response action leads the inventory into a lower level, thus unnecessary inventory holding cost can be eliminated. In Figure 5.5c) we observe that the inventory level of Inv_Kanban system varies a lot in different risk scenarios, while the backlog level of Old_Kanban or Robust_Kanban system remains relatively stable. It is because the Old_Kanban system always holds a constant Kanban number; and the Robust_Kanban system can adjust other machine-capacity parameters instead of the Kanban number to handle the risks. Therefore, their inventory levels are more stable. In the demand++, demand+, supply-, process- risk scenarios, when risks happen to the system, the inventory level decrease or backlog level increase will be incurred as a result. To reduce the impact of risks, the Inv_Kanban system will add more Kanbans into the system. However, the adding-Kanban action might be not useful to mitigate the risk impact, if the risk is severe. Imagine the risk disruption is quite severe, such as the material supply is interrupted for a long period, the processing machine has totally broken down, or the customer demand rate increases rapidly to a high level. In these situations, only to increase the Kanban number cannot effectively mitigate the risk impact and maintain the system performance at a high level. By contrast, to select a backup supplier, set up a new machine, or speed up the machine processing rate could be more effective approaches for reducing the risk impact. Although additional cost must be paid for changing the machine or supplier capacity, the risk of order backlog can be meanwhile reduced and the potential backlog penalty cost is saved, owing to the enhanced service capacity.

Lastly, from Figure 5.5d), we can capture the information about operating cost related to 3-level parameters (including Kanban number, machine service time, server number). The Kanban system using different Kanban number, different machine processing rate, or different server number will certainly generate different operating cost. To set up a new server in a workcell, to speed up the machine process rate by employing more workers or overtime work, will accordingly cause more operating cost than just adjusting the Kanban number. As can be seen from this graph, the operating cost of the Old_Kanban system is identical in all risk scenarios because its 3-level parameter setting is fixed. In the Inv_Kanban system, only the Kanban number operating cost differs among 7 risk scenarios, because only its Kanban number is flexible. Lastly, in the Robust_Kanban system, all operating cost items are varying across different risk scenarios, since all the 3-level parameters can be dynamically adjusted depending on different risk situations.

In most of the scenarios, we can observe that the service time operating cost in the Robust_Kanban system is lower than that in Old_Kanban and Inv_Kanban systems. It is because the Old_Kanban and Inv_Kanban systems adopt a standard machine service time, whereas the Robust_Kanban systems can flexibly adjust the machine service time to a higher level or a lower level depending on different demand requirements. When the demand rate decreases, the robust Kanban system can economically slow down the machine service rate, thus operating cost for abundant service capacities can be saved. Later, when demand increases, the system will switch the machine service rate to a higher level again. The flexible machine service time helps the robust Kanban system work more efficiently in the uncertain environment.

The Kanban number operating cost is found to be lower in the Robust Kanban system than in the other systems, while server-number operating cost is higher in the Robust Kanban system. When severe risk disruption happens, the Robust Kanban system may set up a new server to deal with the risk. The cost of operating a new server could be very expensive; however, comparing to the potential risk of order backlog penalty cost, the action of adding a server can be worthwhile and economical. Due to this reason, higher server-number operating cost is caused in the Robust Kanban system. Usually the severe risk disruption only happen with a low probability, hence the newly added server does not need to work for a long time. When the risk disruption disappears, the server number will be reduced to its normal level for saving unnecessary server-number related operating cost. Meanwhile, in the Robust Kanban system, the Kanban number does not need to be set so large as in the Old_Kanban and Inv_Kanban systems, because other 3-level parameters (like server number and machine service time) can also be flexibly adjusted in response to risks in the robust Kanban system. Sometimes the action of adjusting the machine service time or server number could be more effective and economical than only changing Kanban number, it depends on the risk situation. Therefore, the Kanban number is kept smaller in the Robust Kanban system than in other two Kanban systems.

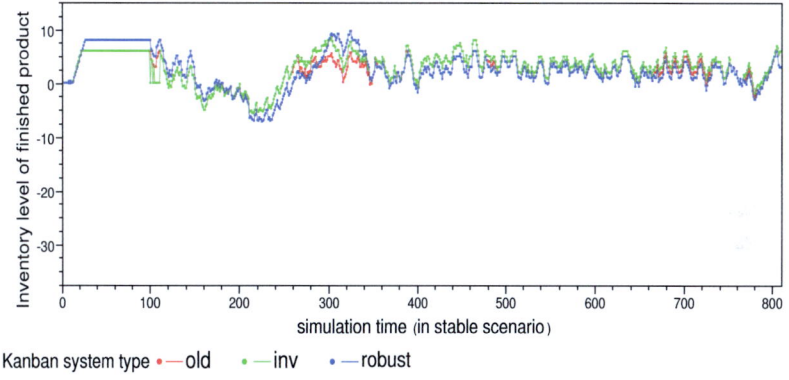

(a) In stable scenario: Real-time inventory and backlog level record of 3 Kanban systems

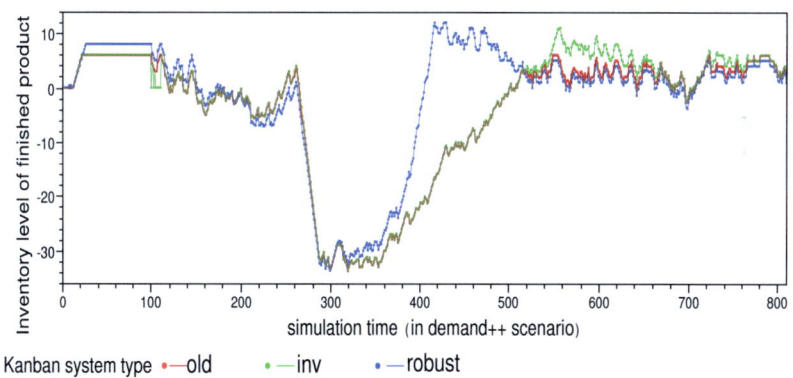

(b) In demand++ scenario: Real-time inventory and backlog level record of 3 Kanban systems

Figure 5.6: Comparison of recovery time of 3 Kanban systems in stable and demand++ scenarios

In Figure 5.5, we have seen the information about the detailed performance measures; they are about subtotal cost items and contribute to the response Netprofit. Nextly, we look into how the Kanban systems recover from the risk disruption. We take some simulation runs as examples to analyze. The operating status of three Kanban systems in stable and demand++ scenarios are shown in Figure 5.6. We choose the inventory and backlog level of finished product (in the customer input buffer) to represent the system operating status. During the simulation, the inventory and backlog level can be constantly recorded. Here in Figure 5.6, we just show a fragment of the whole output data record, it is from time 0 to time 800 (in simulation clock). The entire data record is ranging from time 0 to time 4000.

Figure 5.6a) shows the operating status of three Kanban systems in the stable scenario (without embedded risk events). It is used as a reference and contrast graph for other risk scenarios, such as Figure 5.6b). Figure 5.6b) illustrates the operating status of three Kanban systems in the demand++ scenario, where the customer demand suddenly increased to a higher level for a time length. The data record fragment is also ranging from time 0 to time 800. As can be seen from Figure 5.6b), the demand-increase disruption happened to the system around time 300 (where the inventory level is observed declining), and lasted for a short time. But its impact was severe, the inventory level declined rapidly due to the sudden demand increase. The blue line indicates the inventory level of Robust_Kanban system, and the red line and green line stand for the inventory of Old_Kanban and Inv_Kanban systems, respectively. We can observe that the blue line began to rise up after time 340, which means the Robust Kanban system is taking response actions to recover its inventory level from disruption. Later, after time 360, the other two Kanban systems (red and green lines) began to show the same recover tendency on the inventory level. The inventory level of Robust_Kanban was rising much faster (the curve is steeper) than the other two curves. The Robust_Kanban inventory level (blue line) went back to the normal level at about time 420, whereas the other two are back around time 520. In sum, the observation implies that the robust Kanban system can recover more quickly than the other two Kanban systems when risk disruption happens.

In addition, comparing the behaviors of Old_Kanban and Inv_Kanban systems in Figure 5.6, we also notice that, Inv_Kanban system (green line) generated a higher inventory level than Old_Kanban system (red line) shortly after the operation recovery at about time 520. This is because the Inv_Kanban system has added many Kanban cards to the system during the demand-increase disruption. When the disruption is gone, the system still needs some time to extract the additional Kanbans and go back to the normal operating level. Therefore, a delay of the inventory level's recovery is incurred in the Inv_Kanban system. And the recovery delay can also explain why the inventory level of Inv_Kanban system is higher than other curves in Figure 5.5c).

So far, the comparative experiment for three Kanban systems (Old_Kanban, Inv_Kanban, Robust_Kanban) is completely accomplished. We statistically analyzed the simulation results of three Kanban systems in seven typical risk scenarios. The output data analysis deals with not only the main performance Netprofit, but also many detailed performance measures, such as the inventory and backlog level, changing 3-level parameters cost, and recovery time from disruption. The comparison results are in good agreement with our expectation: the robust Kanban system presented better performance than the traditional and adaptive Kanban systems in a variety of risk situations. The performance improvement made by the robust Kanban system is statistically significant, especially when the environment contains more risks. With using the risk-response mechanism, the robust Kanban system can effectively mitigate the impact of risks, and maintain a high performance level in the uncertain environment.

6 Simulation experiment 2: improve the risk-response mechanism setting

The monitor control parameters of the risk-response mechanism play an important role in the application of the robust Kanban system. The parameters include the safety factor sf, the smoothing weight factors sf_{dt}, sf_{inv}, the safety stock level ss, and so on. If we change their values, the operating status and performance of the robust Kanban system will be inevitably influenced. Recall in Section 4.2, we determined the parameter values using a series of estimation methods, and then this parameter setting was used to run the simulation model of the robust Kanban system in the comparative experiment (see Chapter 5). As shown in Chapter 5, when using the roughly estimated parameter setting in the risk-response mechanism, the robust Kanban system can already generate better performance than the traditional Kanban and adaptive Kanban systems.

However, we still wonder whether the robust Kanban system performance can be further improved. "Are the system performance results sensitive to the changes of the control parameters? Can we find better settings for the control parameters to generate better performance results?" To solve these problems, in this chapter, we investigate the methods for finding better settings of the control parameters used in the risk-response mechanism of the robust Kanban system. The investigation is conducted experimentally based on the robust Kanban system simulation model. We design a factorial experiment using the response surface method (RSM), with the aim of finding optimal (or suboptimal) control parameter settings that can generate better performance results for the robust Kanban system.

The content of this chapter is organized as follows. First, the design of the factorial experiment is introduced in Section 6.1. The experiment is taken to study the effects and interactions of the control parameters on the system performance Netprofit. Later, in Section 6.2, we run a series of simulation experiments following the factorial design tables, and then statistically analyze the output data. At last, we discuss the experiment results and its implication in Section 6.3.

6.1 Design of experiment

6.1.1 Problem statement and experiment planning

When operating the robust Kanban system in an uncertain environment, many factors could influence the system performance. Generally, the factors can be classified as potential design factors and noise factors.

Potential design factors are factors that can be controlled and varied by the experimenter; they can be further divided into design factors and held-constant factors. Held-constant factors, as the name implied, are kept constant in the experiment because their effects are not of interest. On the contrary, the design factors will vary at different levels when performing experiment; the experiment objective is to study their effects on the system performance. In the experiment in Chapter 6, the design factors refer to important control parameters used in the risk-response mechanism of the robust Kanban system. The control parameters include such as sf, sf_{dt}, sf_{inv} and ss.

Noise factors are factors that could influence the experimental response variables (e.g. Netprofit) but are not of interest in the experiment. The noise factors could be either controllable or uncontrollable. The various risk situations the Kanban system could face are considered as noise factors in the factorial experiment.

The robust Kanban system is a complex supply chain system that is operating based on the dual-Kanban control mechanism, and meanwhile controlled by the robustly designed risk-response mechanism. If we adopt proper control parameter settings, the risk-response mechanism can be implemented effectively to reduce the impact of various risks. In the comparative experiment of Chapter 5, we saw that the risk-response mechanism of the robust Kanban system performed well with using a roughly estimated control parameter setting. Nevertheless, we still wonder whether the robust Kanban system's performance can be further improved if other control parameter settings are adopted. Therefore, we design and develop a new factorial experiment in this chapter. The objective of the factorial experiment is to find better control parameter settings for implementing the risk-response mechanism. With using the new control parameter settings, we hope to further improve the performance of the robust Kanban system (higher Netprofit) when facing various risks in the uncertain environment.

Since the Netprofit is a final-integrated performance measure and it is of great interest and importance in the robust Kanban system, we select the time-averaged Netprofit ($Netprofit_{mean}$) as the main response variable of the factorial experiment.

Among the various factors, some factors may have crucial influence on the performance Netprofit while others may play less important roles. Therefore, to select the more-important factors as design factors is the first step of the factor choice. As illustrated in Figure 6.1, we list all the factors that could contribute to the response Netprofit in a cause-and-effect diagram. The factors include the design factors, held-constant factors, or noise factors; and each primary type of factors can be further divided into secondary types.

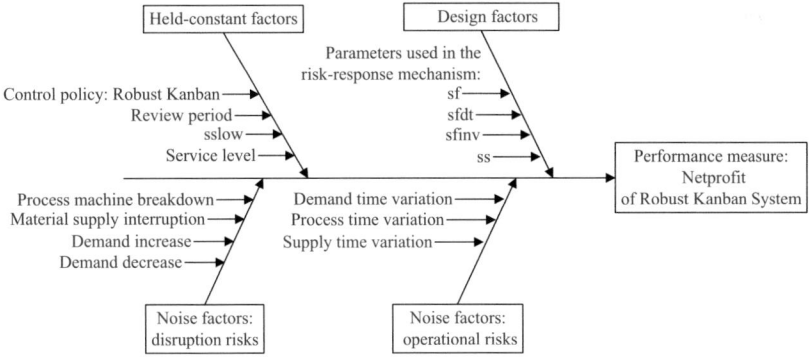

Figure 6.1: The cause-and-effect diagram of factors contributing to robust Kanban system performance

Recall the three steps of applying the risk-response mechanism. We use two monitor items, mi_rate and mi_inv, to monitor the system operating status. In Step 1, when calculating the monitor values, smoothing weight factors such as $sf_{dt}, sf_{su}, sf_{pr}, sf_{inv}$ are used in the formulas. Later, when comparing the obtained monitor values with corresponding control limits, control limit related parameters (such as sf, ss, ss_{low}, and ss_{high}) are adopted and will affect the final adjusting decision. Therefore, the factors $sf_{dt}, sf_{su}, sf_{pr}, sf_{inv}$, sf, ss, ss_{low}, and ss_{high} are initially selected as potential design factors.

The noise factors of the robust Kanban system are the risks from the uncertain environment. We suppose that random risks will happen to the system when the robust Kanban system is operating. The risks cannot be well predicted or controlled, but they will strongly influence the system performance. Hence, we consider risks as noise factors in the factorial experiment. According to the risk measure parameters (extent, duration, frequency, location), we further classified the risks as operational risks and disruption risks. Operational risks refer to slight but frequent risks, such as daily demand fluctuation. And disruption risks happen with a low probability but the consequence is severe, such as the processing machine breakdown. More instances of noise-factor can be found in the noise factor branches in Figure 6.1.

Too many design factors will dramatically increase the complexity of the factorial experiment; hence, we first make efforts to reduce the number of factors. We sort out factors that are more important and keep other potential design factors constant if possible.

The smoothing weight factors ($sf_{dt}, sf_{su}, sf_{pr}, sf_{inv}$) are used in the exponential smoothing calculation of monitor values. For the sake of simplicity, we assume the values of $sf_{dt}, sf_{su}, sf_{pr}$ are identical, because their calculation methods are all based on counting the number of accomplished service tasks. On the other side, the factor sf_{inv} is calculated in continuous time. Therefore, two factors sf_{dt} and sf_{inv} are selected (out of the above smoothing weight factors) to be the control factors of the factorial experiment.

ss, ss_{low}, and ss_{high} are control limit parameters for mi_inv. From the former simulation results, we found that to set $ss_{low}=0$ will cause obviously better results than other values, therefore we fix the ss_{low} value at 0. The ss_{high} value should be set above the ss value. Here we assume $ss_{high}=ss+1$, which indicates the upper bound ss_{high} is dependent on the baseline-safety stock level ss. Now we just need to decide the ss value for judging mi_inv.

A safety factor sf is also used in the risk-response mechanism. We need to check whether $mi\_rate = \frac{demand\ rate}{service\ rate} \leq \frac{1}{sf}$ is true in each review period. Here sf is supposed to be a positive value slightly above 1 ($sf=1+\varepsilon$, ε is a small positive).

Design factors	Notation	Used value*	Domain
Safety factor	sf	1.1	$sf > 1$
Smoothing weight factor for demand/process/supply time	sf_{dt}	0.96	$0 \leq sf_{dt} \leq 1$
Smoothing weight factor for inventory and backlog level	sf_{inv}	0.8	$0 \leq sf_{inv} \leq 1$
Baseline safety stock level	ss	4	$ss > 0$

Table 6.1: Design factors in the factorial experiment (*:Value used in Chapter 5 the comparative experiment)

After the above simplifying work, we select four control parameters as the design factors for the factorial experiment: sf, sf_{dt}, sf_{inv} and ss. The basic information of design factors is summarized in Table 6.1.

In the factorial experiment, we aim to study the effects of design factors on the response variable Netprofit. The risks from the uncertain environment are considered as noise factors. As we know, in real world the risks usually occur randomly and the situations are various, which makes it difficult to describe or control the risks. Therefore, we select some typical risk scenarios to represent the risks.

The typical risk scenarios, such as stable, demand+, demand++ scenarios used in Chapter 5, are supposed to occur in the uncertain environment with specific probabilities. In each risk scenario, we set identical input conditions (including random variable data series) to run the robust Kanban system simulation model for several times. Each time we try a different setting for the design factors. We first investigate the factor-setting problem in individual risk scenarios, then we decide the final factor setting in a comprehensive view with considering integrated risk scenarios. The objective of the experiment is to find the optimal control parameter settings (that can generate the maximum response Netprofit) for the risk-response mechanism. With the obtained factor setting, the performance of the robust Kanban system is expected to be further improved.

6.1.2 Choice of factor ranges and levels: a pilot test

In Table 6.1, the domains of design factors are given based on the factor definition. However, the given domains are too wide for the factorial experiment to find the optimal factor setting. Some values in the domains are apparently far from the optimal factor value. For example, the domain of sf_{dt} is theoretically $0 \leq sf_{dt} \leq 1$; but usually sf_{dt} is set around 0.8 in the exponential smoothing method for generating good results. If we set $sf_{dt}=0.1$, it can be easily found that the decided response action is not so suitable if using this value in monitor calculation, and the caused Netprofit result is far from optimum. Hence, narrower ranges of the design factors should be decided to make the generated Netprofit close to the optimum.

To determine suitable ranges and levels for the design factors, we first perform a preliminary experiment using the robust Kanban system simulation model, it is called the pilot test. We try many different design factor settings in simulation to see what kind of factor values can generate better Netprofit results. Referring to the simulation results, we select a close-to-optimum region (the factor ranges causing the better Netprofit results) for the factor setting, we call it the refined range. Then, we can set suitable levels for each factor in the refined factor setting range, which reduces the complexity of implementing the factorial experiment.

In Table 6.1, we also listed the old values of the four design factors; they are used by the robust Kanban system in the comparative experiment of Chapter 5. In the pilot test, we use the old factor setting (the baseline setting) as a starting point for searching for new suitable ranges of the design factors.

The procedures of doing the pilot test are as follows. We first run the robust Kanban system simulation model using the baseline factor setting. Then, based on the baseline setting, we change one factor at a time, to

RunNo.	sf	sf_{inv}	sf_{dt}	ss	Netprofit (average)
0	1.1	0.8	0.96	4	91.9268
1	1.1	0.8	0.94	4	94.5355
2	1.1	0.8	0.97	4	85.1182
3	1.1	0.8	0.95	4	93.9090
4	1.1	0.8	0.94	4	94.5355
5	1.1	0.8	0.93	4	92.9350
6	1.1	0.8	0.92	4	92.5773
7	1.1	0.8	0.9	4	90.7139
8	1.1	0.9	0.94	4	93.1263
9	1.1	0.7	0.94	4	95.3458
10	1.1	0.6	0.94	4	95.2936
11	1.1	0.5	0.94	4	94.8021
12	1.05	0.8	0.94	4	96.3755
13	1.01	0.8	0.94	4	98.0845
14	1.005	0.8	0.94	4	98.2973
15	1.001	0.8	0.94	4	98.2460
16	1	0.8	0.94	4	97.9256
17	1.1	0.8	0.94	3	93.7411
18	1.1	0.8	0.94	3.5	93.7411
19	1.1	0.8	0.94	4.5	94.2371
20	1.1	0.8	0.94	5	93.0442
21	1.005	0.7	0.94	4	99.0081

Table 6.2 a) Input factor setting and response Netprofit results (mean value of 5 replications)

observe what Netprofit result will be caused. Through analyzing a set of Netprofit results under different factor settings, we can basically know about the relationship between the four design factors and the experimental response Netprofit. The pilot test provides useful information to define the refined factor setting range.

Take the risk situation "stable scenario" as an example to show how to do the pilot test. First, with the baseline factor setting, we run the robust Kanban system simulation model in the stable scenario in 5 replications, then collect output Netprofit results. In the first row (RunNo=0) of Table 6.2, we can see the baseline factor values (sf, sf_{dt}, sf_{inv}, ss) and the corresponding response Netprofit result. Note that the presented

Run No.	Netprofit (average)	R1	R2	R3	R4	R5
0	91.9268	95.5304	87.8022	81.5237	91.6155	103.1623
1	94.5355	95.9979	90.0803	88.7655	91.7759	106.0577
2	85.1182	90.2346	88.6755	76.3072	71.9591	98.4148
3	93.9090	94.5763	90.2066	87.6621	92.1917	104.9082
4	94.5355	95.9979	90.0803	88.7655	91.7759	106.0577
5	92.9350	93.9025	91.9578	83.3592	90.6295	104.8260
6	92.5773	96.5769	91.8774	82.0915	87.6277	104.7129
7	90.7139	94.7049	87.9070	80.3497	92.6301	97.9780
8	93.1263	95.3144	89.6977	85.8201	90.4905	104.3086
9	95.3458	95.7565	91.0608	89.9549	93.3902	106.5665
10	95.2936	96.9219	90.8160	88.0581	93.8630	106.8091
11	94.8021	96.0585	91.0775	88.4252	92.4272	106.0220
12	96.3755	100.6868	91.0190	87.2954	95.3647	107.5115
13	98.0845	98.7208	94.9687	90.4888	97.0266	109.2177
14	98.2973	98.7141	95.7484	90.6363	96.7828	109.6049
15	98.2460	97.3006	97.3468	90.6000	96.2071	109.7754
16	97.9256	96.6268	97.5186	90.6555	96.2071	108.6202
17	93.7411	94.2715	90.6866	86.4203	90.8508	106.4765
18	93.7411	94.2715	90.6866	86.4203	90.8508	106.4765
19	94.2371	95.5622	90.2879	89.2572	90.7219	105.3561
20	93.0442	91.3756	92.2624	87.5687	90.5396	103.4744
21	99.0081	100.8091	97.2249	89.7101	98.3121	108.9842

Table 6.2 b) Netprofit results from 5 replications

Table 6.2: Pilot test results

Netprofit value is the average Netprofit value of 5 replications. Nextly, we change some factors' values in a wide range while keeping other factors unchanged, then run the simulation 5 times and calculate the mean Netprofit result. Similarly, we change another factor's value and keep other factors constant to examine the Netprofit result. In summary, we will try different factor settings on the principle "change one factor at a time" in simulation and collect Netprofit results. Besides the baseline-setting simulation run (RunNo.0), we did another 21 runs with different factor settings. Except the four design factors, the other input conditions are kept unchanged in the 22 runs of the pilot test. The obtained Netprofit results of the 22 runs are listed in Table 6.2. From the results, we can get a general understanding of how the design factors will affect the response Netprofit. The results of the pilot test are also illustrated in 6.2, as a visual description.

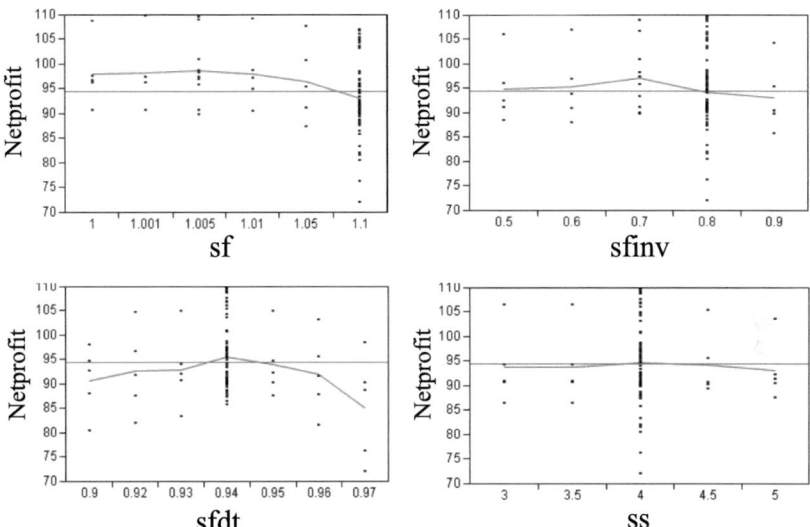

Figure 6.2: Scatter plots and connect-means curves of four design factors $sf, sf_{inv}, sf_{dt}, ss$ (data points from pilot test)

From Figure 6.2, we find that the relationships between the factors sf, sf_{dt}, sf_{inv}, ss and response Netprofit are obviously nonlinear. All the connect-means curves in the four plots present an "arch" shape, which can be approximately modeled by the second-order polynomial. The observation makes sense in real world experience. For example, it is natural that neither a too high nor a too low safety stock level (ss) can cause the best Netprofit result, because too much inventory will cause more inventory holding cost and too little inventory will incur high backlog penalty cost. There must exist a middle level between the two extreme levels that can generate a better result. Hence the curve "Netprofit vs. ss" forms an arch in Figure 6.2.

And for the factors sf_{dt} and sf_{inv}, we consider two extreme situations as well. If the smoothing weight factors are set close to 1, which means the exponentially smoothed data have more weights on historical data, thus the latest change of inventory level or demand time cannot be reflected timely by the monitor mi_rate and mi_inv. This will cause response-action delay. On the contrary, when the smoothing weight factors are set close to 0, indicating the exponentially smoothed data are almost equal to the current data, then the smoothed inventory level or demand time might be too fluctuant so that we cannot tell the unusual changes from normal fluctuation. Thus, if we decide response actions depending on the almost newest data, unnecessary risk response actions might be taken due to distorted monitor information, then much operating cost of the 3-level parameters will be incurred. Similar to the factor ss, a middle value for the smoothing weight factor sf_{dt} or sf_{inv} must exist between 0 and 1 as well to cause a better Netprofit result. Therefore, it can be explained why the curves of Netprofit vs. sf_{dt}, and of Netprofit vs. sf_{inv} are also nonlinear and show an "arch" shape.

For the safety factor sf, the Netprofit vs. sf curve also show an arch shape. We think this is a reasonable phenomenon, because if we set sf value too high, the control limits of mi_rate will tend to adjust a higher-level parameter out of the 3-level parameters as the response action. For example, suppose the currently observed mi_rate value is 0.95. When we set $sf =1.01$, then $mi\_rate=0.95$ is found above UCL_K, indicating the decision of adding a Kanban. By contrast, if we set $sf =1.1$, then $mi\_rate=0.95$ will be found above UCL_{Ts} , indicating the decision of reducing the machine service time. The action of reducing machine service time takes more cost than the action of adding a Kanban. In summary, setting sf too high will cause unnecessary cost of taking over-reactive response actions. On the other side, if we keep the sf value too low, like $sf =1$, then the rate constraint $\frac{supplytime}{demandtime} \leq \frac{1}{sf} \leq 1$ will become too tight (too close to 1). This is not a good setting for sf either, because the response action will be taken only when the risk impact is quite severe, such as the supply rate is obviously lower than the demand rate. In this situation, when risks happen to the system, it will be too late to take the response action; at this moment, larger impact could be already caused by the risks. Based on the above analysis, we reason that a better sf value must exist between 1 and $1+\varepsilon$ (ε is a small positive value). With a middle sf value, the rate ratio is controlled to be strictly less than 1, and the generated Netprofit result should be better than using a too high or too low sf value.

After obtaining the pilot test results, we can then decide suitable ranges and levels for design factors. As seen from Figure 6.2, in the given factor ranges, the effect of factor sf_{dt} is much more significant than the effects of other three factors. This implies the current range of sf_{dt} is too wide for searching for an optimal value, we should further restrict sf_{dt} in a close-to-optimum region. On the contrary, the range of ss is found too narrow, because the curve "Netprofit vs. ss" is quite flat, the Netprofit change is not obvious in the given ss region. Similar observation can be also found in sf_{inv} and sf plots. Therefore, based on the pilot test results, we refine the value ranges of the four design factors. With the refined factor ranges, it is more convenient and probable to search for the optimum region of the design factor setting (that can generate the best Netprofit results) in the factorial experiment.

The finally determined ranges and levels of the four design factors are illustrated in Figure 6.3. The range of sf_{dt} is from 0.92 to 0.96; ss value is set between 2 and 6; sf_{inv} value is set between 0.5 and 0.9; and sf value can vary from 1.001 to 1.021. Considering that the relationships between the four design factors and the response Netprofit are nonlinear, we select three levels for each factor in the factorial experiment. The three levels are denoted by low, middle, and high (level) in each design factor's range.

As introduced above, the pilot test is just an exploratory experiment. With its help, we can get a general understanding of the relationship between the design factors and the response Netprofit, and select suitable ranges and levels for design factors. To further study how to find the optimal factor settings, we need to perform more well-defined factorial experiments and analyze their output results. Since all design factors are continuous variables, we consider adopting the response surface method to search for optimal factor settings that can generate the best Netprofit results. The details of the response surface model and its application will be discussed in the next section.

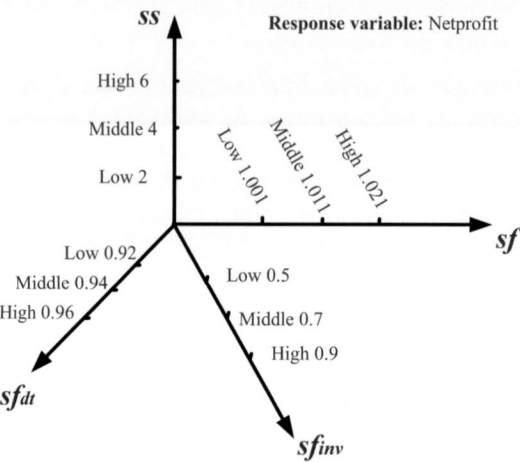

Figure 6.3: Refined ranges and levels of 4 design factors (based on pilot test results)

6.1.3 Design of response surface model

In this section, we further investigate the effects of four design factors (sf, sf_{dt}, sf_{inv}, ss) on the experimental response Netprofit. Based on the pilot test, we have refined the range of each factor. Thus, in a relatively small and close-to-optimum region, we can adopt the response surface models to analyze the relationship between the four design factors and the response Netprofit, and find optimal factor settings.

As can be seen from Figure 6.2, the relationships between the design factors and the response Netprofit are not linear. Hence, to select two levels for each factor is not suitable for this experiment. Since the curves in the factor effect plots (Figure 6.2) have the arch-shape, and all the design factors vary in continuous ranges, we choose a second-order response surface model to approximate the relationship between Netprofit and four control parameters sf, sf_{dt}, sf_{inv}, and ss.

$$y = \beta_0 + \sum_{i=1}^{i=4} \beta_i x_i + \sum_{i=1}^{i=4} \beta_{ii} x_i^2 + \sum_{i<j} \beta_{ij} x_i x_j + \varepsilon \qquad (6.1)$$

The second-order response surface model is presented in Formula 6.1, where y signifies the response Netprofit. For the sake of simplicity, we denote the four control parameters sf, sf_{dt}, sf_{inv}, ss by x_i (i=1,2,3,4) respectively. And the remaining β-series parameters are deterministic coefficients. The robust Kanban system working under the risk-response mechanism is a quite complex system. It is unlikely that a polynomial response surface model, like Formula 6.1, can accurately represent the relationship between the Netprofit and the factors over the entire region of factor values. However, when the factor-value region is sufficiently small, the response surface model can work very well to describe the relationship (Montgomery 2007). The refined factor ranges have been presented in Figure 6.2 based on the pilot test results. In the following study, the response surface model will be applied within the refined factor ranges.

We develop a single-replication central composite inscribed (CCI) design table (refer to NIST/SEMATECH (2012)) to conduct the factorial experiment. In the CCI design, the experiment contains 4 design factors, and each factor has 5 levels. We need to run the simulation model 26 times (RunNo.=1,...,26) for trying different factor values combinations. The 26 runs include 2 center-point runs (RunNo.25 and 26) and other 24 runs with different factor settings. In each run, we can obtain a Netprofit result as response; the response is the average of Netprofit results from 5 replications. Take the stable scenario as an example. Based on the refined factor ranges (obtained from the pilot test), the single-replication CCI design table for the response surface model in the stable scenario, is summarized in Table 6.3.

Following the design table, we can perform the factorial experiment to search for the optimal control parameter settings used in the risk-response mechanism. The factorial experiment is carried out using the simulation model of the robust Kanban system. We try different input factor value combinations one by one as the CCI design table planned, then run the simulation model to collect corresponding Netprofit results. The other simulation input conditions of the factorial experiment are identical to the conditions used in Chapter 5. The 26 Netprofit results of the factorial experiment in the stable scenario is given in Table 6.3, too.

So far, we have introduced the steps of performing the factorial experiment in the stable scenario. Subsequently, we will use response sur-

RunNo.	Pattern	sf	sf_{inv}	sf_{dt}	ss	Netprofit
1	$----$	1.006	0.93	0.6	3	99.4810
2	$---+$	1.006	0.93	0.6	5	99.9708
3	$--+-$	1.006	0.93	0.8	3	99.1097
4	$--++$	1.006	0.93	0.8	5	99.1246
5	$-+--$	1.006	0.95	0.6	3	101.3698
6	$-+-+$	1.006	0.95	0.6	5	100.7389
7	$-++-$	1.006	0.95	0.8	3	99.6940
8	$-+++$	1.006	0.95	0.8	5	99.5688
9	$+---$	1.016	0.93	0.6	3	99.3137
10	$+--+$	1.016	0.93	0.6	5	99.9654
11	$+-+-$	1.016	0.93	0.8	3	98.7033
12	$+-++$	1.016	0.93	0.8	5	99.6988
13	$++--$	1.016	0.95	0.6	3	100.4620
14	$++-+$	1.016	0.95	0.6	5	98.7949
15	$+++-$	1.016	0.95	0.8	3	99.5962
16	$++++$	1.016	0.95	0.8	5	98.4388
17	a000	1.001	0.94	0.7	4	100.1685
18	A000	1.021	0.94	0.7	4	100.0603
19	0a00	1.011	0.92	0.7	4	98.8730
20	0A00	1.011	0.96	0.7	4	99.3438
21	00a0	1.011	0.94	0.5	4	100.2418
22	00A0	1.011	0.94	0.9	4	99.0846
23	000a	1.011	0.94	0.7	2	99.6388
24	000A	1.011	0.94	0.7	6	100.3108
25	0000	1.011	0.94	0.7	4	101.1023
26	0000	1.011	0.94	0.7	4	101.1023

Table 6.3: Response surface model-CCI design table and Netprofit results (in stable scenario, with refined factor ranges)

face methods and related statistical tools to analyze the output results and determine suitable factor settings to optimize the response Netprofit. The optimization procedures and result analysis will be discussed in the next section.

6.2 Result analysis

6.2.1 Optimization with response surface model

Using the factorial experiment results, we nextly build a response surface model to find the optimal response Netprofit. The factor setting that can generate maximum Netprofit will be derived as the solution of the Netprofit optimization problem. Referring to the pilot test results, we choose a second-order response surface model, as shown in Formula 6.1, to model the functional relationship between the response Netprofit and four factors sf, sf_{dt}, sf_{inv}, ss. The statistical software JMP 8.0 is applied to develop the fitted response surface model.

To determine the β-series coefficients in Formula 6.1, we need to perform the following procedures.

First, based on the output data of the factorial experiment, we employ the second-order response surface model to do ANOVA (Analysis of Variance) and effect tests. The analysis results are summarized in Figure 6.4, and illustrated with effect plots in Figure 6.5.

From the results of effect tests in Figure 6.4, we find that some p-values ("Prob>F" value) are below 0.05 (marked with asterisk). Such p-value result indicates the corresponding factor effect is significant. Meanwhile, some other p-values are found quite large (>0.05), which means the factor effects are not obvious enough. Based on the observation, the full second-order model (Formula 6.1) can be refined by removing the nonsignificant-effect factor terms. Only the factor terms with significant effects are kept in the refined response surface model.

The main effect and interaction effect plots in Figure 6.5 visually present the results of the effect tests. It can be observed that, the factor terms showing significant effects in the graphs are consistent with the factor terms marked with asterisks ("Prob>F" value <0.05) in the effect tests. From the graphs, we can directly see the effect of each factor term included in the second-order response surface model.

Referring to the effect test results, we plan to refine the full second-order response surface model given in Formula 6.1. The factor terms with nonsignificant main or interaction effects should be removed from the second-order model. We use the Stepwise-Fit tool (provided by the

Analysis of Variance

Source	DF	Sum of Squares	Mean Square	F Ratio
Model	14	13.247185	0.946228	6.2093
Error	11	1.676283	0.152389	**Prob > F**
C. Total	25	14.923469		0.0022*

Effect Tests

Source	Nparm	DF	Sum of Squares	F Ratio	Prob > F
sf	1	1	0.7706909	5.0574	0.0460*
sfdt	1	1	0.7482630	4.9102	0.0487*
sfinv	1	1	2.9939907	19.6470	0.0010*
ss	1	1	0.0002985	0.0020	0.9655
sf*sf	1	1	1.1954129	7.8445	0.0173*
sf*sfdt	1	1	1.0378406	6.8105	0.0243*
sfdt*sfdt	1	1	4.5968470	30.1651	0.0002*
sf*sfinv	1	1	0.2412184	1.5829	0.2344
sfdt*sfinv	1	1	0.2433444	1.5969	0.2325
sfinv*sfinv	1	1	2.4480445	16.0644	0.0021*
sf*ss	1	1	0.0535596	0.3515	0.5653
sfdt*ss	1	1	2.0538147	13.4774	0.0037*
sfinv*ss	1	1	0.0488691	0.3207	0.5826
ss*ss	1	1	1.5354363	10.0757	0.0089*

Figure 6.4: ANOVA effect tests results for the second-order response surface model

statistical software JMP 8.0) to screen stepwise the factor terms in the full second-order model. The result of Stepwise-Fit is presented in Figure 6.6. The entered parameter (with a check mark in the "Entered" option) implies that it has a relatively significant effect on the response Netprofit, so it should remain in the refined surface response model. Observing the Stepwise-Fit results, we can find that the entered parameters are almost the same with the parameters which have significant effects (p-values<0.05) in effect tests. The only exception is the factor *ss*.The factor *ss* does not show a significant effect in the effect tests, but it is kept as an entered parameter in the Stepwise-Fit result. This is because all first-order factor terms will be contained in the Stepwise-Fit method

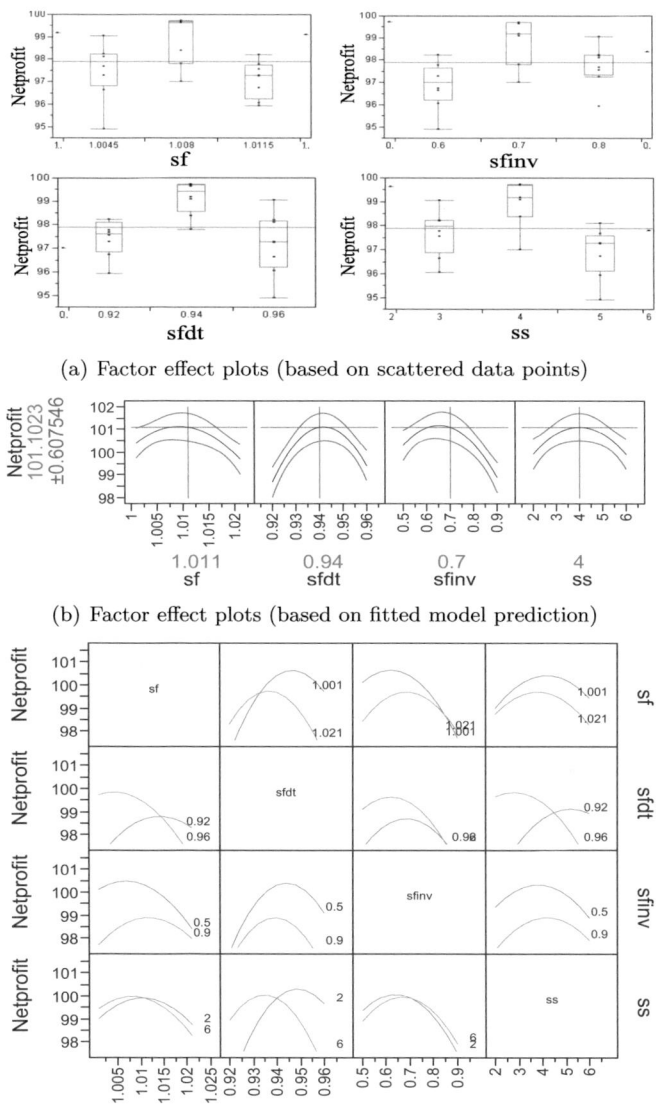

(a) Factor effect plots (based on scattered data points)

(b) Factor effect plots (based on fitted model prediction)

(c) Factor interaction effect plots (based on fitted model prediction)

Figure 6.5: Main effects and interaction effects plots (Factor: $sf, sf_{dt}, sf_{inv}, ss$; Response: Netprofit)

195

regardless of its p-value, thus all factors' main effects are included in the response surface model.

Stepwise Fit

Response: Netprofit

Stepwise Regression Control

Prob to Enter   0.100   Enter All
Prob to Leave   0.100
Direction: Forward   Remove All
Rules: Combine

Go   Stop   Step   Make Model

Current Estimates

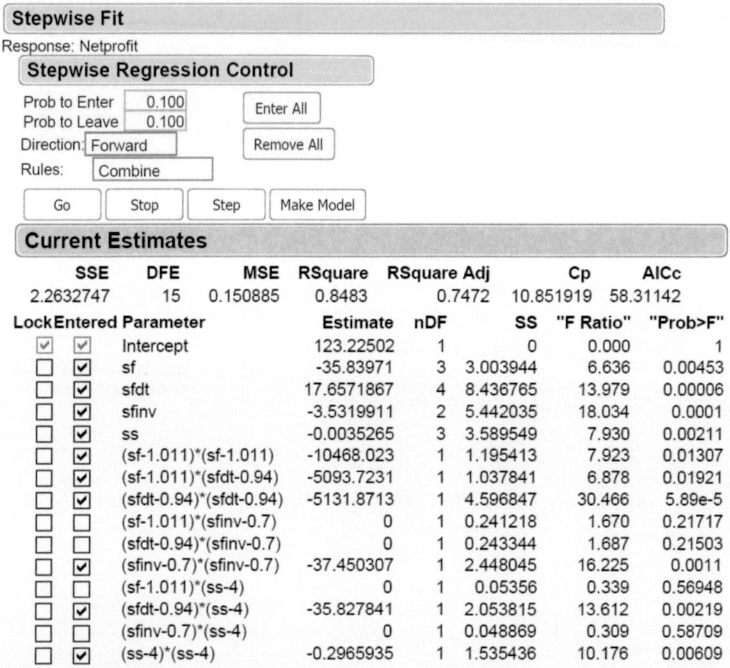

SSE	DFE	MSE	RSquare	RSquare Adj	Cp	AICc
2.2632747	15	0.150885	0.8483	0.7472	10.851919	58.31142

Lock	Entered	Parameter	Estimate	nDF	SS	"F Ratio"	"Prob>F"
☑	☑	Intercept	123.22502	1	0	0.000	1
☐	☑	sf	-35.83971	3	3.003944	6.636	0.00453
☐	☑	sfdt	17.6571867	4	8.436765	13.979	0.00006
☐	☑	sfinv	-3.5319911	2	5.442035	18.034	0.0001
☐	☑	ss	-0.0035265	3	3.589549	7.930	0.00211
☐	☑	(sf-1.011)*(sf-1.011)	-10468.023	1	1.195413	7.923	0.01307
☐	☑	(sf-1.011)*(sfdt-0.94)	-5093.7231	1	1.037841	6.878	0.01921
☐	☑	(sfdt-0.94)*(sfdt-0.94)	-5131.8713	1	4.596847	30.466	5.89e-5
☐	☐	(sf-1.011)*(sfinv-0.7)	0	1	0.241218	1.670	0.21717
☐	☐	(sfdt-0.94)*(sfinv-0.7)	0	1	0.243344	1.687	0.21503
☐	☑	(sfinv-0.7)*(sfinv-0.7)	-37.450307	1	2.448045	16.225	0.0011
☐	☐	(sf-1.011)*(ss-4)	0	1	0.05356	0.339	0.56948
☐	☑	(sfdt-0.94)*(ss-4)	-35.827841	1	2.053815	13.612	0.00219
☐	☐	(sfinv-0.7)*(ss-4)	0	1	0.048869	0.309	0.58709
☐	☑	(ss-4)*(ss-4)	-0.2965935	1	1.535436	10.176	0.00609

Figure 6.6: Stepwise screening of factors for the second-order response surface model

Based on the Stepwise-Fit result, the full second-order response surface model can be refined in a simpler form. The factor terms with nonsignificant effects are eliminated from the full second-order model, such as $sf \cdot sf_{inv}, sf_{dt} \cdot sf_{inv}, sf \cdot ss,$, and $sf_{inv} \cdot ss$. Nextly, we will use the refined response surface model as approximation for the relationship between the response Netprofit and four design factors sf, sf_{dt}, sf_{inv}, and ss.

Having refined the response surface model, we further explore the coefficients of the selected factor terms to complete the response surface function. We adopt the Standard Least Square approach (using software

JMP 8.0) to estimate the coefficients of factor terms in the response surface function. The finally obtained function is shown in Table 6.4. Using the response surface function, we can easily find the factor setting solution that generates the maximum Netprofit. Note that the derived factor setting is just an optimal solution for the response surface function; it cannot be proved that the response surface model solution is absolutely optimal over the entire space of factor values. However, based on the practical simulation results, the solution is found much better than most of other factor settings. Moreover, the solving method using the response surface model is practical to implement. Due to these reasons, we think the solution derived from the response surface model is an adequately good solution for the design factor setting. We consider the solution as an approximate optimal (or suboptimal) factor setting for the risk-response mechanism.

Fitted response surface model (second-order form)	$Netprofit = 123.2250 - 35.8397sf + 17.6571sf_{dt}$ $-3.5320sf_{inv} - 0.0035ss$ $-10468.0233(sf - 1.011)^2 - 0.2966(ss - 4)^2$ $-5131.8713(sf_{dt} - 0.94)^2 - 37.4503(sf_{inv} - 0.7)^2$ $-5093.7231(sf - 1.011)(sf_{dt} - 0.94)$ $-35.8278(sf_{dt} - 0.94)(ss - 4)$
Optimal factor setting	sf=1.0083, sf_{dt}=0.9438, sf_{inv}=0.6528, ss=3.7600
Predicted response value	Netprofit= 101.2678 (Maximum, obtained at the above factor-setting solution)

Table 6.4: Fitted function and optimal solutions of the response surface model (in stable scenario)

The optimal solution derived from the response surface model is also presented in Table 6.4. As shown in the table, we should set sf =1.0083, sf_{dt}=0.9438, sf_{inv}=0.6528 and ss =3.7600 when applying the robust Kanban system in the stable scenario. And the Netprofit result given by the fitted response surface model is 101.2678, which is an absolute maximum over the refined factor setting range of the response surface model.

As a confirm test, we adopt the optimal factor setting given in Table 6.4 to run the robust Kanban system simulation model again. We intend

197

to test whether the calculated optimal solution works well in a practical simulation environment. The Netprofit result obtained from simulation is 101.1042. Although the simulation result is slightly lower than the Netprofit prediction given by the response surface model (101.2678), the difference between them is quite small. Moreover, the simulation Netprofit result using this factor setting is still found to be better than most of the simulation Netprofit results using other factor settings. Therefore, it is reasonable to conclude that the factor setting solution obtained from the response surface model is adequately good (optimal or suboptimal), and can be used as a suitable control parameter setting for the risk-response mechanism in the robust Kanban system. With the new factor setting, we can further improve the operation of the risk-response mechanism, and help the robust Kanban system generate better Netprofit results than in the comparative experiment of Chapter 5.

We briefly introduced the optimal solution obtained from the response surface model in this section. Using the response surface method, we have found out suitable design factor settings that can optimize the response Netprofit. More results and details about the response surface model application will be discussed in the next section. A set of statistical approaches are used to analyze the experiment output data.

6.2.2 Statistical analysis

In this section, we will first visually present the results obtained from the response surface model. Then, we will use a set of statistical methods to evaluate how well the response surface model fits the data points of the simulation experiment.

First, based on the refined response surface model where nonsignificant factor terms are removed, we draw the main effect plots and interaction effect plots of design factors in Figure 6.7. From the main effect plots, we can see why a second-order model is necessary for defining the response surface model. And the interaction effect plots show why interaction factor terms are needed (parallel lines indicate no interaction) in the response surface model, such as the interaction terms sf vs. sf_{dt}, sf_{dt} vs. ss.

Nextly, we draw the response surface plots and contour plots for the refined response surface model. Since there are four design factors included in the model, we fix two factors' values and vary the other two factors' values, to construct the 3D response surface plots. In Figure 6.8, we just show the plots of two possible varying-factor combinations: sf_{dt} vs. sf on Netprofit, and sf_{dt} vs. sf_{inv} on Netprofit. The complete six combinations results are illustrated in Appendix B. From the response surface plots in Figure 6.8, we can directly observe the maximum point in the response surface, which also confirms the results obtained in Table 6.4.

Besides the above descriptive graphs, we also apply numerical methods to measure how well the response surface model fits the real data points from simulation experiment.

First, we calculate the goodness-of-fit statistics for the refined response surface model (given in Table 6.4) to examine how well the response surface model is fitting the real data points. The results can be found in Figure 6.9. Here we obtained R-square=0.8483 and R-square Adjusted=0.7472. If the R-square and Adjusted R-square values are close to 1, it indicates the proposed function is a good fit for the relationship between Netprofit and factors. This can be seen in this model. Besides, we observe that the data points in the plot "actual Netprofit value vs. predicted Netprofit value" are scattering randomly along the diagonal line; this indicates a good residual distribution. Therefore, we conclude that the refined response surface model is a suitable fitting model for the relationship between the response Netprofit and four design factors.

Secondly, we use the ANOVA method to gain some statistical inferences for the refined response surface model. The ANOVA results are summarized in Figure 6.10. After removing the nonsignificant-effect factor terms from the stepwise factor screening, the refined response surface model includes only important factor terms. From Figure 6.10, we can see that all the factor terms remaining in the refined model show significant effects with low "Prob>F" p-values (except the single factor ss which is held because it is a first-order factor). The result is consistent with the predicted result of the former effect tests. It should be noted that when we apply the ANOVA (Analysis of Variance), the statistical inferences will make sense only when required assumptions are satisfied (such as the data normality). ANOVA is applicable with the following

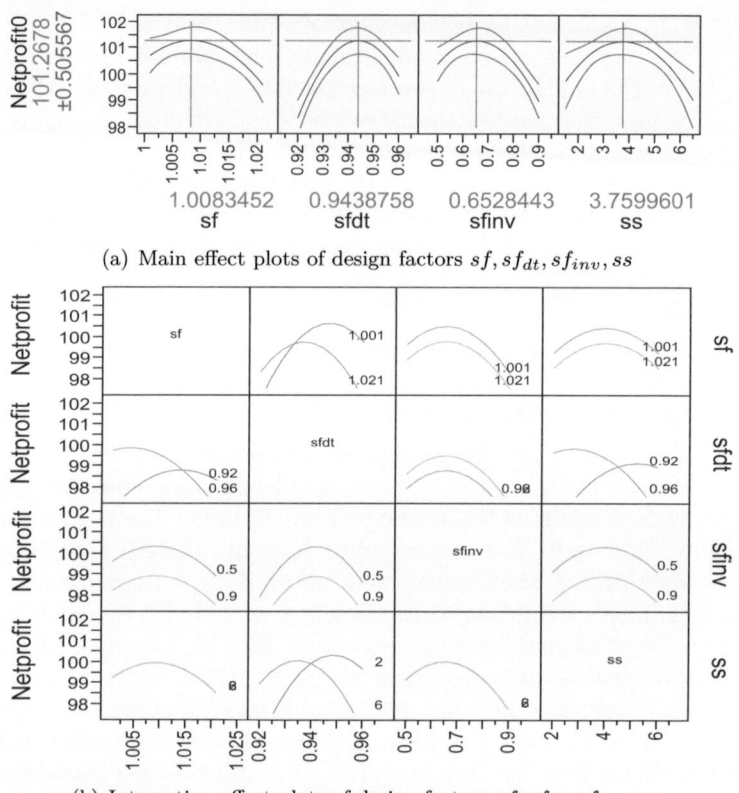

(a) Main effect plots of design factors $sf, sf_{dt}, sf_{inv}, ss$

(b) Interaction effect plots of design factors $sf, sf_{dt}, sf_{inv}, ss$

Figure 6.7: Based on the refined response surface model (in stable scenario): Main effects and interaction effects plots (Factor: $sf, sf_{dt}, sf_{inv}, ss$; Response: Netprofit)

assumptions of data (Montgomery 2007): 1) Independence; 2) Normality; 3) Homogeneity of variances. For the sample data in the factorial experiment (in Table 6.3), the data independence condition is satisfied, because different simulation runs are independent. The normality of data has been analyzed in Section 5.2.2. Then we focus on examining the equality of variances. We did residual analysis on the 26 data samples from Table 6.3, the results can be found in Figure 6.11. Three types of residual plots

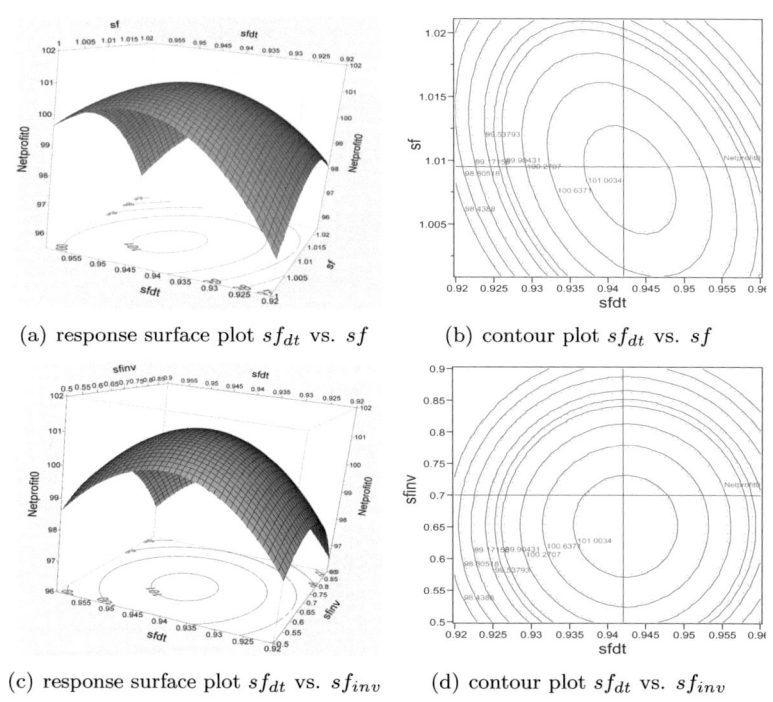

(a) response surface plot sf_{dt} vs. sf

(b) contour plot sf_{dt} vs. sf

(c) response surface plot sf_{dt} vs. sf_{inv}

(d) contour plot sf_{dt} vs. sf_{inv}

Figure 6.8: Response surface and contour plots of fitted model (in stable scenario)

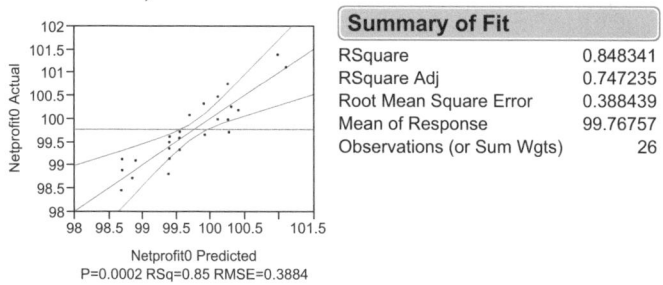

Summary of Fit	
RSquare	0.848341
RSquare Adj	0.747235
Root Mean Square Error	0.388439
Mean of Response	99.76757
Observations (or Sum Wgts)	26

Figure 6.9: Goodness of Fit results for the refined response surface model (in stable scenario)

Analysis of Variance

Source	DF	Sum of Squares	Mean Square	F Ratio
Model	10	12.660194	1.26602	8.3906
Error	15	2.263275	0.15088	**Prob > F**
C. Total	25	14.923469		0.0002*

Effect Tests

Source	Nparm	DF	Sum of Squares	F Ratio	Prob > F
sf	1	1	0.7706909	5.1078	0.0391*
sfdt	1	1	0.7482630	4.9592	0.0417*
sfinv	1	1	2.9939907	19.8429	0.0005*
ss	1	1	0.0002985	0.0020	0.9651
sf*sf	1	1	1.1954129	7.9227	0.0131*
sf*sfdt	1	1	1.0378406	6.8784	0.0192*
sfdt*sfdt	1	1	4.5968470	30.4659	<.0001*
sfinv*sfinv	1	1	2.4480445	16.2246	0.0011*
sfdt*ss	1	1	2.0538147	13.6118	0.0022*
ss*ss	1	1	1.5354363	10.1762	0.0061*

Figure 6.10: ANOVA results of the refined response surface model (in stable scenario)

are included here: normal probability plot of residuals, residuals vs. run order, and residuals vs. fitted values. Observing "slight departures from the diagonal line" in the normal probability plot, we can infer the error distribution is approximately normal in the ANOVA data samples. And unrelated scatter points observed in Plot b) and c) imply respectively the data are independent, and the residuals are structureless (namely without unusual relationship with the fitted values). Based on the residual analysis results, we therefore conclude that it is reasonable to accept the variance homogeneity assumption for the data samples. Thus, all three assumptions for applying ANOVA are ensured in the factorial experiment; it implies that the statistical inferences obtained from ANOVA are useful for reference.

In this section, we used both graphical and numerical methods to analyze the results about the response surface model. Through various data analysis, we can reason that the response surface model is a good model

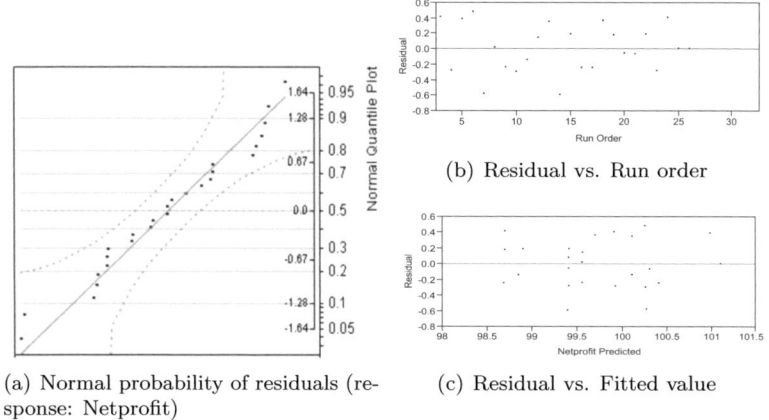

(a) Normal probability of residuals (response: Netprofit)

(b) Residual vs. Run order

(c) Residual vs. Fitted value

Figure 6.11: Residual analysis results of refined response surface model (in stable scenario)

for fitting the relationship between Netprofit and the four design factors. Using the response surface model, we can find suitable factor settings to optimize the response Netprofit. Comparing with the Netprofit obtained in the comparative experiment (where a roughly estimated factor setting was used), we can see that the performance of the robust Kanban system is significantly improved in this factorial experiment with the new factor setting.

6.3 Result discussion

In the former sections, we have presented how to determine the factor setting (design factors sf, sf_{dt}, sf_{inv}, ss) for the robust Kanban system through using response surface methods. Note that the given example is for a specific risk situation "stable scenario", where only the customer demand interarrival time is supposed to have uncertainty($t_d \sim exp(1/2)$, see Table 5.2a) for the scenario details). Besides the stable scenario, we also consider using other typical risk scenarios in simulation, under which the robust Kanban system model has to operate and select response actions to handle the risks. When used in other risk scenarios, the factor setting determined in the stable scenario could be not so suitable and cannot generate good Netprofit results. Hence, we perform similar factorial experiments in other risk scenarios to observe the operation and performance of robust Kanban system under different conditions. Then, we use the response surface methods to determine suitable factor settings for each scenario. Finally, in a comprehensive view, we determine a suitable factor setting for the integrated risk scenarios.

In the following work, we present an example that considers 3 risk scenarios in the environment when the robust Kanban system is working. We select another 2 risk scenarios (demand+, demand++) in addition to the "stable scenario" to compose the entire uncertain environment. The 3 risk scenarios are assumed to happen with different probabilities, and the sum is 1. For example, the probability of stable scenario is assumed to be 0.7, of demand+ scenario is 0.2, of demand++ scenario is 0.1. We suppose that the stable scenario, which indicates a normal environment, should occur the most frequently. Therefore we set a high probability for it. And for other risk scenario (demand++, demand+ scenarios), which may have larger effects on the system operation and performance, we assume it occurs with a low probability. Here we consider the factor ranges defined in the pilot test for the stable scenario (see Section 6.1.2) as the factor ranges for response surface models in other scenarios, because the stable scenario is the most weighted risk situation, most of the time the Kanban system will operate in the stable scenario.

Thus, we first study the factor setting problem for a single risk scenario (stable, demand+, demand++ scenario), then for the integrated risk scenario that consists of the single scenarios with different probabilities. More details about the factorial experiments in other risk scenarios can be found in Appendix B. Here we just summarize some results as below.

Figure 6.12 displays the predicted effects of four design factors on the response Netprofit, the prediction is given by the fitted response surface models obtained in three risk scenarios (stable, demand+, demand++ scenarios). The curves can visually present the relationship between the response Netprofit and design factors sf, sf_{dt}, sf_{inv}, ss in each scenario.

Table 6.5 lists the estimated coefficients of the response surface model in each risk scenario. Similar to the parameter estimation in the stable-scenario, the Least-Square approach is used again to estimate the coefficients of each risk scenario.

Table 6.6 summarizes the optimal factor settings determined by the response surface model in each risk scenario and predicted Netprofit results. The probability (weight) of each risk scenario is listed in the table, too.

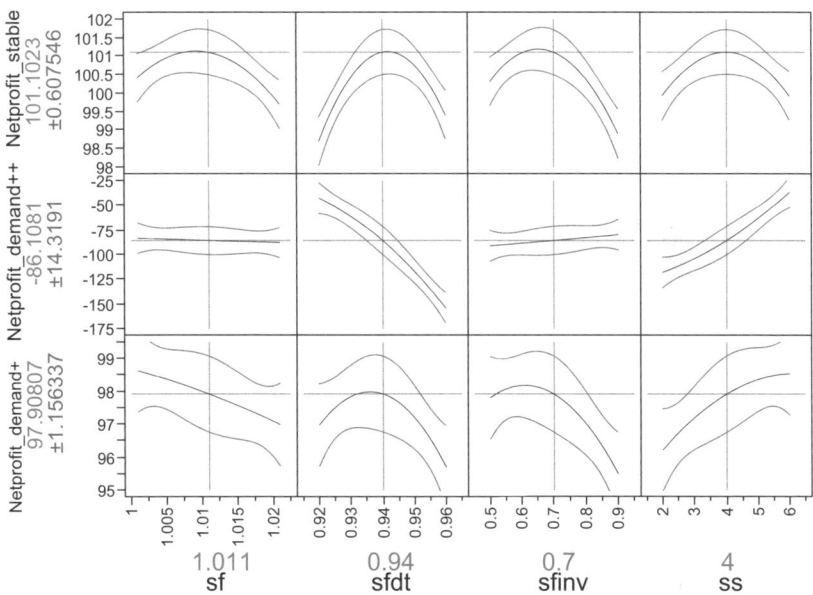

Figure 6.12: Predicted effects of design factors $sf, sf_{dt}, sf_{inv}, ss$ in different risk scenarios (stable, demand+, demand++)

After analyzing the results from the various scenarios, we can draw some useful implications for the factor setting problem.

As can be seen from the effect plots in stable scenario (see Figure 6.12), for each factor, there exists a medium value in the given range which can cause the optimal Netprofit. In comparison, the factor sf_{dt} has a more significant effect than other factors; and the factor sf affects the response Netprofit more slightly. But when comparing with the effect plots in demand+ and demand++ scenarios, the varying range of each factor's effect in the stable scenario differs not so much.

Index	Factor terms in the response surface model	Coefficients of factor terms in specified risk scenario		
		stable	demand++	demand+
1	Intercept	123.2250	2454.1942	212.0942
2	sf	-35.8397	0	-81.7605
3	sf_{dt}	17.6571	-2786.1040	-31.9682
4	sf_{inv}	-3.5319	0	-5.7577
5	ss	-0.0035	20.2952	0.5780
6	$(sf - 1.011)^2$	-10468.0230	0	0
7	$(sf - 1.011)(sf_{dt} - 0.94)$	-5093.7231	0	0
8	$(sf_{dt} - 0.94)^2$	-5131.8713	-37010.1460	-3434.1200
9	$(sf - 1.011)(sf_{inv} - 0.7)$	0	0	774.0829
10	$(sf_{dt} - 0.94)(sf_{inv} - 0.7)$	0	0	0
11	$(sf_{inv} - 0.7)^2$	-37.4503	0	-26.4474
12	$(sf - 1.011)(ss - 4)$	0	0	0
13	$(sf_{dt} - 0.94)(ss - 4)$	-35.8278	793.3181	0
14	$(sf_{inv} - 0.7)(ss - 4)$	0	0	0.1988
15	$(ss - 4)^2$	-0.2966	0	0

Table 6.5: Coefficients of the response surface model in different risk scenarios

In demand++ scenario (see Figure 6.12), we can see that sf_{dt} and ss have much more significant effects than other factors; a lower sf_{dt} value and a higher ss value (comparing with the setting in stable scenario) can lead to better Netprofit results. It can be explained as below. When the customer demand increases rapidly to a great extent, to hold more safety

Factor	Range	Optimal value setting in risk scenario		
		Stable	Demand++	Demand+
sf	[1.001,1.021]	1.008	1.001	1.001
sf_{dt}	[0.92,0.96]	0.944	0.92	0.935
sf_{inv}	[0.5,0.9]	0.653	0.7	0.5
ss	[2,6]	3.76	6	6
Response Netprofit		101.2678	-20.8409	100.9442
Scenario probability (weight)		0.7	0.1	0.2

Table 6.6: Optimal factor-setting solutions in different risk scenarios

stocks (a high ss value) can reduce the risk and cost of order backlog. Also, to put less weight on the historical demand time data (a low sf_{dt} value) can help the Kanban system detect unstable demand change more quickly. The observation is in accordance with the practical experience.

Similar observation can be also obtained in the demand+ risk scenario (see Figure 6.12), where the customer demand just increases slightly for a time length. Comparing with the factor setting in stable scenario, when in the demand+ scenario, a lower sf_{dt} value and a higher ss value can result in the higher Netprofit result, but the factor setting is not so extreme as in the demand++ scenario. To sum up, in the demand+ scenario, the factor sf_{dt} and ss affect the response more significantly than sf_{inv}, and the effect of sf is the smallest.

The coefficient estimation given in Table 6.5 confirms indirectly the observation from effect plots. We can see that the factors that have significant effects own substantial coefficient values, while the nonsignificant factors are suggested taking 0 as the coefficient value.

From the solution table (Table 6.6), we can clearly see the optimal factor values determined for each risk scenario. In the stable scenario, all factors are suggested to take some medium values within the factor ranges to generate the maximum Netprofit result. On the other hand, in the demand++ and demand+ scenarios, both sf values are set at the lower bound 1.001, indicating a more close-to-1 ratio of demand rate to service rate. And both ss values are set at the upper bound 6, which implies we should keep more safety stocks to mitigate the impact of sudden demand-increase risk. The optimal sf_{dt} value in the demand++ scenario is found to be the lowest among three scenarios (sf_{dt}=0.92), in the stable scenario is the highest (sf_{dt}=0.944), in the demand+ scenario is inbetween (sf_{dt}=0.935); it is consistent with our observations in Figure 6.12.

At last, Figure 6.13 shows a combined contour plot about the response surface models in the three risk scenarios. The response is Netprofit; the more significant factors sf_{dt} and ss are set as x- and y-axis; and the other factors sf and sf_{inv} are kept constant (sf =1.011, sf_{inv}=0.7) to draw the contour plot.

Comparing the results of different scenarios, we notice that the effects of factors in stable and demand+ scenarios remain in a relatively

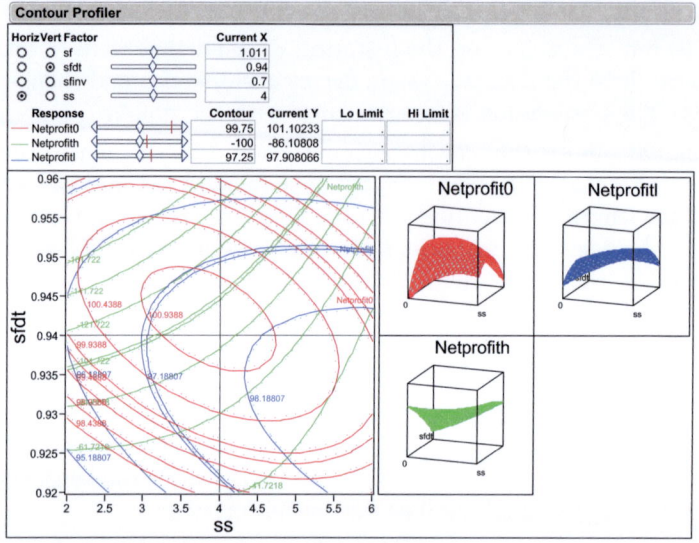

Figure 6.13: Contour plot of response surface models in 3 risk scenarios (stable, demand++,demand+), Varying factors: sf_{dt} vs. ss; Response: Netprofit

narrow range, whereas in demand++ scenario some factors' effects are much more significant, such as factor sf_{dt}, ss. This implies that the response Netprofit is sensitive to some of the factors (like sf_{dt} and ss), especially in the unstable risk scenarios. Therefore, we must determine these factor settings carefully when implementing the risk-response mechanism in the robust Kanban system. On the contrary, other factors, like sf and sf_{inv}, have relatively stable influences on the response Netprofit. Furthermore, in the unstable scenarios most of factors are suggested to take the value at the edge of the domain (lower or upper bound of the factor range). This implies that the current factor setting determined depending on the given range might not be optimal if we extend the range; better factor settings could exist in a wider range of the factor values. However, since most of the time the Kanban system is operating in a stable scenario (with a high probability), the stable scenario is the most weighted scenario we need to consider for decide the factor setting, we therefore define the factor setting range used in the stable scenario as the range of the integrated risk scenarios.

The above analysis sheds light on our further work. The work is how to find suitable factor settings for a robust Kanban system in the integrated risk scenarios (including 3 single risk scenarios). We develop a mathematical programming model to solve the parameter setting problem. The model is summarized as below.

Maximize (the objective):

$$meanNetprofit = \sum_{sc \in ScenariosSet} Prob_{sc} \cdot Netprofit_{sc} \tag{6.2}$$

Subject to:

$$Netprofit_{sc} = \beta_0^{sc} + \sum_{i=1}^{i=4} \beta_i^{sc} x_i + \sum_{i=1}^{i=4} \beta_{ii}^{sc} x_i^2 + \sum_{i<j} \beta_{ij}^{sc} x_i x_j \quad \forall sc \in ScenariosSet$$

$$\tag{6.3}$$

$$LB_i \le x_i \le UB_i, \quad i, j = 1, 2, 3, 4 \tag{6.4}$$

Decision variables: x_i, $i = 1, 2, 3, 4$

For the sake of readability, in the mathematical programming model, we use x_i variables to denote the four design factors $x_1 = sf$, $x_2 = sf_{dt}$, $x_3 = sf_{inv}$, $x_4 = ss$. In this example, we suppose that the Scenarios Set ($sc \in ScenariosSet$) include stable, demand++, and demand+ scenarios; sc is the index of risk scenarios. The parameters $\beta_i^{sc}, \beta_{ii}^{sc}, \beta_{ij}^{sc}$ are the coefficients of related factor terms, their values are obtained from the response surface models, as shown in Table 6.5. And UB_i and LB_i are the upper and lower bounds of factor x_i (here we use the refined factor-value ranges from the stable scenario as the bounds). The parameter $Prob_{sc}$ is the probability that the indexed-sc risk scenario will occur in the environment; the probability values are given in Table 6.6.

We build the mathematical programming model using AIMMS software, and solve it by the nonlinear programming solver. The factor setting solution (for the four design factors sf, sf_{dt}, sf_{inv}, ss) generated by the mathematical programming model is summarized in Table 6.7. The solution is determined with considering the Netprofit results in 3 risk scenarios simultaneously. Using this factor setting, we believe that

209

the risk-response mechanism can be applied appropriately in the robust
Kanban system.

Factor (index x_i)	Range	Optimal value setting for integrated scenario		
		Stable	Demand++	Demand+
sf (x_1)	[1.001,1.021]		1.010	
sf_{dt} (x_2)	[0.92,0.96]		0.930	
sf_{inv}(x_3)	[0.5,0.9]		0.641	
ss (x_4)	[2,6]		6	
Response Netprofit		99.97	-34.59	99.15
Scenario probability (weight)		0.70	0.10	0.20

Table 6.7: Optimal factor-setting solution for integrated risk scenario

Comparing the Netprofit results in Table 6.7 (for integrated risk scenarios) with results in Table 6.6 (for individual risk scenarios), we can
see that the Netprofit generated from each risk scenario in Table 6.7 is
not as optimal as the corresponding Netprofit given in Table 6.6. This is
because the Netprofit result of each risk scenario in Table 6.6 is derived
from individual optimization; so the optimal factor settings for the 3 risk
scenarios are different. We cannot make the system achieve the best performance simultaneously over the 3 risk scenarios. Therefore, we need to
consider some trade-off between the solutions of different risk scenarios.
We suppose each scenario will occur with a specific probability (weight),
then in the calculation of total Netprofit, we put different weight parameters on each scenario's Netprofit result. The objective of the factor
setting decision is to maximize the total Netprofit, which is the sum of the
weighted Netprofit results from different risk scenarios. After executing
the mathematical programming model, we finally get a balanced solution
for the factor setting in the integrated risk scenarios. The balanced factor
setting is a proper setting, which is robust to the assumed risk scenarios
simultaneously. Therefore the robust Kanban system using this factor
setting can perform well in the overall uncertain environment.

So far, we have accomplished the factorial experiment for the parameter setting improvement. We found out suitable control parameter
settings of the risk-response mechanism, this setting can cause better (optimal or suboptimal) Netprofit results in the robust Kanban system. The

optimal factor setting for each single-risk scenario is determined with using the response surface methods. Then a balanced factor setting solution is determined by a mathematical programming model that considers the integrated risk scenarios. With the well-defined risk-response mechanism, the robust Kanban system would perform more robustly and efficiently when facing various risks. After analyzing the experiment output results in different risk scenarios, we can draw the conclusion that the response-surface model is a good method for optimizing the factor setting (control parameter setting) of the robust Kanban system. With the factor setting solution, the risk-response mechanism can be implemented successfully; thus the robust Kanban system can perform well when facing a variety of risks in an uncertain environment.

7 Concluding remarks

7.1 Work summary

Modern supply chains are operating in an uncertain environment, subject to various risks and disruptions. Therefore, to design a robust supply network to hedge against the uncertainties is of great value and importance. The traditional supply chain management pursues cost-effective features. As a typical policy in this direction, the Kanban-controlled system works quite well in a stable environment. However, when the environment is uncertain, the Kanban system cannot take effective response actions to mitigate the impact of risks. This restricts the application of Kanban systems in the uncertain environment. The traditional Kanban system calls for improvement to cope with the various risks in the modern uncertain environment.

Many robust methods are developed to improve the supply chain performance when facing risks. The methods can be classified into three types based on the decision level: strategic, tactical, and operational levels. For each decision level, we can find many risk response methods in the literature. However, we notice that most of the methods just focus on an individual decision level. Few methods consider combining three decision levels simultaneously to deal with the risks, especially in the scope of a Kanban-controlled system.

Therefore, in this dissertation we proposed a robustly designed supply chain model based on the Kanban control mechanism. A risk-response mechanism is developed to help the Kanban system reduce the impact of various risks and remain at a high performance level in an uncertain environment. The robust Kanban system can dynamically adjust a series of system parameters as risk response actions (from the operational, tactical, or strategic level), depending on the degree of different risk situations.

In Chapter 3, we designed a conceptual model of the robust Kanban system, and then built a simulation model to study its behavior and performance in the uncertain environment. The robust Kanban system can systematically change its parameters from a strategic level (backup supplier, new server), tactical level (single machine service time), or operational level (Kanban number), to deal with a variety of risk situations. The severe material supply shortage from the upstream supplier, the slight demand fluctuation from downstream customer, or the short-time machine breakdown from a process stage, are all typical risk situations considered in this study.

The newly developed risk-response mechanism is the main feature of the robust Kanban system. Hence, the parameter setting of the risk-response mechanism is crucial to the final success of the robust Kanban system application. In order to implement the robust Kanban system effectively, we need to define related parameter settings appropriately. Hence in Chapter 4, we developed a mathematical programming model to determine the 3-level adjustable parameters. The parameter setting in the stable scenario is used as the baseline setting for adjusting the 3-level parameters. Meanwhile, some simple estimation methods were adopted to decide the initial setting of the monitor control parameters used in the risk-response mechanism, such as control limits for monitor mi_rate and mi_inv.

After the model formulation and parameter setting, we further performed two experiments based on simulation of related Kanban system models. The first experiment is a comparative experiment (Chapter 5). We compared three Kanban systems based on simulation, to examine the performance improvement made by the robust Kanban system in a variety of risk scenarios. After a statistical analysis of the experiment output results, we concluded that robust Kanban system performed better than the other two Kanban systems (traditional Toyota Kanban system, inventory-based adaptive Kanban system) in the uncertain environment. The improvement was statistically significant, especially in the scenarios with severe risks.

The second experiment is a factorial experiment (Chapter 6). It aims to further improve the robust Kanban system performance through optimizing the control parameter setting of the risk-response mechanism, because the control parameter setting were just roughly estimated in

Chapter 4. Four control parameters $(sf, sf_{dt}, sf_{inv}, ss)$ used in the risk-response mechanism are selected as the design factors in the factorial experiment. The experimental response is Netprofit. We designed and performed a series of tests under different risk scenarios, then employed response surface models to determine optimal factor settings. At last, we formulated a mathematical programming model to find a suitable balanced factor setting over the integrated risk scenarios.

To sum up, this study contributes to the development of Kanban-controlled systems from three aspects. First, we propose a new robust model for the Kanban-controlled supply chain system, which is named the robust Kanban system. The main feature of the robust Kanban system is a risk-response mechanism, with which the Kanban system can systematically and dynamically adjust 3-level (strategic, tactical, operational level) parameters to deal with a variety of risks in an uncertain environment. Second, we build simulation models to test and implement the design ideas of robust Kanban system. The robustly designed risk-response mechanism is executed through computer programming in the simulation model, and the performance of the robust Kanban system is verified through simulation-based comparative experiment. Third, we develop a series of practical and effective methods for determining the parameter settings for the robust Kanban system. The parameters include 3-level adjustable parameters that configure the system structure, and control parameters used by the risk-response mechanism. The methods used for determining the parameter settings contain both analytical methods (MINLP model) and simulation methods (response surface model).

In addition, the robust Kanban model and its application methods proposed in this study are not problem-specific and practical to apply, hence they can be easily implemented in a wide range of applications.

Although we believe that this study provides a practical and meaningful framework for operating the Kanban system robustly, there is much room for improvement on the robust Kanban system model. For example, the studied robust Kanban system has a serial-line shape. Although this is the basic shape of a supply chain, the supply network is a more general and realistic shape in real life. When considering supply networks, the system structure could be extended to more variations, such as an assembly type, a converge type, or an assembly-converge-mixed type, or even a general network without specific structure. The network structure will make the model of the robust Kanban system more complex and realistic. Besides, in this work we assumed that only a single-product is produced by the system; hence, to develop a multi-product robust Kanban system will be also a promising direction.

7.2 Application guidelines for the robust Kanban system

There are some instructive points to be noted when applying the robust Kanban system model in practice. In Figure 7.1, we summarize the procedures for designing and implementing the robust Kanban system in a realistic problem.

Before applying the robust Kanban system model, two preconditions should be checked to make sure that it is the suitable situation for the model application. First condition, the environment should contain some uncertainty in the demand, process, or supply side. Second condition, the system service capacity should be flexible. The capacity parameters are supposed to be able to change in a specified range. Only when both preconditions are satisfied, it is suitable to apply the robust Kanban system. Otherwise, if the environment is quite stable or repetitive, the traditional Toyota Kanban system could already perform very well, then there is no need considering a more complex robust Kanban system. Also, if the Kanban system is not allowed to change its capacity parameters (such as Kanban number, machine process time), it is not possible to apply the risk-response mechanism which need to adjust service capacities. Therefore, before applying the robust Kanban system model, we should consider the environment and the system characteristics to check whether the two preconditions are satisfied. Only when the conditions are assured, it is reasonable to continue the robust Kanban system application.

As shown in Figure 7.1, the first step of applying the robust Kanban system is to collect input data. Many kinds of data need to be collected as background information for the model formulation.

216

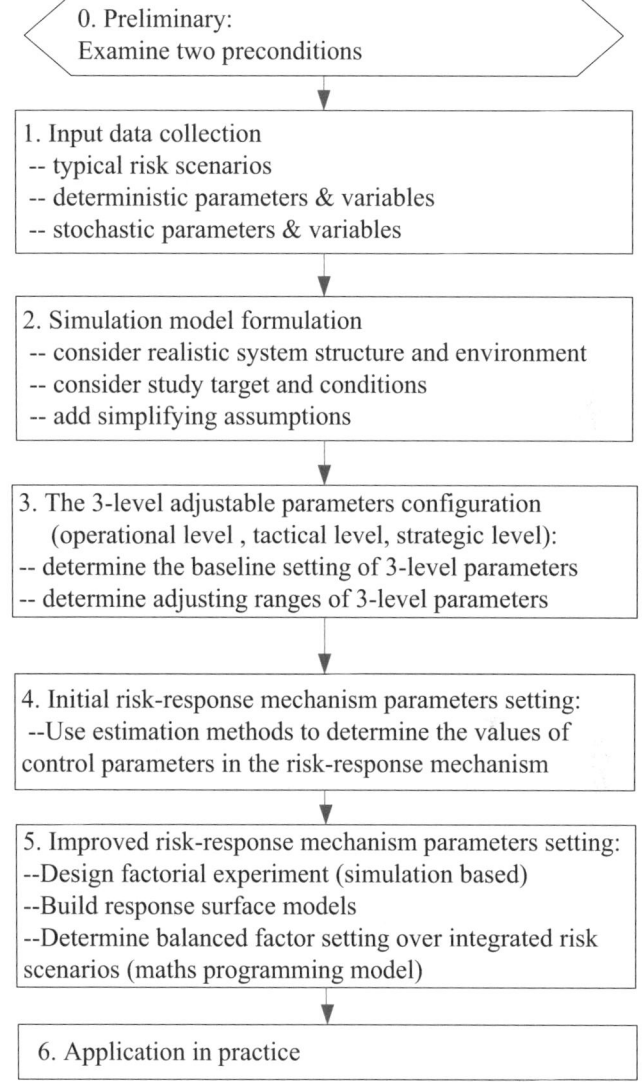

Figure 7.1: Flow chart of Robust Kanban System application

For example, we need the information about system configuration. The parameters with respect to the system structure, capacity and operation sequence should be figured out so that the model can reflect the realistic situation of the system. The number and location of stages in the supply chain, the process time, machine number, transport capacity at each stage, the allowable adjusting ranges of process or transport capacity, and related cost for operating the service equipment, all the parameters should be specified properly depending on the information.

Besides, since a variety of risks may happen to the system, we need to collect the information about the risk events to know the risk probability or occurring rules. Suppose the customer demand interarrival time is stochastic, then we should collect demand time data as much as possible to know its probability distribution. When the occurring rules of risk events are difficult to conclude, we can select some typical risk scenarios to represent the uncertain environment. Namely, the overall risk environment is divided into several simpler typical risk scenarios that can be easily described by parameters. We first study the application problem in each scenario, then integrate the individual results to draw a final solution. The selection and specification (location, extent, duration, and probability) of the typical risk scenarios have large influence on the following study, they should be selected carefully.

The input parameters group into two types: deterministic and stochastic parameters. If we know the system feature with certainty, it can be measured by deterministic parameters. Otherwise, if the feature may realize in different forms randomly, we use stochastic parameters to describe it. For example, we suppose that the single-machine process time at a non-bottleneck stage is constant, then it can be defined by a constant parameter. By contrast, the customer demand arrives in the system randomly, then we consider the demand interarrival time as a stochastic variable. For some known probability distribution types (e.g. the demand interarrival time follows an exponential distribution), related deterministic parameters, like mean or variance, are also employed to specify the stochastic variables.

When all the required background information and data are prepared, we can do the second step. It is to build a simulation model of the robust Kanban system, to study the system behavior through simulation-based experiments. The simulation model should be built at a proper detail level considering the study objective, realistic situation, and the study conditions. Some simplifications and assumptions can be included in the simulation model. Try to make the model as simple as possible, but not simpler: this is the basic principle of building the simulation model. Following this rule, we first need to make clear the objective of the simulation-based study. Then, with a clear goal, we can build the simulation model at a proper detail level. Then we can collect relevant simulation output data to do further analysis.

Take the simulation model given in Chapter 4 as an example. In this example, we were interested in the operation details of the proposed risk-response mechanism. Hence, we built a simulation model that can record the value change data of 3-level parameters. Other performance measures, such as Netprofit, inventory level in each buffer, customer waiting time, and backlog order level, are also data of interest; and the simulation model is able to collect or calculate these data too. After the simulation model construction, the verification and validation work should be conducted as well, to examine the correctness and usability of the simulation model.

Step 3 deals with the configuration of 3-level adjustable parameters in the robust Kanban system. We first use analytical methods to optimize the settings of 3-level parameters in the stable scenario. We think of the stable-scenario parameter setting as a baseline setting for the 3-level parameters. Based on the baseline setting, we can further decide suitable adjusting ranges for the 3-level parameters. The functional relationships between the performance measure "order backlog level" and the 3-level parameters are a crucial part of applying the analytical methods. In Chapter 4 we introduced two methods for formulating the backlog level function: the analytical method and the simulation method. The simulation method is a more general approach that can be applied in a wide range of problems; but to build the simulation model and carry out simulation experiments is to some extent time-consuming. By contrast, the analytical method is problem-specific, some specific features of system structure or environment are required when using analytical methods. For example, if the demand time and process time are exponentially distributed in a serial line Kanban system, it is efficient to find solutions using analytical methods. Both analytical and simulation methods have pros and cons for developing the backlog level function, which method is better depends on the features and requirements of the problem.

In Step 4 and 5, we come to decide suitable values for the control parameters used in the risk-response mechanism. The smoothing weight factors for calculating *mi_rate*, the control limits for comparing monitor values, are examples of control parameters. In the example given in Chapter 4, we first provided a set of simple estimation methods to decide suitable control parameter settings. The roughly estimated setting is named the initial setting in Step 4. Later, we use response surface models in simulation experiment to find improved control parameter settings (Step 5), which can generate better Netprofit results.

Some points should be noticed when applying the response surface models to optimize the Netprofit results. For example, a factor screening test can be carried out before we start building the response surface model. Through the factor screening, we can select important factors which have larger effects on the response, thus simplify the factorial experiment to a reasonable detail level. Especially, when there are many factors existing in the experiment, to include all the factors is not applicable. After the factor screening, the experiment will be more economical and practical to perform in realistic problems.

Besides the factor screening test, another pilot test should be conducted as well for the factorial experiment. It is used to refine the searching region of optimal factor values for the response surface model. A response surface model usually takes the form of a 1, 2 or 3-order polynomial in engineering application (Montgomery 2007). The results of response surface models will be sufficiently accurate and effective, only when the factor-value searching region is relatively small and close to optimum. Therefore, we need to do a pilot test before using the response surface methods. We first perform a series of simulation runs (pilot test) to get a general understanding of the factor effects. With knowing the factor effects or tendency basically, we can quickly find a smaller and close-to-optimum region as the factor-setting domain for the response surface model. Within the small region, we can do the factorial experiment then use the response surface methods to find the optimal factor setting. In the example given in Chapter 6, a unique response variable "Netprofit" was selected for the factorial experiment. Netprofit refers to the time-averaged net profit obtained from operating the robust Kanban system. In other study cases, the manager may be interested in other performance measures, more than one response variables can be then selected. We should follow the principle "choose direct and important response measures other than indirect response" for the response variable (performance measure) selection. For example, to choose demand time and service time as two individual responses is better than taking the ratio of demand time to service time as a single response. In addition, we can also put reasonable weights on response variables according to their importance or the decision maker's opinion, then draw an integrated decision for the factor setting.

Lastly, as listed in Step 6, when all the configuration of the risk-response mechanism and the Kanban system is finished, we can apply the robust Kanban system model in the realistic problem. To implement the system successfully, the designer should listen to the voices from various aspects. For example, we should consider both the customer's requirement (e.g. service level and waiting time) and the manufacturer's expectation (e.g. target inventory level and backlog level, Netprofit or total cost). Besides, the realistic production capacity and flexibility of the factory, and the real risk situations in the environment should be also carefully observed and considered when making decisions on adjusting the 3-level parameters.

As a supplement, when we design experiment and analyze the output data, the experiment type and data analysis methods should be selected appropriately, too. Related information, such as system operation features, environment conditions, the target of doing the experiment, should be considered carefully. For example, in the comparative experiment given in Chapter 5, we used the paired-t test with sample size=40 to compare the Netprofit results of different Kanban systems. The paired test and the sample size 40 were determined after analyzing the distribution and related statistics (mean, variance) of the sample data. When using statistical techniques to analyze the output data, we should pay attention to the preconditions or assumptions of applying the statistical method. We should check whether the required assumptions are satisfied in the study, such as the normality assumption required for t-test and ANOVA. If the assumptions are not satisfied, the statistical inferences drawn from the analysis will not make much sense, then we should consider using other techniques for data analysis.

Glossary of Notation

Symbols for Kanban system model configuration

i	Index of stage in the supply chain system
sc	Index of risk scenarios
T	Total system operating time
t	Current time
ρ	Traffic intensity of a queueing system, $\rho = \lambda/k\mu$
	λ is demand rate; μ is service rate; k is server number
t_d (t_d^{mean})	Customer demand interarrival time (mean value)
K_i	Number of Kanban (*Production Kanban, Trans-
$(*Kp_i, Kt_i)$	port Kanban) at stage i
(K_{min}, K_{max})	Adjusting range of K_i (lower, upper bounds)
Ts_i	Single machine service time at stage i
$(Ts_{min},$	Adjusting range of Ts_i (lower, upper bounds, base-
$Ts_{max}, Ts_0)$	line value)
ts_i	Disrupted single-machine service time (stochastic)
Ns_i	Server number at stage i
$(Ns_{\min}, Ns_{\max})$	Adjusting range of Ns_i (lower, upper bounds)
tsu_{main}	Material supply time of the main supplier
tsu_{backup}	Material supply time of the backup supplier
pr_{backup}	Material supply proportion from the backup sup-
	plier
T_{su}	Actual material supply time at the supplier stage
(pr_{low}, pr_{high})	Adjusting range of pr_{backup} (lower, upper bounds)
h_i	Inventory holding cost at stage i
b_i	Order backlog penalty cost at stage i
cK_i	Cost of keeping a Kanban (*Production Kanban,
$(*cKp_i, cKt_i)$	Transport Kanban) cyclic at stage i for one time
	unit

$cStime_i$	Cost coefficient of using the given machine process speed per time unit at stage i
$cServer_i$	Cost of operating a server per time unit at stage i
$cSupplier$	Cost of changing the backup supplier supply proportion each time
$cost_{Kanban}$	Time-averaged operating cost of Kanban
$cost_{stime}$	Time-averaged operating cost of machine service rate
$cost_{server}$	Time-averaged operating cost of in-use servers
$cost_{supplier}$	Time-averaged operating cost of changing supplier proportions
$cost_{change3level}$	Time-averaged operating cost of 3-level adjustable parameters
	$cost_{change3level} = cost_{Kanban} + cost_{stime} + cost_{server} + cost_{supplier}$
$pricein_{main}$	Material purchase price per product unit from the main supplier
$pricein_{backup}$	Material purchase price per product unit from the backup supplier
$priceout$	Sell price of finished product per product
sl_0 (*$sl(t)$)	Target service level (*actual service level calculated at time t)
$I_i(t)$ (*$\overline{I}_i$)	Inventory level at stage i at time t (*time-averaged value)
$B_i(t)$ (*$\overline{B}_i$)	Order backlog level at customer stage at time t (*time-averaged value)
$cost_{inventory}$	Time-averaged inventory holding cost of the entire system
$cost_{backlog}$	Time-averaged backlog penalty cost of the entire system
$cost_{purchase}$	Time-averaged cost of purchasing material from suppliers
$Income_{mean}$	Time-averaged total income, from selling finished product to customers, $Income_{mean} = priceout \cdot [N(t) - B(t)]/T$

$Netprofit_{mean}$	Time-averaged total net profit of operating the robust Kanban system, $Netprofit_{mean} = Income_{mean} - cost_{purchase} - cost_{change3level} - cost_{inventory} - cost_{backlog}$

Symbols for Risk-response mechanism

mi_rate	Rate-balance monitor
$mi_{rate}(t)$	Value of mi_rate observed at time t
mi_inv	Inventory-balance monitor
$mi_{inv}(t)$	Value of mi_inv observed at time t
t_{review}	Review period length used in the risk-response mechanism
$\widetilde{T}_{demand}(t)$	Exponentially smoothed value of demand interarrival time, for calculating mi_rate
$\widetilde{T}_{supplier}(t)$	Exponentially smoothed value of supplier material supply time, for calculating mi_rate
$\widetilde{T}_{process}(t)$	Exponentially smoothed value of bottleneck-stage process time, for calculating mi_rate
$\widetilde{T}_{transport}(t)$	Exponentially smoothed value of bottleneck-stage transport time, for calculating mi_rate
$\widetilde{I}(t)$	Exponentially smoothed value of inventory level at customer stage, for calculating mi_inv
$\widetilde{B}(t)$	Exponentially smoothed value of backlog level at customer stage, for calculating mi_inv
sf	Safety factor used to control the rate balance ($sf = 1 + \varepsilon \geq 1$, ε is a small positive value)
sf_{dt}	Smoothing weight factor of demand interarrival time, $sf_{dt} \in [0,1]$
sf_{pr}	Smoothing weight factor of single-machine service time, $sf_{pr} \in [0,1]$
sf_{su}	Smoothing weight factor of supplier material supply time, $sf_{su} \in [0,1]$
sf_{inv}	Smoothing weight factor of inventory and backlog level, $sf_{inv} \in [0,1]$
ss	Safety stock level, baseline control limit of mi_inv
ss_{low}	Lower bound of ss, lower control limit of mi_inv

ss_{high}	Upper bound of ss, upper control limit of mi_inv
LCL_K	Lower control limit of mi_rate for changing Kanban number
UCL_K	Upper control limit of mi_rate for changing Kanban number
LCL_{Ts}	Lower control limit of mi_rate for changing machine service time
UCL_{Ts}	Upper control limit of mi_rate for changing machine service time
LCL_{Ns}	Lower control limit of mi_rate for changing server number
UCL_{Ns}	Upper control limit of mi_rate for changing server number
LCL_{su}	Lower control limit of mi_rate for changing backup supplier proportion
UCL_{su}	Upper control limit of mi_rate for changing backup supplier proportion

Abbreviations

CCI	Central Composite Inscribed Design (for response surface model)
i.i.d	Identically independently distributed
MINLP	Mixed Integer Nonlinear Programming
M,D,unif,gam	Exponential, constant, uniform, gamma distribution type
RSM	Response surface method
Stable	Stable scenario for Kanban system operating environment
Demand++	Risk scenario with severe demand rate increase
Demand+	Risk scenario with slight demand rate increase
Demand−−	Risk scenario with severe demand rate decrease
Demand−	Risk scenario with severe demand rate decrease
Process−	Risk scenario with longer machine process time
Supply−	Risk scenario with longer supplier material supply time

References

Akturk, M. S. and F. Erhun (1999). An overview of design and operational issues of kanban systems. *International Journal of Production Research 37*(17), p. 3859–3881.

Allen, A. (1990). *Probability, Statistics, and Queueing Theory: With Computer Science Applications.* Academic Press.

Arnold, D. and K. Furmans (2006). *Materialfluss in Logistiksystemen.* Springer.

Askin, R. and J. Goldberg (2002). *Design and analysis of lean production systems.* Wiley.

Askin, R. G., M. George Mitwasi and J. B. Goldberg (1993). Determining the Number of Kanbans in Multi-Item Just-in-Time Systems. *IIE Transactions 25*(1), p. 89–98.

Askin, R. G. and S. Krishnan (2009). Defining inventory control points in multiproduct stochastic pull systems. *International Journal of Production Economics 120*(2), p. 418–429.

Axsaeter, S. (2000). *Inventory control.* Kluwer Academic.

Ballou, R. (1992). *Business Logistics Management.* Prentice Hall.

Baynat, B., Y. Dallery, M. Di Mascolo and Y. Frein (2001). A multiclass approximation technique for the analysis of kanban-like control systems. *International Journal of Production Research 39*(2), p. 307–328.

Beamon, B. (1999). Measuring supply chain performance. *International Journal of Operations & Production Management 19*(3), p. 275–292.

Berkley, B. (1992). A review of the kanban production control research literature. *Production and Operations Management 1*(4), p. 393–411.

Berkley, B. J. (1991). TANDEM QUEUES AND KANBAN-CONTROLLED LINES. *International Journal of Production Research 29*(10), p. 2057–2081. Berkley, bj.

Bitran, G. and L. Chang (1987). A mathematical programming approach to a deterministic kanban system. *Management Science*, p. 427–441.

Bonvik, A. M., C. E. Couch and S. B. Gershwin (1997). A comparison of production-line control mechanisms. *International Journal of Production Research 35*(3), p. 789–804.

Boonlertvanich, K. (2005). *Extended-CONWIP-Kanban System: Control and Performance Analysis*. Phd dissertation. very good.

Buzacott, J. (1989a). QUEUEING MODELS OF KANBAN AND MRP CONTROLLED PRODUCTION SYSTEMS*. *Engineering Costs and Production Economist, 17 (1989) 3-20*.

Buzacott, J. A. (1989b). QUEUING MODELS OF KANBAN AND MRP CONTROLLED PRODUCTION SYSTEMS. *Engineering Costs and Production Economics 17*(1-4), p. 3–20. Buzacott, ja.

Cachon, G. P. and M. A. Lariviere (2005). Supply Chain Coordination with Revenue-Sharing Contracts: Strengths and Limitations. *Management Science 51*(1), p. 30–44.

Chopra, S. and M. Sodhi (2004). Managing Risk to avoid Supply-Chain Breakdown. *MIT Sloan management review*.

Clark, A. and H. Scarf (1960). Optimal policies for a multi-echelon inventory problem. *Management Science 6*(4), p. 475–490.

Company, P. (2011). P&G 2011 Annual Report.

Dallery, Y. and S. Gershwin (1992). Manufacturing flow line systems: a review of models and analytical results. *Queueing Systems 12*(1), p. 3–94.

Dallery, Y. and G. Liberopoulos (2000). Extended kanban control system: combining kanban and base stock. *IIE Transactions 32*(4), p. 369–386. Dallery, Y Liberopoulos, G.

Deleersnyder, J.-L., T. J. Hodgson, H. Muller-Malek and P. J. O'Grady (1989). Kanban Controlled Pull Systems: An Analytic Approach. *Management Science Vol. 35,*(No. 9 (Sep., 1989)), p. 1079–1091.

DiMascolo, M., Y. Frein and Y. Dallery (1996). An analytical method for performance evaluation of kanban controlled production systems. *Operations Research 44*(1), p. 50–64. DiMascolo, M Frein, Y Dallery, Y.

Dupont, W. and W. Plummer Jr (1990). Power and sample size calculations:: A review and computer program. *Controlled Clinical Trials 11*(2), p. 116–128.

Duri, C., Y. Frein and M. Di Mascolo (2000). Comparison among three pull control policies: kanban, base stock, and generalized kanban. *Annals of Operations Research 93*, p. 41–69. Duri, C Frein, Y Di Mascolo, M International Workshop on Performance Evaluation and Optimization of Production Lines May 19-22, 1997 Samos island, greece.

Frein, Y., M. Di Mascolo and Y. Dallery (1995). On the design of generalized kanban control systems. *International Journal of Operations & Production Management 15*(9), p. 158–184.

Geraghty, J. and C. Heavey (2005). A review and comparison of hybrid and pull-type production control strategies. *OR Spectrum 27*(2-3), p. 435–457.

Graves, S. and B. Tomlin (2003). Process flexibility in supply chains. *Management Science*, p. 907–919.

Groenevelt, H. (1993). The just-in-time system.

Gross, D. and C. Harris (1998). *Fundamentals of queueing theory*. Wiley.

Gunasekaran, A., C. Patel and R. McGaughey (2004). A framework for supply chain performance measurement. *International Journal of Production Economics 87*(3), p. 333–347.

Holt, C. (2004). Forecasting seasonals and trends by exponentially weighted moving averages. *International Journal of Forecasting 20*(1), p. 5–10.

Hopp, W. J., S. M. R. Iravani and W. L. Xu (2010). Vertical Flexibility in Supply Chains. *Management Science 56*(3), p. 495–502.

Huang, C.-C. and A. Kusiak (1996). Overview of Kanban systems. *International Journal of Computer Integrated Manufacturing 9*(3), p. 169–189.

Huang, P., L. Rees and B. Taylor (1983). A SIMULATION ANALYSIS OF THE JAPANESE JUSTéĹěæÄŽNéĹěæÄšIME TECHNIQUE (WITH KANBANS) FOR A MULTILINE, MULTISTAGE PRODUCTION SYSTEM. *Decision Sciences 14*(3), p. 326–344.

Jordan, W. and S. Graves (1995). Principles on the benefits of manufacturing process flexibility. *Management Science*, p. 577–594.

Karaesmen, F. and Y. Dallery (2000). A performance comparison of pull type control mechanisms for multi-stage manufacturing. *International Journal of Production Economics 68*(1), p. 59–71. good 4 types of Kanban systems extended generalized.

Kimball, G. (1988). General principles of inventory control. *Journal of manufacturing and operations management 1*(1), p. 119–130.

Kimura, O. and H. Terada (1981). Design and analysis of Pull System, a method of multi-stage production control. *THE INTERNATIONAL JOURNAL OF PRODUCTION RESEARCH 19*(3), p. 241–253.

Kleindorfer, P. and G. Saad (2005). Managing disruption risks in supply chains. *Production and Operations Management 14*(1), p. 53–68.

Kleinrock, L. (1976). *Queueing Systems: Theory*. Wiley.

Krafcik, J. (1988). Triumph of the lean production system. *Sloan Management Review 30*(1), p. 41–52.

Krajewski, L., B. King, L. Ritzman and D. Wong (1987). Kanban, MRP, and shaping the manufacturing environment. *Management Science*, p. 39–57.

Kumar, C. S. and R. Panneerselvam (2007). Literature review of JIT-KANBAN system. *International Journal of Advanced Manufacturing Technology 32*(3-4), p. 393–408. 140EP Times Cited:12 Cited References Count:104.

Law, A. (2007). *Simulation modeling and analysis*. McGraw-Hill.

Lee, H. (2004). The triple-A supply chain. *Harvard Business Review 82*(10), p. 102–113.

Lee, H., V. Padmanabhan and S. Whang (1997). Information distortion in a supply chain: the bullwhip effect. *Management Science*, p. 546–558.

Liberopoulos, G. and Y. Dallery (2000). A unified framework for pull control mechanisms in multi-stage manufacturing systems. *Annals of Operations Research 93*, p. 325–355. 309TB Times Cited:44 Cited References Count:22.

Lim, M. K. (2009). *Supply Chain Network Design in the Presence of Disruption Risks*. Phd dissertation.

Lucas, J. and M. Saccucci (1990). Exponentially weighted moving average control schemes: properties and enhancements. *Technometrics*, p. 1–12.

Martinez de Albeniz, V. and D. S. Levi (2005). A portfolio approach to procurement contracts. *Production and Operations Management 14*(1), p. 90–114.

Mathworks (2012). Mathworks Product Documentation: Simulink.

Moeeni, F., S. M. Sanchez and A. J. Vakha Ria (1997). A robust design methodology for Kanban system design. *International Journal of Production Research 35*(10), p. 2821–2838.

Monden, Y. (1983). *Toyota production system: practical approach to production management.* Industrial Engineering and Management Press, Institute of Industrial Engineers, 1983.

Montgomery, D. (2007). *Design and Analysis of Experiments, 6th Edition Set.* John Wiley & Sons, Limited.

NIST/SEMATECH (2012). e-Handbook of Statistical Methods.

Ohno, T. (1988). *Toyota production system: beyond large-scale production.* Productivity Press.

Parlar, M. (1997). Continuous-review inventory problem with random supply interruptions. *European Journal of Operational Research 99*(2), p. 366–385. Xe640 Times Cited:52 Cited References Count:17.

Philipoom, P. R., L. P. Rees, B. W. Taylor and P. Y. Huang (1987). An Investigation of the Factors Influencing the Number of Kanbans Required in the Implementation of the Jit Technique with Kanbans. *International Journal of Production Research 25*(3), p. 457–472. G2740 Times Cited:44 Cited References Count:0.

Rees, L. P., P. R. Philipoom, B. W. Taylor and P. Y. Huang (1987). Dynamically Adjusting the Number of Kanbans in a Just-in-Time Production System Using Estimated Values of Leadtime. *IIE Transactions 19*(2), p. 199–207. H7942 Times Cited:52 Cited References Count:8.

Schmidt, G. and W. Wilhelm (2000). Strategic, tactical and operational decisions in multi-national logistics networks: a review and discussion of modelling issues. *International Journal of Production Research 38*(7), p. 1501–1523.

Sivakumar, G. D. and P. Shahabudeen (2009). Algorithms for the design of a multi-stage adaptive kanban system. *International Journal of Production Research* 47(23), p. 6707–6738.

Snyder, L. V. and M. S. Daskin (2006). Stochastic p-robust location problems. *IIE Transactions* 38(11), p. 971–985. 081YC Times Cited:16 Cited References Count:45.

Spearman, M. L. (1992). CUSTOMER SERVICE IN PULL PRODUCTION SYSTEMS. *Operations Research* 40(5), p. 948–958. Spearman, ml.

Spearman, M. L., D. L. Woodruff and W. J. Hopp (1990). Conwip - a Pull Alternative to Kanban. *International Journal of Production Research* 28(5), p. 879–894. Dd900 Times Cited:298 Cited References Count:0.

Spearman, M. L. and M. A. Zazanis (1992). PUSH AND PULL PRODUCTION SYSTEMS - ISSUES AND COMPARISONS. *Operations Research* 40(3), p. 521–532. Spearman, ml zazanis, ma.

Takahashi, K. (2003). Comparing reactive Kanban systems. *International Journal of Production Research* 41(18), p. 4317–4337.

Takahashi, K. and N. Nakamura (1999). Reacting JIT ordering systems to the unstable changes in demand. *International Journal of Production Research* 37(10), p. 2293–2313.

Tang, C. and B. Tomlin (2008). The power of flexibility for mitigating supply chain risks. *International Journal of Production Economics* 116(1), p. 12–27.

Tang, C. S. (2006a). Perspectives in supply chain risk management. *International Journal of Production Economics* 103(2), p. 451–488.

Tang, C. S. (2006b). Robust strategies for mitigating supply chain disruptions. *International Journal of Logistics: Research and Applications* 9(1), p. 33–45.

Tanner, M. (1995). *Practical queueing analysis.* McGraw-Hill.

Tardif, V. and L. Maaseidvaag (2001). An adaptive approach to controlling kanban systems. *European Journal of Operational Research* 132(2), p. 411–424. Tardif, V Maaseidvaag, L.

Tomlin, B. (2006). On the Value of Mitigation and Contingency Strategies for Managing Supply Chain Disruption Risks. *Management Science* 52(5), p. 639–657.

Tomlin, B. and Y. Wang (2005). On the Value of Mix Flexibility and Dual Sourcing in Unreliable Newsvendor Networks. *Manufacturing and Service Operations Management* 7(1), p. 37–57.

Wang, S. J. and B. R. Sarker (2006). Optimal models for a multistage supply chain system controlled by kanban under just-in-time philosophy. *European Journal of Operational Research* 172(1), p. 179–200. Wang, SJ Sarker, BR.

Womack, J., D. Jones, D. Roos and M. I. o. Technology (1990). *The machine that changed the world: based on the Massachusetts Institute of Technology 5-million dollar 5-year study on the future of the automobile*. Rawson Associates.

Zipkin, P. (1989). A kanban-like production control system: analysis of simple models. *Technical Report, Research Working Paper* (89-1).

Zipkin, P. (1991). Does manufacturing need a JIT revolution. *Harvard Business Review* 69(1), p. 40–50.

List of Figures

1.1   3-level adjustable parameters   7

2.1   Robust approaches from 4 aspects   13
2.2   Variations of Kanban Systems   17

3.1   Real-world Kanban systems   28
3.2   5-stage Kanban system model   29
3.3   Working-mechanism flow chart   35
3.4   Risk-response mechanism   50
3.5   Control logic of the risk-response mechanism   51
3.6   Three cases of calculating $cost_{notchange}$ 65
3.7   Simulation model of Robust Kanban System   71
3.8   Typical simulation output data of Robust Kanban System   78
3.9   Value change records of monitors and parameters   81
3.10 Simulation output results of validation test 2   85

4.1   Backlog level in M/D/k type Kanban system   109
4.2   Backlog level in G/G/k type Kanban system Part1   112
4.2   Backlog level in G/G/k type Kanban system Part2   113
4.3   G/G/k queue model for transport module   119
4.4   Queue length L_q vs. Server number k in an M/M/k queue   121
4.5   Smoothed demand interarrival time   140
4.6   Smoothed inventory and backlog level   141

5.1   General model of the robust Kanban system operation process   144
5.2   Comparison of 3 Kanban systems in 7 risk scenarios . . .   152
5.3   Netprofit comparison in stable scenario   159
5.4   Netprofit comparison in other scenarios   163

5.5   Performance measure results of 3 Kanban systems in 7 scenarios 171

5.6   Recovery time comparison of 3 Kanban systems 175

6.1   Cause-and-effect diagram 181

6.2   Scatter plots of 4 design factors in pilot test 187

6.3   Refined ranges of 4 design factors 190

6.4   ANOVA results for the second-order response surface model 194

6.5   Main and interaction effects plots of 4 factors 195

6.6   Stepwise screening of factors for the second-order response surface model 196

6.7   Factor main and interaction effects plots in the refined model 200

6.8   Response surface and contour plots in stable scenario . . . 201

6.9   Goodness of Fit test results 201

6.10 ANOVA results of the refined response surface model (in stable scenario) 202

6.11 Residual analysis of the refined model 203

6.12 Predicted effects of design factors in different risk scenarios 205

6.13 Contour plot of 3 risk scenarios 208

7.1   Flow chart of Robust Kanban System application 217

A.1   Paired difference test results of Netprofit between 3 Kanban systems in stable scenario 242

A.2   Paired difference test results of Netprofit between 3 Kanban systems in Demand++ scenario 244

A.3   Paired difference test results of Netprofit between 3 Kanban systems in Demand+ scenario 246

A.4   Paired difference test results of Netprofit between 3 Kanban systems in Process− scenario 248

A.5   Paired difference test results of Netprofit between 3 Kanban systems in Supply− scenario 250

A.6   Paired difference test results of Netprofit between 3 Kanban systems in Demand−− scenario 252

A.7   Paired difference test results of Netprofit between 3 Kanban systems in Demand− scenario 254

List of Tables

3.1   Risk-response actions in model vs. in real life   34
3.2   Four risk-measure parameters   40
3.3   Three risk sources   41
3.4   Summary of performance measures   48
3.5   Simulation input data 1: random variables   73
3.6   Simulation input data 2: deterministic parameters   74
3.7   Simulation output data   75
3.8   Results comparison for traditional Kanban system   88
3.9   Results comparison for adaptive Kanban system   88

4.1   Curve fitting results for the backlog level function 110
4.2   Curve fitting results of Mean waiting queue length $L_q(k)$ vs. Server Number k in an M/M/k queue 120
4.3   Input parameters of the MINLP numerical example 125
4.4   Output solutions of the MINLP numerical example 126
4.5   Optimal solutions of MINLP model when the service time is fixed (without service level constraint) 128
4.6   Summary of adjusting ranges of 3-level parameters 133
4.7   Specification of control limit parameters for mi_rate . . 137

5.1   Comparison of three Kanban system models 146
5.2   Input factor design in the comparative experiment 149
5.3   Response variables used in the comparative experiment . 151
5.4   Simulation input data 1: cost coefficient parameters . . . 154
5.5   Simulation input data 2: 3-level parameters 155
5.6   Simulation input data 3: scenarios and output performance measures 156
5.7   Simulation input data 4:risk-response mechanism parameters 157
5.8   Netprofit comparison results in stable scenario 160
5.9   Netprofit comparison results in other scenarios 164

6.1 Design factors in the factorial experiment 183
6.2 Pilot test results 186
6.3 Response surface model-CCI design table and Netprofit
     results (in stable scenario, with refined factor ranges) . . . 192
6.4 Fitted function and optimal solutions of the response sur-
     face model (in stable scenario) 197
6.5 Coefficients of the response surface model in different risk
     scenarios 206
6.6 Optimal factor-setting solutions in different risk scenarios 206
6.7 Optimal factor-setting solution for integrated risk scenario 210

A.1 Detailed cost results of 3 Kanban systems in 7 risk scenarios 240
A.2 Netprofit comparison results of 3 Kanban systems in stable
     scenario 241
A.3 Netprofit comparison results of 3 Kanban systems in De-
     mand++ scenario 243
A.4 Netprofit comparison results of 3 Kanban systems in De-
     mand+ scenario 245
A.5 Netprofit comparison results of 3 Kanban systems in
     Process− scenario 247
A.6 Netprofit comparison results of 3 Kanban systems in
     Supply− scenario 249
A.7 Netprofit comparison results of 3 Kanban systems in
     Demand−− scenario 251
A.8 Netprofit comparison results of 3 Kanban systems in
     Demand− scenario 253

B.1 CCI table and Netprofit results in 3 risk scenarios 255

A Appendix for Chapter 5

Detailed performance measures comparison for 3 Kanban systems

See Table A.1.

Netprofit paired comparison for 3 Kanban systems

See Table A.2 to Table A.8, Figure A.1 to Figure A.7 for the comparison results in 7 scenarios.

Scenario	Kanban system type	Netprofit	Order Backlog	Inv Stage0	Inv Stage1	Inv Stage2	Inv Stage3	Customer service level	Cost of Server	Cost of Stime	Cost of Kanban
stable	old	76.9531	0.2036	4.7143	5.1812	3.7902	2.8813	0.8668	120.0000	243.9024	84.0000
	inv	78.1903	0.1646	5.7647	6.2668	4.3716	3.6021	0.9015	120.0000	243.9024	98.7595
	robust	85.3638	0.2144	4.4373	4.9492	3.4396	2.5922	0.8155	122.2163	238.3656	80.1312
Demand++	old	-344.4320	2.8786	4.6656	5.1433	3.4548	2.4446	0.7111	120.0000	243.9024	84.0000
	inv	-329.0220	2.7207	6.5384	7.0572	4.4583	3.2097	0.7454	120.0000	243.9024	110.0838
	robust	-250.8250	2.2577	4.9570	5.4356	3.6393	2.5888	0.7346	124.1588	239.1655	88.2508
Demand+	old	38.3777	0.4658	4.6857	5.1603	3.6403	2.7173	0.8231	120.0000	243.9024	84.0000
	inv	45.9516	0.3817	6.0242	6.5374	4.3760	3.5118	0.8672	120.0000	243.9024	102.8300
	robust	78.4515	0.2480	4.4571	4.9778	3.4289	2.5594	0.8072	122.7825	240.8508	80.8824
Process-	old	-398.9060	3.1997	4.7114	5.1785	3.3843	2.3112	0.6967	120.0000	243.9024	84.0000
	inv	-376.5620	3.0158	6.8304	7.3212	4.5030	3.0288	0.7333	120.0000	243.9024	113.3527
	robust	34.4454	0.5071	4.4780	4.9831	3.3879	2.5167	0.7924	124.4063	239.7174	81.0263
Supply-	old	-221.5350	2.0955	4.1517	4.7476	3.3778	2.4941	0.7520	120.0000	243.9024	84.0000
	inv	-160.4000	1.5281	5.3367	6.1676	4.2447	3.3242	0.8093	120.0000	243.9024	106.8795
	robust	-97.0472	1.2817	3.8743	4.4936	3.2141	2.5066	0.7639	127.4738	239.0022	87.3814
Demand-	old	64.9668	0.1246	4.9702	5.3462	3.4985	2.5444	0.8810	120.0000	243.9024	84.0000
	inv	64.7613	0.1089	5.6736	6.0472	4.5727	3.9191	0.9036	120.0000	243.9024	92.4315
	robust	74.4996	0.1750	4.6890	5.0967	3.8960	3.1759	0.8247	121.0200	232.7931	79.9518
Demand-	old	70.0979	0.0555	5.0265	5.3905	4.5320	3.7279	0.9215	120.0000	243.9024	84.0000
	inv	70.5327	0.0540	5.1498	5.4999	4.3586	3.6507	0.9287	120.0000	243.9024	84.6563
	robust	89.6012	0.0886	4.5947	4.9841	4.0093	3.2642	0.8780	120.6863	229.0083	78.0675

Table A.1: Detailed cost results of 3 Kanban systems in 7 risk scenarios

	In stable scenario		
No.	Netprofit_Old	Netprofit_Inv	Netprofit_Robust
1	91.2342	89.4543	92.9516
2	93.5024	96.7944	96.9218
3	14.3929	27.0197	44.9798
4	79.1866	87.0104	105.0413
5	95.2477	92.7152	101.2111
6	-6.1904	-8.4779	-26.1421
7	72.7773	72.2602	90.4127
8	62.5625	61.1925	72.1571
9	92.0551	89.8820	71.9022
10	78.0213	77.0070	96.8206
11	-30.3960	-29.4169	44.4168
12	61.3204	58.6740	73.4434
13	92.2454	94.6947	91.6685
14	38.3790	80.0359	81.6186
15	95.7178	96.3722	97.7307
16	100.0080	100.5576	98.6197
17	93.7895	95.9194	89.3830
18	69.9298	77.4169	74.3054
19	77.8979	80.1945	81.2184
20	99.8149	97.7156	107.8556
21	85.0541	83.2301	104.1168
22	90.5965	88.3291	58.7755
23	77.7463	74.9701	91.3346
24	100.2708	99.5743	94.4277
25	96.8689	95.3517	92.9409
26	96.1637	93.7876	97.2121
27	100.6682	99.0692	91.7538
28	93.3322	91.9494	104.8650
29	93.2597	90.9025	96.2337
30	19.1044	24.8161	85.0538
31	88.6554	87.6364	100.6737
32	67.1713	61.9460	84.7238
33	82.5265	80.5565	90.5447
34	97.1726	95.8360	102.8715
35	97.6835	96.5617	99.3200
36	96.2045	95.9104	88.1140
37	95.3684	94.9825	95.6696
38	56.2538	58.8237	69.4531
39	90.2837	90.8926	93.3049
40	82.2460	85.4679	86.6479
Mean	76.9532	78.1904	85.3638

Table A.2: Netprofit comparison results of 3 Kanban systems in stable scenario

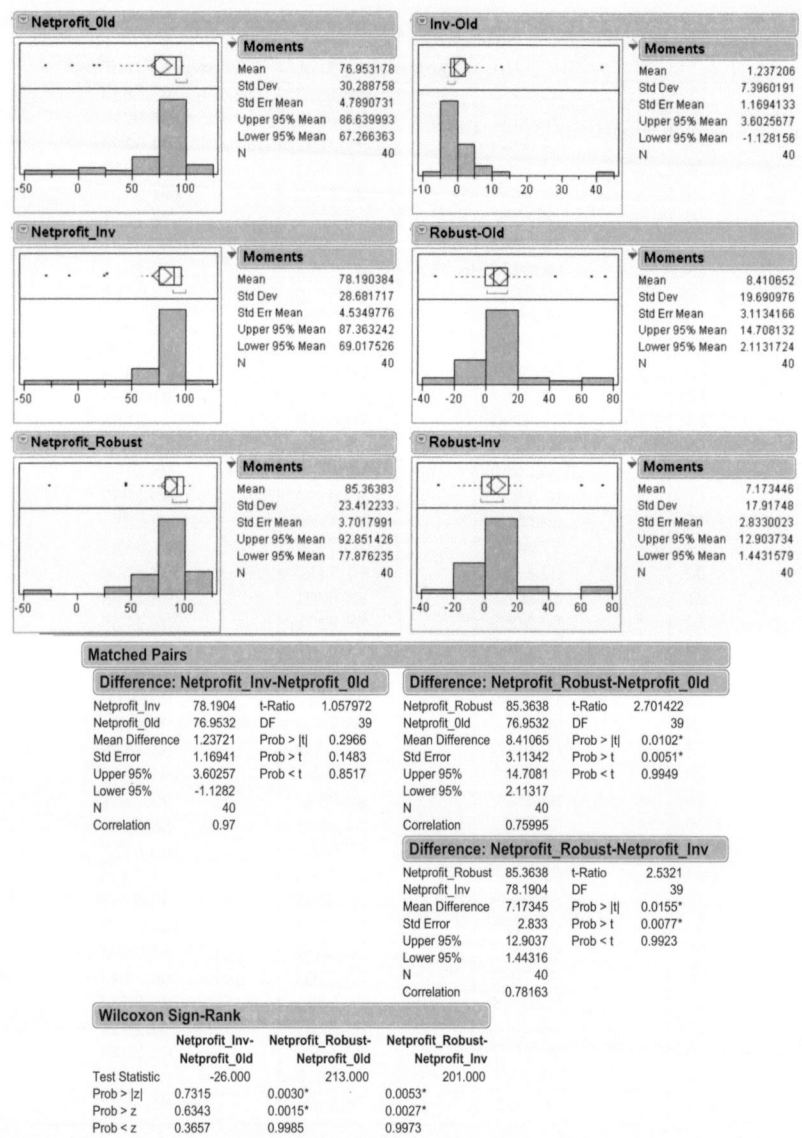

Figure A.1: Paired difference test results of Netprofit between 3 Kanban systems in stable scenario

	In Demand++ scenario		
No.	Netprofit_Old	Netprofit_Inv	Netprofit_Robust
1	-304.9718	-306.8301	-154.6765
2	-269.3062	-271.6045	-234.9415
3	-347.9497	-321.0208	-161.3619
4	-244.7640	-237.1276	-236.4190
5	-275.4073	-254.9275	-151.5239
6	-1023.2186	-988.6052	-300.3163
7	-296.0363	-300.1170	-95.1307
8	-252.6776	-201.8003	-149.2935
9	-372.4326	-354.1810	-212.5440
10	-277.6790	-260.4666	-265.0315
11	-572.0107	-552.6302	-636.1595
12	-240.9008	-241.2838	-185.8721
13	-374.7047	-378.9249	-549.4831
14	-769.8017	-753.8818	-517.8601
15	-360.2601	-331.5577	-261.5250
16	-307.3150	-265.2903	-120.2247
17	-198.2311	-190.8804	-132.5458
18	-223.1352	-189.9306	-101.9791
19	-417.3477	-421.7664	-393.7813
20	-389.2169	-358.8232	-560.2741
21	-194.1453	-201.6655	-344.0620
22	-369.8286	-361.6170	-682.5342
23	-343.5128	-325.9804	-332.1536
24	-186.3129	-136.8305	-169.8686
25	-322.1822	-329.4883	-53.3413
26	-246.1030	-253.1087	-403.7278
27	-498.8631	-504.5791	-99.7916
28	-336.6220	-306.7913	-303.7212
29	-121.9158	-117.2835	-105.9248
30	-330.8018	-292.1479	18.4222
31	-152.1673	-151.0583	-123.8972
32	-441.2652	-413.7162	-450.5831
33	-362.2964	-333.1453	-310.0294
34	-109.6215	-101.2167	-175.8187
35	-257.3598	-234.7493	-108.7470
36	-552.3666	-539.4026	-306.2187
37	-335.2910	-340.1081	-81.4415
38	-449.8217	-433.9854	-252.0563
39	-240.6540	-223.1308	-68.7045
40	-408.7686	-379.2428	-257.8386
Mean	-344.4317	-329.0224	-250.8245

Table A.3: Netprofit comparison results of 3 Kanban systems in Demand++ scenario

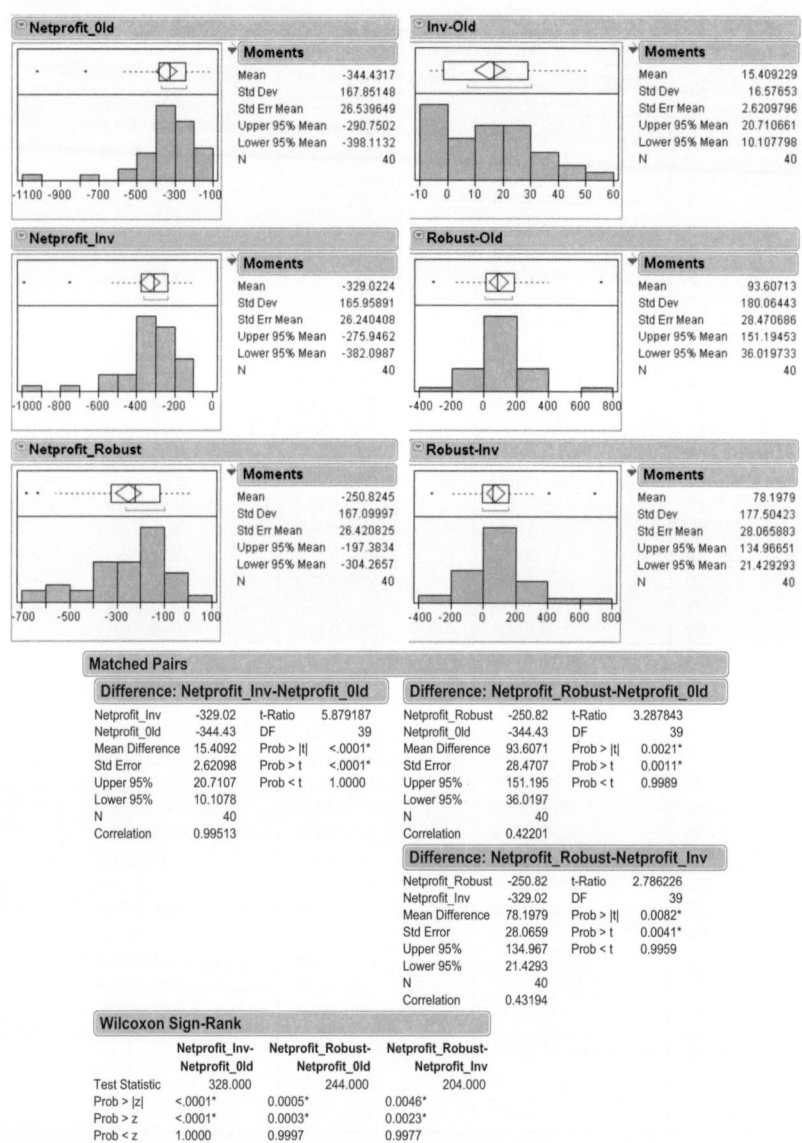

Figure A.2: Paired difference test results of Netprofit between 3 Kanban systems in Demand++ scenario

In Demand+ scenario			
No.	Netprofit_Old	Netprofit_Inv	Netprofit_Robust
1	88.0894	86.9024	86.3152
2	89.9997	96.3503	90.0115
3	-137.2772	-99.9642	20.0056
4	33.6031	47.5491	98.4272
5	89.0296	87.1156	92.0817
6	-300.7801	-303.7624	-11.8286
7	38.0139	38.4577	88.4938
8	62.8663	61.1755	74.3388
9	81.9710	94.5113	71.8170
10	62.5387	73.2870	83.4488
11	-61.6015	-45.1513	48.9733
12	15.9557	18.8856	72.9689
13	65.7435	80.8264	89.0820
14	-132.6174	-93.6026	69.9177
15	82.8242	83.1432	92.5912
16	100.3472	100.3820	94.2412
17	79.2752	88.6388	90.0371
18	69.0516	78.4276	70.3534
19	1.1400	2.7576	49.4163
20	94.4536	91.9470	104.3459
21	84.8768	83.7258	101.4171
22	3.2636	42.5883	91.1611
23	27.1684	37.1069	83.7473
24	87.6229	89.9557	86.7060
25	88.7460	97.8080	88.0450
26	77.2010	75.2681	92.0086
27	-5.5553	8.5252	80.4234
28	93.2736	91.6776	101.7118
29	60.2920	71.3360	-22.5351
30	-39.1005	-6.8110	80.4531
31	79.4669	79.4717	96.4402
32	61.7883	56.5929	85.6830
33	43.9109	62.2095	92.1729
34	91.9336	90.1203	98.4711
35	70.1155	68.2383	93.8760
36	59.7369	66.1457	89.5209
37	94.3652	94.6423	92.5209
38	-21.0007	-24.4010	55.2297
39	82.2755	83.0755	89.3175
40	72.1029	82.9135	86.6513
Mean	38.3778	45.9516	78.4515

Table A.4: Netprofit comparison results of 3 Kanban systems in Demand+ scenario

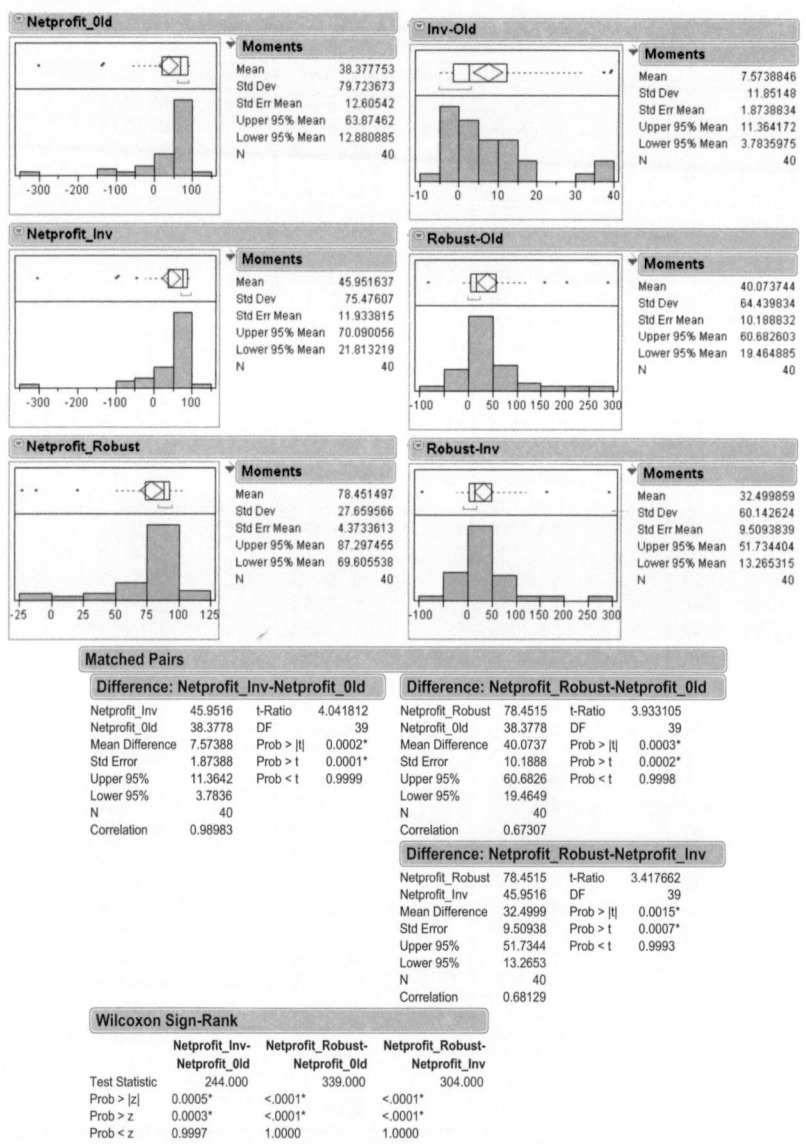

Figure A.3: Paired difference test results of Netprofit between 3 Kanban
systems in Demand+ scenario

	In Process-- scenario		
No.	Netprofit_Old	Netprofit_Inv	Netprofit_Robust
1	-64.9877	-63.9269	6.8918
2	-515.2107	-501.9719	83.6970
3	-993.2621	-940.0293	89.8630
4	-596.0968	-563.5968	98.1597
5	11.2335	18.2701	98.3364
6	-590.0160	-563.9295	-13.0390
7	-353.2979	-333.8444	0.7669
8	-109.2742	-106.2351	69.8927
9	-450.3078	-429.1137	84.2582
10	-457.3063	-411.5812	-162.1767
11	-329.2708	-294.4688	-8.4441
12	-579.8243	-584.2517	58.6548
13	-420.9248	-373.7318	87.2533
14	-629.3506	-587.7255	73.7571
15	-627.5360	-549.0484	-106.5056
16	-138.8939	-131.4466	80.0528
17	-95.8657	-70.9914	9.8503
18	-353.5840	-338.9250	71.3914
19	-103.8118	-72.9365	32.7558
20	-617.4154	-609.8234	95.3328
21	-96.8720	-100.6885	96.4859
22	-534.6403	-495.7538	48.9806
23	-539.2762	-521.7194	84.7297
24	-247.8282	-202.9775	17.2056
25	-462.6755	-438.8960	16.8945
26	-366.4100	-344.9859	94.0939
27	-290.9528	-293.4579	83.5629
28	-693.8788	-699.4636	-149.0973
29	-346.9144	-351.0479	12.3604
30	-376.3319	-359.1453	-5.7389
31	-60.8962	-63.3178	92.3723
32	-344.9084	-348.8201	80.6703
33	-955.8770	-770.9828	85.3189
34	-408.0263	-412.5552	18.3340
35	-354.1185	-352.7197	89.4200
36	-563.6217	-540.1418	-267.0191
37	-82.3175	-66.5483	52.0439
38	-297.8510	-279.1779	11.9361
39	-251.7528	-243.3032	83.4498
40	-666.0859	-667.4502	81.0645
Mean	-398.9060	-376.5615	34.4454

Table A.5: Netprofit comparison results of 3 Kanban systems in Process--scenario

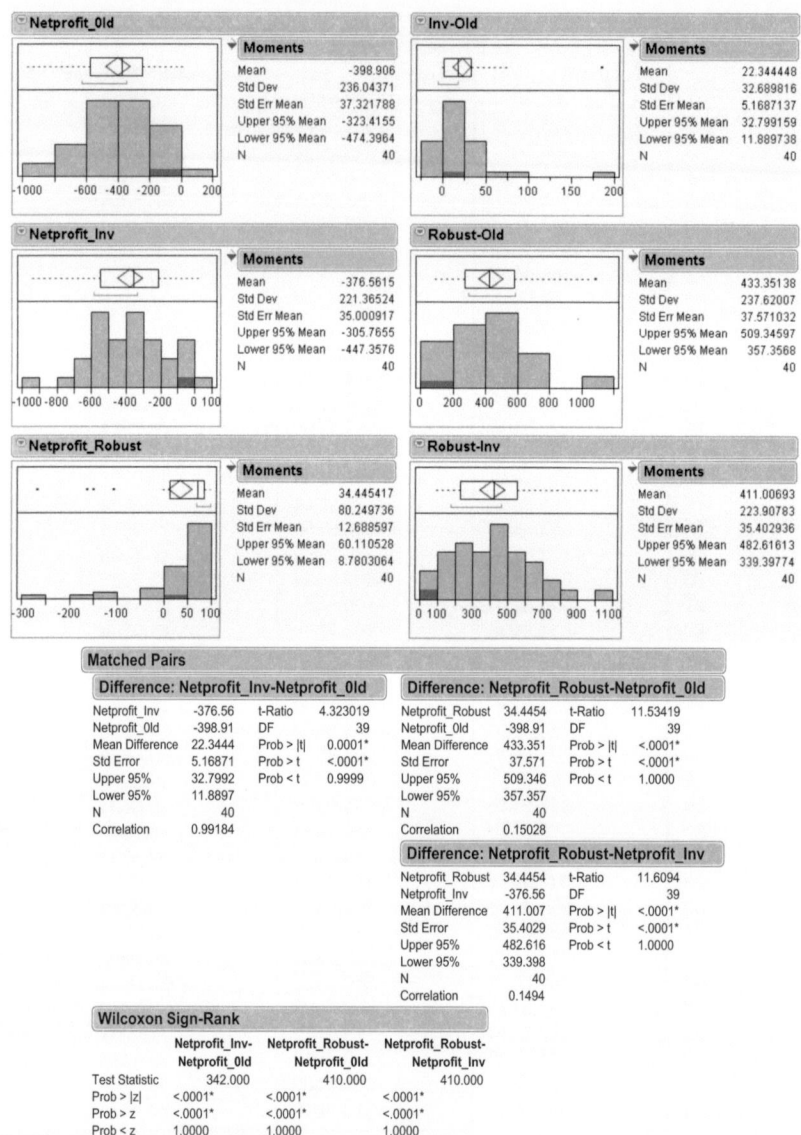

Figure A.4: Paired difference test results of Netprofit between 3 Kanban systems in Process— scenario

	In Supply-- scenario		
No.	Netprofit_Old	Netprofit_Inv	Netprofit_Robust
1	-23.0608	23.9141	8.8959
2	-421.9243	-333.2498	-39.1163
3	-846.2549	-581.9388	-255.6826
4	-478.7209	-392.0528	-147.5170
5	87.2949	73.0338	62.2908
6	-350.9933	-313.5892	-225.4997
7	-91.8004	-95.0198	-159.1164
8	-24.9401	13.2754	-51.7349
9	-212.3581	-28.6106	-66.8419
10	-255.2012	-204.4313	-134.3748
11	-246.7253	-182.7780	-118.4038
12	-349.9054	-337.4865	-238.4250
13	-241.3644	-40.4179	-71.2024
14	-439.5109	-389.3618	-222.5858
15	-263.2580	-234.5651	-122.2664
16	-10.0203	9.4080	-16.5864
17	57.0378	38.3940	36.1370
18	-120.8362	-61.5040	-103.4488
19	46.1802	55.7129	68.2614
20	-471.0808	-490.9750	-262.3719
21	41.7174	21.5575	58.7297
22	-243.4352	32.3423	-100.4587
23	-337.9006	-249.9213	-134.0819
24	-52.1233	85.1598	1.5214
25	-378.2589	-213.3804	-147.1397
26	-224.8577	-149.8665	-58.7969
27	-50.4271	-41.1143	-78.6273
28	-172.9916	-195.3982	-125.3512
29	-214.5518	-166.8818	-136.6982
30	-195.3455	-219.8653	-10.4371
31	31.8160	29.8908	70.7947
32	-268.7941	-293.4048	-138.9518
33	-613.0938	-514.8576	-196.6678
34	-206.5553	-178.4559	-52.0845
35	-268.1098	-54.9297	-108.7835
36	-437.5678	-381.2930	-275.6142
37	33.6586	25.1124	55.4912
38	-203.6662	-222.3430	-133.0401
39	1.9614	35.9622	21.1506
40	-445.4363	-292.0623	-333.2527
Mean	-221.5351	-160.3998	-97.0472

Table A.6: Netprofit comparison results of 3 Kanban systems in Supply--scenario

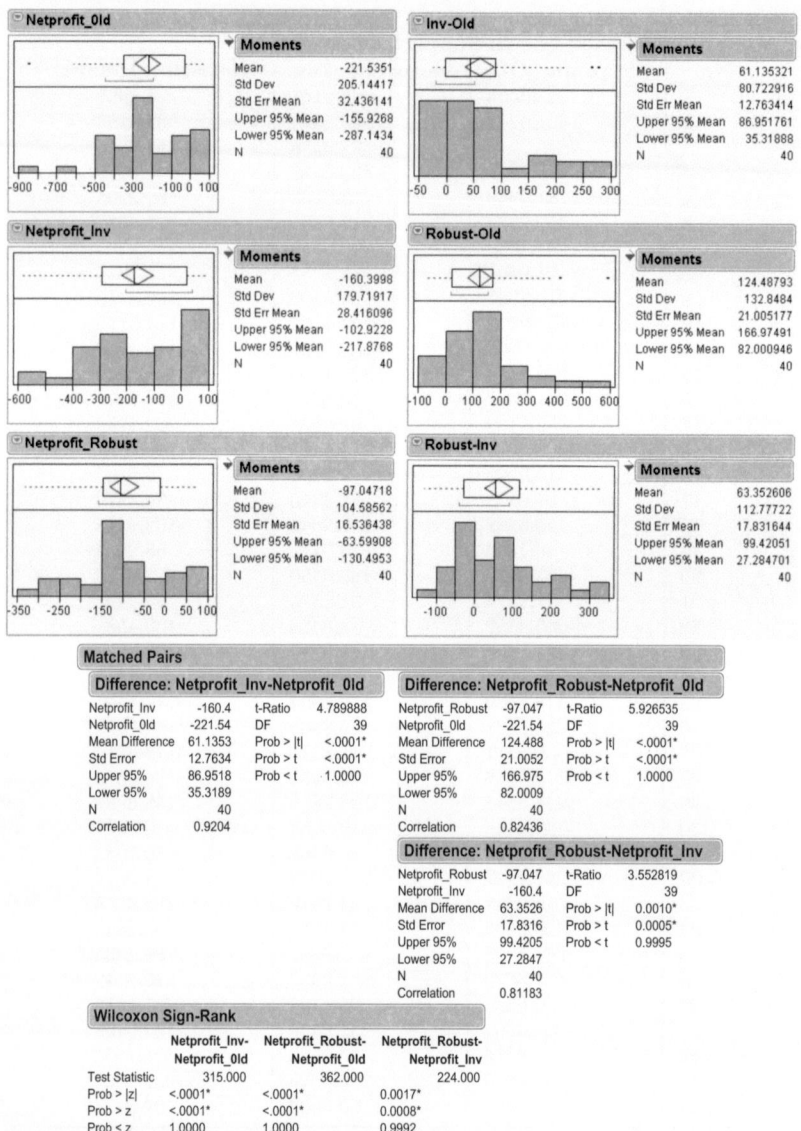

Figure A.5: Paired difference test results of Netprofit between 3 Kanban systems in Supply− scenario

	In Demand-- scenario		
No.	Netprofit_Old	Netprofit_Inv	Netprofit_Robust
1	67.7196	67.2651	62.7154
2	72.9226	76.5006	82.1748
3	-6.5676	-8.8084	34.6771
4	58.9119	57.2905	96.4548
5	73.4190	71.4219	78.1625
6	55.7980	54.4933	56.4016
7	70.3698	69.7525	77.2191
8	68.6396	68.2958	77.0803
9	69.6920	68.1169	49.5153
10	56.3818	54.7504	74.4598
11	74.0065	74.5534	84.2037
12	40.3821	37.3783	60.6216
13	70.5346	71.9964	59.3562
14	16.2983	58.4571	57.3044
15	74.4704	75.1781	81.5156
16	76.9172	77.2690	86.7925
17	73.2021	75.7750	80.3575
18	49.4565	57.6767	51.6746
19	76.5529	76.7728	73.8396
20	79.2818	76.9466	72.9737
21	76.0492	75.5217	94.4298
22	72.1856	70.2529	86.8039
23	59.4677	55.1744	83.4103
24	78.8789	72.2870	84.4024
25	74.6640	71.1420	81.7528
26	73.9870	69.7387	84.1428
27	79.0088	79.2911	77.5409
28	73.3384	71.0711	94.9659
29	69.6664	61.0602	82.0775
30	63.4594	62.4241	86.4495
31	67.5353	57.4185	94.3903
32	47.2421	38.3552	16.7795
33	61.7897	60.6759	74.5692
34	75.1656	73.1241	91.3997
35	77.0217	77.0403	93.6350
36	77.8870	73.3142	47.2795
37	73.8672	73.9475	81.9967
38	42.8261	40.1734	55.0937
39	72.5290	73.4857	86.4944
40	63.7164	73.8732	84.8727
Mean	64.9669	64.7613	74.4997

Table A.7: Netprofit comparison results of 3 Kanban systems in Demand-- scenario

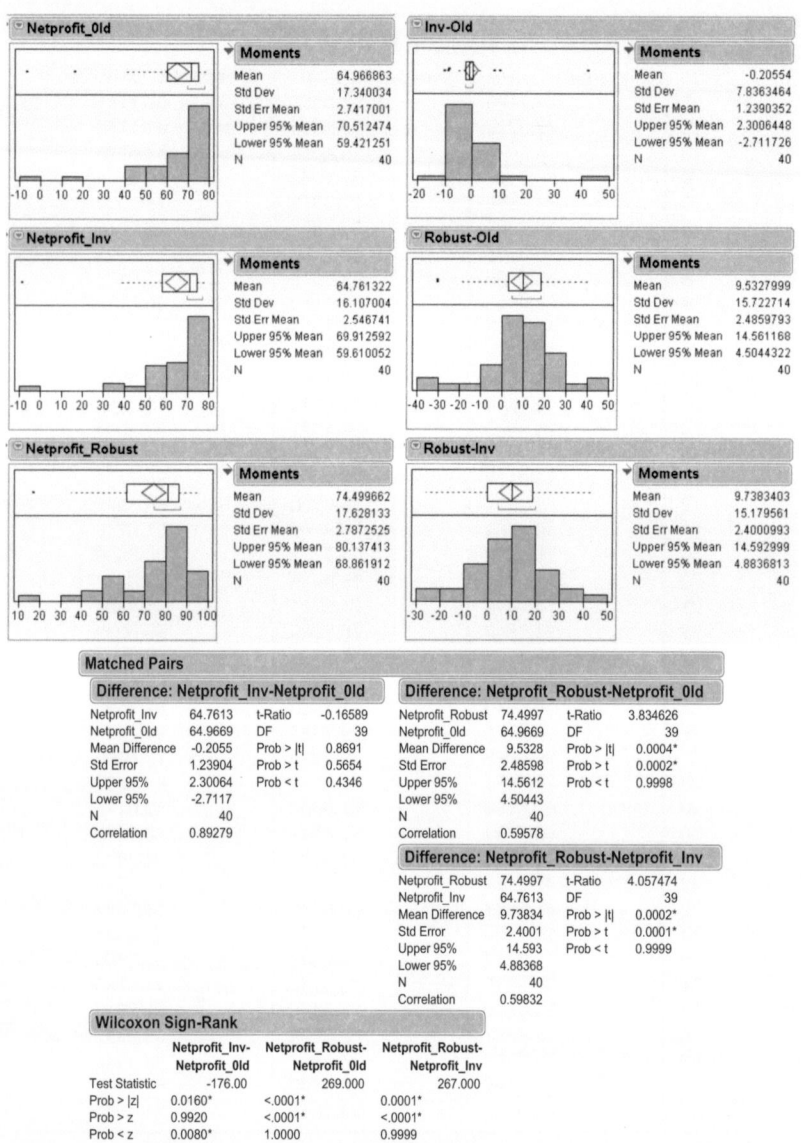

Figure A.6: Paired difference test results of Netprofit between 3 Kanban systems in Demand—— scenario

	In Demand– scenario		
No.	Netprofit_Old	Netprofit_Inv	Netprofit_Robust
1	64.7582	65.8986	88.5620
2	71.0671	74.2001	83.9154
3	80.1485	79.9615	102.4858
4	76.0222	77.1881	103.8515
5	70.7527	70.5601	92.8091
6	78.9442	79.1463	97.6609
7	67.5650	64.8290	89.2494
8	62.8033	66.5798	70.1489
9	73.7031	74.6500	94.3879
10	68.8731	70.3077	90.2390
11	71.5264	74.8224	81.9277
12	65.8839	59.3078	86.2793
13	75.4072	77.0804	95.7979
14	71.2673	64.1989	64.7145
15	69.1726	71.2656	91.3140
16	73.1980	75.7739	84.9294
17	69.1586	73.1553	88.8933
18	47.0151	48.9252	68.3768
19	74.1157	78.7706	81.0120
20	75.5406	75.8724	94.1554
21	68.2604	69.5852	91.2094
22	76.7614	77.2899	103.5469
23	72.8865	72.2614	97.7846
24	76.7426	77.3624	98.1773
25	73.0585	73.8954	92.5272
26	67.3796	65.7252	95.0008
27	81.9575	81.8123	100.4611
28	66.8725	66.6475	89.7223
29	73.9526	73.2087	92.5813
30	65.7027	58.7534	74.1183
31	63.1156	64.3587	93.5486
32	40.4072	42.7709	78.8351
33	61.9936	61.9593	89.6052
34	70.0099	71.2276	96.7045
35	76.1776	77.4543	99.0115
36	74.7133	75.6794	94.5950
37	69.4198	70.5773	93.0536
38	75.3853	75.4980	90.8596
39	71.4986	71.8341	83.3810
40	70.7004	70.9163	78.6154
Mean	70.0980	70.5328	89.6012

Table A.8: Netprofit comparison results of 3 Kanban systems in Demand– scenario

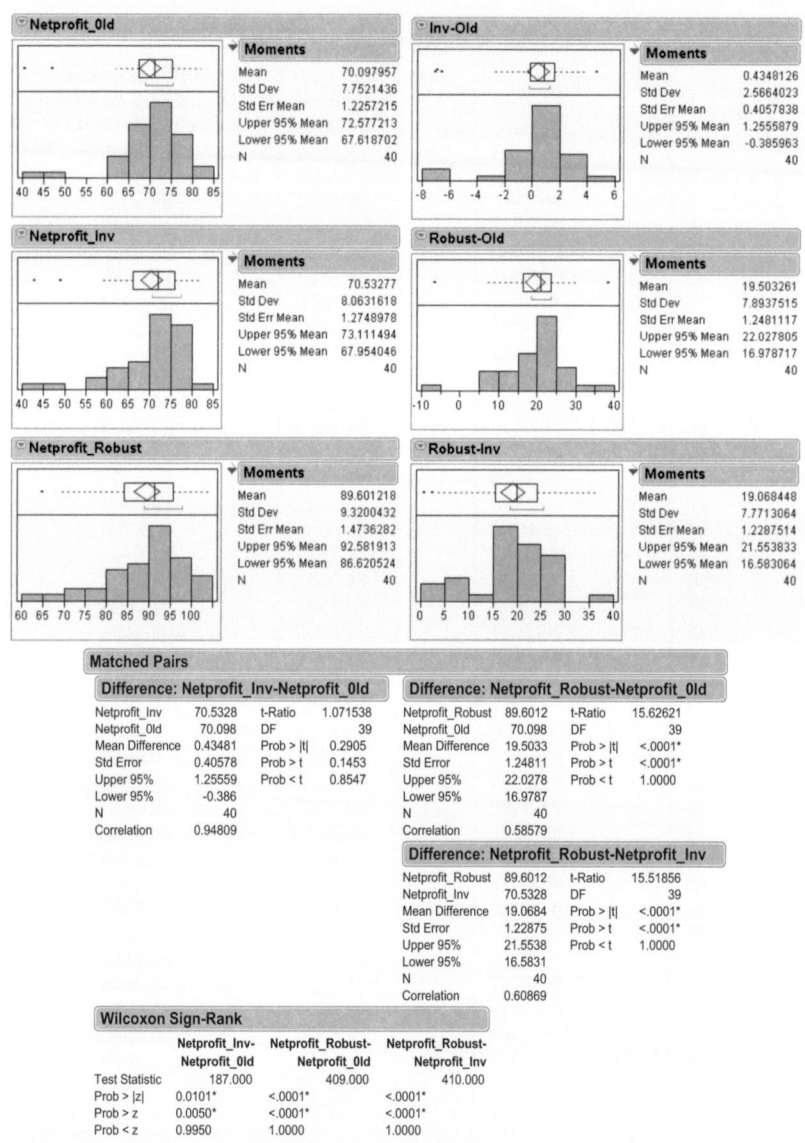

Figure A.7: Paired difference test results of Netprofit between 3 Kanban systems in Demand– scenario

B Appendix for Chapter 6

No.	Pattern	Factor				Response: Netprofit		
		sf	sf_{dt}	sf_{inv}	ss	Stable	Demand++	Demand+
1	$----$	1.006	0.93	0.6	3	99.4810	-84.0266	97.8495
2	$---+$	1.006	0.93	0.6	5	99.9708	-44.2284	99.4707
3	$--+-$	1.006	0.93	0.8	3	99.1097	-64.2392	95.9855
4	$--++$	1.006	0.93	0.8	5	99.1246	-43.2468	98.3858
5	$-+--$	1.006	0.95	0.6	3	101.3698	-139.5758	97.1661
6	$-+-+$	1.006	0.95	0.6	5	100.7389	-89.0789	99.1968
7	$-++-$	1.006	0.95	0.8	3	99.6940	-143.2461	95.3293
8	$-+++$	1.006	0.95	0.8	5	99.5688	-92.6810	96.0579
9	$+---$	1.016	0.93	0.6	3	99.3137	-91.6491	96.4523
10	$+--+$	1.016	0.93	0.6	5	99.9654	-53.6188	98.3496
11	$+-+-$	1.016	0.93	0.8	3	98.7033	-72.1574	95.7991
12	$+-++$	1.016	0.93	0.8	5	99.6988	-51.4441	98.0585
13	$++--$	1.016	0.95	0.6	3	100.4620	-151.1959	95.8215
14	$++-+$	1.016	0.95	0.6	5	98.7949	-76.4302	96.4271
15	$+++-$	1.016	0.95	0.8	3	99.5962	-144.4346	95.1881
16	$++++$	1.016	0.95	0.8	5	98.4388	-73.7973	96.2729
17	a000	1.001	0.94	0.7	4	100.1685	-79.7122	98.5849
18	A000	1.021	0.94	0.7	4	100.0603	-86.3490	97.2155
19	0a00	1.011	0.92	0.7	4	98.8730	-30.3040	96.1271
20	0A00	1.011	0.96	0.7	4	99.3438	-161.7218	96.7367
21	00a0	1.011	0.94	0.5	4	100.2418	-88.8592	97.7881
22	00A0	1.011	0.94	0.9	4	99.0846	-77.3313	95.7071
23	000a	1.011	0.94	0.7	2	99.6388	-105.2267	97.1576
24	000A	1.011	0.94	0.7	6	100.3108	-44.6837	97.7798
25	0000	1.011	0.94	0.7	4	101.1023	-86.1081	97.9081

Table B.1: Central composite design (Inscribed) table and response Netprofit results in 3 risk scenarios (stable, demand++, demand+)